MACRO-ECONOMICS

The Measurement, Analysis, and Control

of Aggregate Economic Activity

Second Edition

McGRAW-HILL BOOK COMPANY

New York   San Francisco   Toronto   London

MACRO-ECONOMICS

The Measurement, Analysis, and Control
of Aggregate Economic Activity

THOMAS F. DERNBURG

Associate Professor of Economics,   *Oberlin College*

DUNCAN M. McDOUGALL

Associate Professor of Economics,   *Purdue University*

MACRO-ECONOMICS

Preface

This second and substantially revised edition has the same twofold purpose as the first edition. First, we hope that we have provided a fairly comprehensive survey of the subject matter included in a junior- or senior-level course in aggregative economics. Second, we hope that we have spanned the gap between the elementary and the professional level, providing a framework for more advanced study.

This new edition is both revised and enlarged. In Part I the same conceptual framework is used, and the statistical materials have been updated. In the interim the Department of Commerce has revised its method of reporting, but we have retained the older accounting procedures for analytical reasons.

In Part II we have undertaken substantial revision. Chapter 5 now includes the recent empirical findings and theories that have done much to improve our understanding of the determinants of aggregate consumption spending. Chapter 8 incorporates recent developments in the theory of the demand for money and also developments in the newly revived theory of the money supply. Chapter 9 is now graced by the addition of a method of identifying disturbances that cause income to change, developed by J. L. Stein. The inclusion of this material provides the student with an additional means of familiarizing himself with the Hick-Hansen model that forms the basis of the analysis of the book, and it permits us to make use of the concept of velocity in a significant way. The material on the effectiveness of monetary and fiscal policy in Chapter 10 has been supplemented by a discussion of the possibility that monetary policy may be ineffective, not because of an interest-elastic demand for money, but, due to the behavior of banks, because of an interest-elastic money supply. We are indebted to George Horwich of Purdue University for suggesting to us that the liquidity trap of the 1930s may have been a supply phenomenon. Chapter 11 has been completely rewritten and now includes a more extensive discussion of the role of money illusion. Chapter 12, which we regarded as our lone original contribution, remains intact. In Chapter 13 we have tried to atone for the glaring omission of Metzler's analysis of wealth and the rate of interest. Chapter 14 has been revised to present a clearer demonstration of the incompatibility of the goals of full employment, price stability, balance-of-payments equilibrium, and fixed exchange rates; and to relate the conflict between these goals to the policy dilemma in which the United States now finds itself.

There are also extensive changes in Parts III and IV. We have added a chapter on statics, dynamics, and the correspondence principle, and we believe that it provides a useful transition from the static models of Part II to the dynamic analysis of Part III. Chapter 17 has been rewritten and is now confined entirely to an analysis of excess-demand inflation. A new chapter (Chapter 21) on cost inflation, structural unemployment, and other pressing current problems has been added to Part IV.

Finally, we have placed all the mathematical appendices together in one omnibus appendix at the end of the book.

As before, our debts are far too numerous to permit us to present a complete list. The intellectual debt we owe our past teachers is enormous. Among these, Evsey Domar, William Fellner, Simon Kuznets, Arthur Okun, and James Tobin head the list. In addition, our colleagues and students at Oberlin College and Purdue University have contributed much in the way of helpful suggestion. R. K. Davidson, George Horwich, V. L. Smith, Rubin Saposnik, and the late J. A. Estey of Purdue University; and Kenneth Strand of Oberlin College must be cited as persons who have read and contributed to the manuscript. This edition has benefited greatly from the influence of Albert Rees, Zvi Griliches, and especially Joel Segall of the University of Chicago. A huge vote of thanks is owed to Mr. Victor Goldberg, an Oberlin College senior, who contributed both labor and keen insight to the improvement of the book. Finally, we wish to thank all those teachers and students who took the trouble to point out errors and to suggest improvements.

None of the above-mentioned persons is to be blamed in any way for the result.

Thomas F. Dernburg
Duncan M. McDougall

Contents

Part III: Growth and Instability in Economic Activity

Part IV: Problems in the Control of Economic Activity

chapter 1

The framework

1-1   Introduction

The businessman faced with incessant demands for higher wages to "keep up with the cost of living," the retired person trying to live on a fixed income, and the housewife who struggles to put food on the family dinner table in a period of rising food prices need hardly be told that inflation is a serious economic problem. Similarly, the worker who is laid off from an assembly line, the graduating senior who despite his qualifications has difficulty finding a job, and the businessman who finds profits shrinking and orders declining are all too familiar with the evils of recession. Economic ailments affect us all. Allowed to become too severe, they create great physical and psychological hardships and strain the sinews of the social and political structure. The purpose of this book is to promote a better understanding of these ailments, to provide the tools with which to analyze them, and to suggest possible cures.

It may seem curious that an understanding of what is perfectly obvious to those suffering the consequences of an economic disease should require the complex analysis of economic theory. But personal experience is often a poor guide to generalization. For example, the housewife may feel that inflation is reducing her family's well-being when in fact the rise in the cost of living which she observes results from a temporary phenomenon such as a crop failure.

1

While such a crop failure is an unfortunate occurrence, it would be quite erroneous to suppose that the increase in food prices is the result of a general inflationary trend. Similarly, the graduating senior may not find work in his chosen field because consumers no longer choose to buy the product manufactured by the particular industry in which he attempts to gain employment. A similar fate may befall a production worker. When small cars strike the fancy of consumers in preference to large chromium-plated "jewel boxes," it is too bad for some automobile companies and for their employees, but it is not an indication that the economy as a whole is in a slump. It is rather an indication that resources should be shifted from large-car to small-car production. Such shifts in resources are the very essence of economic progress. If we commit the fatal error of bringing policy weapons designed to affect the sum total of economic activity to bear on the particular problem of a declining industry, under the illusion that general economic activity is less than it should be, we not only obstruct the shift of resources but, as we shall soon see, give rise to inflationary pressures as well. Conversely, we may be so paralyzed by the fear of inflation that we are prevented from taking effective antirecessionary action.

It is clear then that a method of obtaining an over-all picture of economic activity is essential. This is the function of the national income accounts which we shall study in the first part of the book. In addition, we need a theoretical superstructure within which to analyze this picture. On the theoretical level, it is again true that what is valid in a specific instance may not be true of the sum total. If we could simply analyze the operation of a single firm and assume that the economy as a whole is really only one big firm, there would be no need to study macro-economics or to develop theories of macro-economic behavior. But macro-economics is set apart as a separate discipline with its own rules because aggregate economic behavior does not correspond to the summation of individual activities. We may, for example, find that if wages, and therefore production costs, fall, a single firm will find it profitable to expand output and therefore hire more workers. For the economy as a whole it does not follow that a wage cut will lead to a general expansion of employment. Similarly, one individual, in borrowing from another, borrows a claim over real resources which he must pay back at some future date by giving up a claim over real resources. The community as a whole cannot borrow real resources from itself in one year and pay these resources back in another year. Yet despite this obvious truth the fiction persists that World War II remains to be paid for and that the economic product of future generations is mortgaged to the follies of the past.[1] Similarly, if one individual plans to increase his savings

---

[1] There is some truth to the notion that our grandchildren will be less well off because of our extravagances. Insofar as the resources that went into the war effort could have been utilized to build up the productive capacity of the nation, the product of the future will be reduced.

by consuming less, he will, given the necessary self-control, be successful. But if the community as a whole makes such an effort, the reduction in total consumption expenditures may lead to such a shrinkage in income that aggregate savings may be less than before.

Many similar examples could be given. Most of these cases, which seem paradoxical at first, stem from the fact that what is true for an individual is true only if other things remain equal. This is an assumption which is legitimate in micro-economic (partial equilibrium) analysis. But in macro-economics this so-called *ceteris paribus* assumption is not justified; therefore an entirely different approach to the analysis of macro-economic problems must be developed.

1-2   The Record of the American Economy

In order to introduce some of the concepts which will be used throughout the book, the remainder of this orientation chapter is devoted to a statistical description of the behavior of the American economy since 1929. Although the precise definition and measurement of the descriptive aggregates are complicated matters, for the time being little harm is done if we content ourselves with a fairly loose notion of the meanings of the terms.

A concept which has become practically a household word is that of gross national product, or *GNP*. *GNP* is the market value of the newly produced goods and services that are not resold in any form during the year. The national income statistician divides the goods produced into those purchased by consumers, by government, by business (investment goods), and by foreigners. In addition to producers' durable equipment and new construction, investment goods include net changes in inventory, i.e., changes in the stock of unsold production. Net changes in inventory are included because *GNP* is a measure of production. Failure to include changes in the stock of unsold goods would make *GNP* a measure of sales rather than production. Similarly, because foreigners sell goods to us, *GNP* includes what is called the "net export of goods and services," i.e., total exports minus total imports. This is a necessary inclusion because sales to Americans include goods produced in foreign countries. The value of these goods must be subtracted if a measure of American production only is to be derived.

It is useful to divide the purchases of the various sectors into different groups according to commodity classes. Personal consumption expenditures, for example, may be divided into expenditures on nondurable goods (food, clothing, etc.), services (medical attention, laundry, etc.), and durable goods (TV sets, automobiles, etc.). Gross private domestic investment may similarly be broken down into purchases of producers' durable equipment (machines, trucks, etc.), construction activity (both residential and nonresidential), and the change in inventories. Finally, government expenditures on goods and services may be broken down into expenditures by the Federal government and by state and local governments.

From the economist's point of view, a more interesting though more difficult-to-estimate statistic than gross national product is net national product (*NNP*). Since a portion of annual output is used to replace equipment that has been worn out during the production of the year's output, a deduction known as "capital consumption allowance" (familiarly known as "depreciation") is made from *GNP*. The resulting figure is net national product, which may be defined as the net creation of new wealth resulting from the productive activity of the economy during the accounting period.

Any economy produces a great variety of goods and services during a year. The diversity of output dictates that some common measure be used to aggregate it. The most convenient measure is the price of the various things produced. Thus, *GNP* and its components are given in terms of dollars, the sum of the market prices of the goods and services produced. The difficulty with using prices is that they fluctuate over time. Because of this, an increase in *GNP* need not reflect an increase in output; it can, instead, result from an increase in prices. To avoid this difficulty, a measure of "real" *GNP* and its components is frequently given by valuing the output of any year in terms of the prices of a selected year. Changes in *GNP* measured in terms of the prices of a given year reflect, therefore, only changes in the physical output of the economy.

What do these "real" magnitudes look like over a period of time? In Figure 1-1 we plot *GNP* and its major components—personal consumption expenditures, gross private domestic investment, and government expenditures on goods and services—all in terms of 1954 prices. The net export of goods and services, which fluctuates rather closely about zero, is omitted. The first thing to notice about *GNP* is that it grows. During 1929, regarded as a full employment year, *GNP* was $181.8 billion. By 1961 it had grown to $447.9 billion. The second thing to notice is that this growth process does not take place steadily. Thus *GNP* declined after 1929, falling to a low of $126.6 billion in 1933, the worst year of the great depression. Recovery began in 1934 and continued until 1938, when a mild slump again took place. With the coming of the war, *GNP* jumped precipitously and continued to climb until 1946, when a drastic reduction in government expenditures produced a decline. The following decade was marked by fairly even advance. A mild slump developed in 1949 but was soon followed by recovery and, subsequently, the Korean War. Another moderate slump occurred in 1953, and a more serious one in 1958. The recovery from the recession of 1958 has been disappointing, with consumption expenditures being the only component of expenditure to show a consistent increase.

Notice next how the components of *GNP* behave over time. Consumption expenditures rise as *GNP* rises and generally (but not always) fall as *GNP*

Figure 1-1 Gross national product and the expenditure components, 1929–1961 (1954 prices)

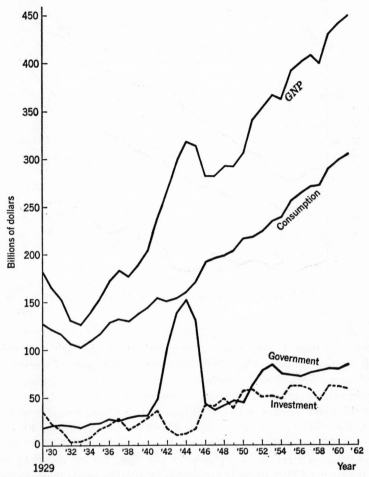

Source: The data in this chart and succeeding charts in this chapter were obtained from U.S. Department of Commerce, *U.S. Income and Output,* Tables I-2, I-5, I-17, I-18, II-1, and II-2, U.S. Government Printing Office, Washington, 1958, and U.S. Department of Commerce, *Survey of Current Business, July, 1962,* Tables 1 to 5, U.S. Government Printing Office, Washington, 1961.

falls. In terms of relative changes, consumption is far more stable than *GNP*, which in turn reflects the extreme volatility of investment expenditures.

Although it is true that consumption expenditures as a whole are fairly stable, the same cannot be said of all the components. The three components of aggregate consumption—durables, nondurables, and services—are plotted in Figure 1-2. Observe the remarkable stability of expenditures for consumer

Figure 1-2   Components of personal consumption expenditures, 1929–1961   (1954 prices)

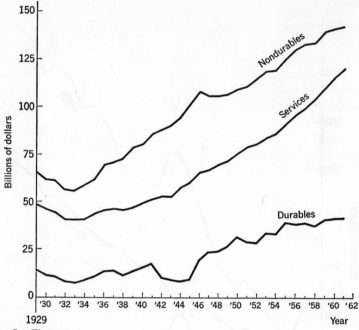

Source: See Figure 1-1.

services over time. Expenditures on nondurables are similarly not subject to significant fluctuations. The same, however, is not true of durable goods expenditures. Since durables include postponable household items, a fall in family income is apt to cut into such expenditures to a greater degree than into nondurables and services, which tend instead to be unpostponable necessities. While, therefore, expenditures on nondurables fell by about 30 per cent between 1929 and 1933, expenditures on durables fell by about 48 per cent. Expenditures on services fell by only 15 per cent. During the 1938 slump a more pronounced fluctuation is noticeable in durable goods than in the other components of consumption expenditures. The war years were, of course, exceptions. The manufacture of major durable consumer goods all but ceased. We therefore observe a decline from 1941 on, and a rapid upsurge in the immediate postwar period when consumers attempted to replace their obsolete and worn-out automobiles, refrigerators, and other durable goods.

Notice the upsurge in durable goods buying in 1950. That was the Korean War period, at which time the war scare apparently gave rise to the expectation of durable goods shortages, with the result that consumers rushed out to stock up on household appliances and other durable goods.

Figure 1-1 suggests that the explanation of fluctuations in *GNP* is largely a matter of explaining fluctuation in investment expenditures. When investment falls, *GNP* falls; when investment rises, *GNP* rises. This is true for all periods except the war years, when investment spending was suppressed by direct control. *GNP*, however, rose sharply during the war years as a result of the vast increase in government expenditures.

It is interesting, though somewhat bewildering, to observe the movement of the components of investment expenditures over time. The components are plotted in Figure 1-3. New construction and the purchase of producers' durable equipment seem to move together fairly closely. During the 1929–1933 period both all but collapsed. The period, moreover, was marked by a considerable reduction in inventories. Again, during the slump of 1938 all components of investment expenditures fell off, though new construction was least affected. The principal change, as frequently happens, was a reduction in inventories. Again in 1947 inventories declined drastically, but in this case the

Figure 1-3 Components of gross private domestic investment, 1929–1961 (1954 prices)

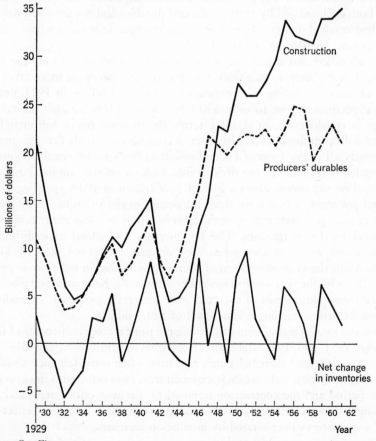

Source: See Figure 1-1.

decline was due to the reduction of stocks of war materials and the acceleration of consumer purchases that took place immediately after the war. Subsequent recessions also showed a reduction in inventories.

A reduction of inventories is a typical manifestation of a recession. Such reductions, moreover, may be a key to the cumulative nature of business contraction and expansion. If entrepreneurs merely reduced their orders by the amount of the decline in sales, there would be no net change in inventories. But typically orders are reduced by more than this, which indicates that production and income payments will also decline by more than the initial fall in sales. This, in turn, causes a further reduction in sales.

During the postwar period new construction and producers' durable equipment expenditures advanced steadily until 1949, at which time the economy entered its first postwar decline. Recovery was, however, bolstered by a high level of consumer buying and by the coming of the Korean War. Until 1955 or 1956 construction and producers' durables expanded fairly evenly but in 1958 both declined and by 1961 producers' durables had not achieved the level they had reached in 1957. In fact, investment expenditure as a whole was the same amount in 1961 as in 1957.

The so-called vast expansion of government expenditures during the 1930s seems, at first glance, to be a figment of the imagination of the more rabid anti-New Dealers. Beginning with expenditures of $18.5 billion in 1929, government expenditures rose to only $30.1 billion by 1939. Though the relative change is considerable, in absolute terms the increase might legitimately be termed a drop in the bucket. However, a closer look reveals that the increase was nearly all in the form of Federal government expenditures. In Figure 1-4 government expenditures are divided into Federal on the one hand and state and local on the other. From a low of $2.9 billion in 1929, spending by the Federal government rose throughout the decade of the 1930s to a 1939 level of $11.0 billion, at which time Federal spending was still less than spending by state and local governments. The big increase in Federal expenditures, of course, came with the war, when they climbed to a 1944 peak of $138.4 billion. With the close of the war, Federal spending again fell to near prewar levels. But with the postwar foreign-aid programs, the Korean military buildup, and the tremendous drain of the cold war, Federal government expenditures continued to rise, reaching a 1961 level of $44.5 billion.

State and local spending remains among the most stable components of *GNP*. Between 1931 and 1933 state and local governments, behaving like most businesses, tightened their belts and, at a time when some felt they should be expanding activities, reduced their expenditures. However, with the exception of this period and the contraction imposed by the war effort, state and local spending has been extremely stable, though rising at a rate that reflects the added expenditures necessitated by population increases.

Although it is impossible, at this early stage of the investigation, to answer a number of questions that are raised by even a superficial survey of the data, we can nevertheless begin to examine some of the fundamental changes that have taken place in the economy. One of the most interesting phenomena is the changing role of consumption. Notice in Figure 1-1 that the fall in *GNP* between 1929 and 1933 was accompanied by a fall in consumption expenditures. However, *GNP* fell in 1949, and again in 1958, and yet consumption expenditures continued to rise. Here, clearly, is a fundamental change which has taken place in the economy. To see how this has come about, let us introduce some additional national income concepts.

For each dollar spent by consumers, investors, and the government, there must be a receipt of one dollar of income by someone. This dollar will be reflected in an increase in wages, interest, rent, corporate profits, and the incomes of unincorporated enterprises. A portion of the gross receipts of business will be kept as depreciation, and a portion may be kept in the form of retained earnings. The sum of retained earnings and depreciation is called "gross business savings." The remainder, which is not retained by business, is then split between the public, which receives "disposable income," and the government, which receives "net taxes." While the government collects taxes, it also returns negative taxes, or "transfer payments." Such transfers include

Figure 1-4 Components of government expenditures, 1929–1961 (1954 prices)

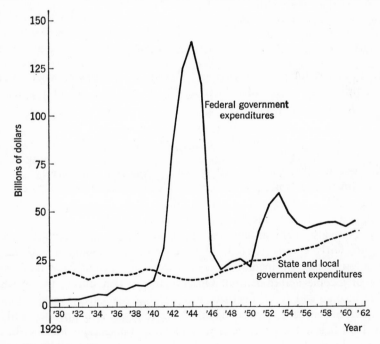

Source: See Figure 1-1.

social security payments, unemployment insurance, and interest on the public debt.

In line with distinctions made in the last paragraph, we may look at the income pie as follows: Dividing the economy into a consuming sector, a business sector, and a government sector and ignoring foreign trade, we have:

	Receives	Spends
The consuming sector	Disposable income (Y_d)	Consumption (C)
The business sector	Retained earnings (S_b)	Net investment (I_r)
The government sector	Taxes net of transfers (T)	Expenditures (G)
All sectors	Net national product (NNP)	Net national product (NNP)
	Depreciation (D)	Depreciation (D)
	Gross national product (GNP)	Gross national product (GNP)

This table represents the model which will be used throughout the analysis in this book. Symbolically, we find that real NNP (which we shall agree to call Y) equals

$$Y = C + I_r + G \tag{1-1}$$

and

$$Y = Y_d + S_b + T \tag{1-2}$$

Since consumers may either spend their disposable income on consumption or save it, we may further write

$$Y = C + S_p + S_b + T \tag{1-3}$$

where S_p stands for personal savings. Writing $S_p + S_b$ as S, where S stands for net private savings, and combining Eq. (1-3) with Eq. (1-1) yields the fundamental accounting identity

$$I_r + G = S + T \tag{1-4}$$

or

$$I_r = S + (T - G) \tag{1-5}$$

which indicates that the national income accountant must always find that net investment equals net private savings plus the government surplus.

In Figure 1-5, series relating to the disposition of income are plotted in current price values. Note that GNP and NNP follow each other rather closely. Note also that consumption and disposable income, except for the war years, are fairly closely related. The notion that consumption is largely dependent on disposable income is one of the fundamental hypotheses of the theory of income determination. Observe finally that during the 1930s disposable income and NNP fluctuate together but that after World War II the correspondence is far less close. While NNP fell in 1949 below the 1948 level, and in 1954 below 1953, the same was not true of disposable income. In 1958, NNP rose by only $1 billion over the level of 1957, but disposable income rose

Figure 1-5 Disposition of income, 1929–1961   (current prices)

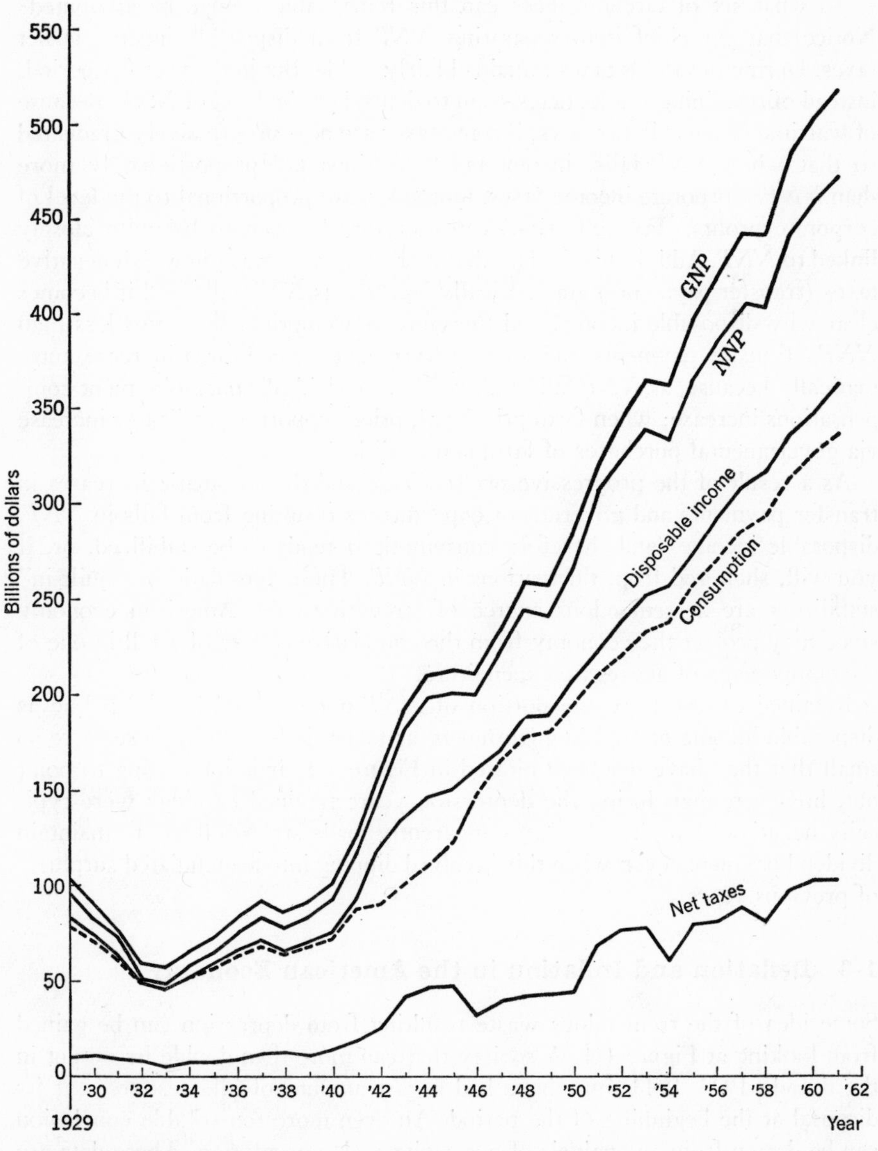

Source: See Figure 1-1.

by $9 billion. If disposable income now fluctuates less than *NNP* and there is a close relationship between disposable income and consumption, it follows that consumption now also fluctuates less than *NNP*. In both 1949 and 1954, when *NNP* fell below the level of the previous year, consumption expenditures actually increased. In 1958, when *NNP* rose by only $1 billion, consumption expenditure rose by $8 billion.

To what set of circumstances can this remarkable change be attributed? Notice that the chief item separating *NNP* from disposable income is net taxes. During the 1930s taxes remained fairly stable. But in the postwar period, instead of remaining stable, taxes seem to depend on the level of *NNP*. Because of wartime changes in tax laws, income taxes are now progressively graduated so that when *NNP* falls, income-tax collections fall proportionately more than *NNP*. Corporate income taxes, moreover, are proportional to the level of corporate profits. Tax collections can therefore be seen to be quite closely linked to *NNP*. Add to this the fact that there are many ways in which negative taxes (transfer payments) automatically increase as *NNP* falls, and it becomes clear why disposable income, and therefore consumption, fluctuates less than *NNP*. Transfer payments and some government expenditures increase automatically because, as *NNP* falls and workers are laid off, unemployment compensations increase; when farm prices fall, price support expenditures increase via governmental purchases of farm commodities.

As a result of the progressive tax structure and the automatic increases in transfer payments and government expenditures resulting from falls in *NNP*, disposable income (and therefore consumption) tends to be stabilized, or, if you will, sheltered from fluctuations in *NNP*. These automatic or "built-in" stabilizers are a tremendous source of strength to the American economy since they protect the economy from the cumulative effects of a fall in one of the components of aggregate expenditure.

Retained earnings are the portion of *NNP* not received by the public as disposable income or by the government as taxes. Before 1950 these were so small that they have not been plotted in Figure 1-5. It is interesting to point out, however, that during the depression years retained earnings were typically negative. American business apparently made strong efforts to maintain dividend payments even when this involved dipping into accumulated surpluses of previous years.

1-3   Deflation and Inflation in the American Economy

Some idea of the tremendous waste resulting from depression can be gained from looking at Figure 1-1. A society that can more than double its output in the decade 1933–1943 must have had a vast amount of idle resources at its disposal at the beginning of the period. An even more remarkable conclusion can be drawn from an analysis of per capita real consumption. These data are plotted in Figure 1-6 where it appears that, despite the wartime suppression of consumption, the average American family was better clothed and better fed during the war than prior to it. This is true despite the fact that in 1942, 1943, and 1944, respectively, 36, 45, and 47 per cent of our total output went into the war effort.

Figure 1-7 records the movement of prices for the United States in conjunction with the movement of real and money *GNP*. The constant-price series of Figure 1-1 and the current-price *GNP* series of Figure 1-5 are included so

Figure 1-6   Per capita consumption, 1929–1961   (1954 prices)

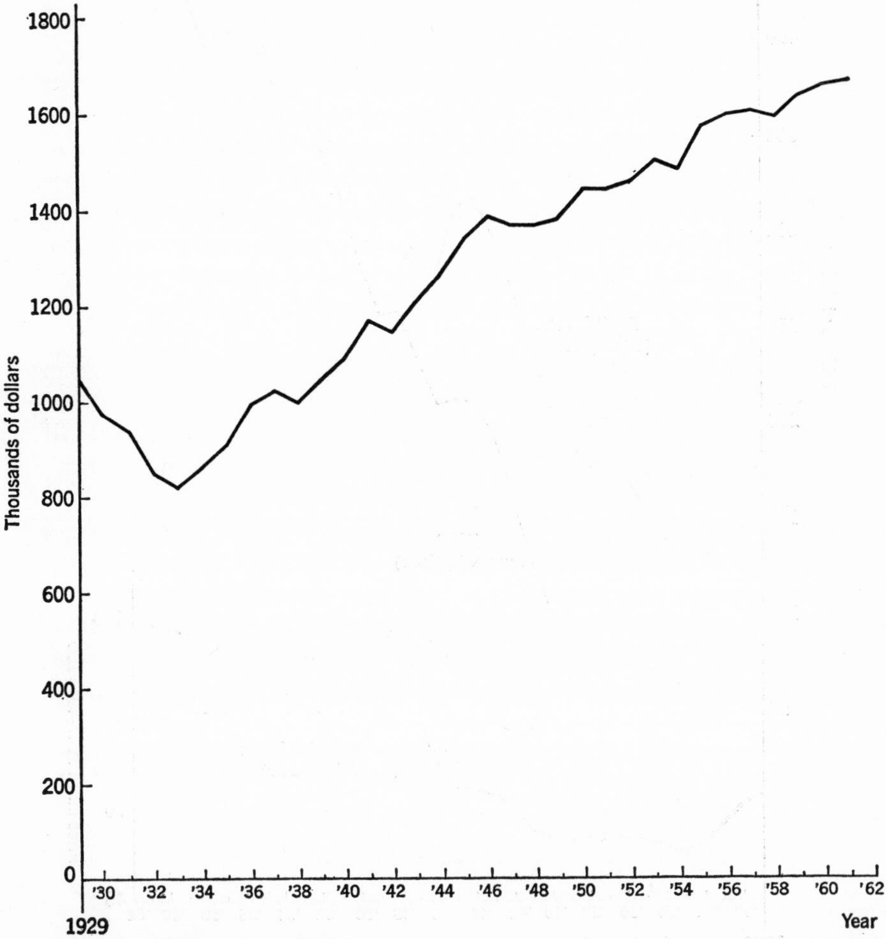

Source: For consumption expenditures, see Figure 1-1. Population refers to total population residing in the United States as of July 1 and is taken from U.S. Department of Commerce, *Statistical Abstract of the United States, 1962,* Table 2, U.S. Government Printing Office, Washington, 1962, p. 5.

Figure 1-7 Real and money gross national product and the consumer price index,1 929–1961

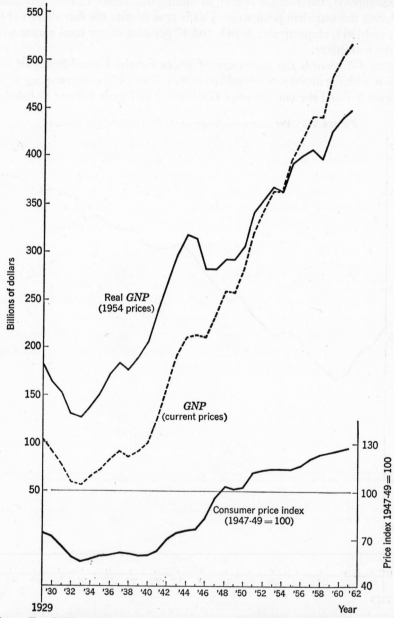

Source: For *GNP*, see Figure 1-1. The price index is prepared by the U.S. Department of Labor and appears in U.S. Department of Commerce, *Statistical Abstract of the United States, 1962*, U.S. Government Printing Office, Washington, 1962, p. 348.

that the behavior of the price index can be compared with changes in the level of economic activity.

From 1929 to 1933 both real and money *GNP* fell; but the fall in the price level during the same period indicates that real *GNP* fell by a greater percentage than money *GNP*. On the other hand, when the economy moved out of the trough of 1933, the percentage increase was greater in money *GNP* than in real *GNP*, as indicated by the rise in the price level.

Both real and money *GNP* marched steadily upward during the war years. The fantastic increase in real output which took place was made possible by the existence of a vast pool of unemployed resources at the start of the war and by the willingness of most Americans to work overtime to make up for the manpower drain to the armed forces. The fact that the price level did not increase as rapidly as might be expected was due to a combination of circumstances: the unemployed resources available at the start of the war; wartime price, credit, and production controls; and the willingness of consumers to save a larger proportion of their disposable income than they normally would.

After 1945 we observe a drastic fall in real *GNP* accompanied by an equally drastic rise in money *GNP*. The conversion from war to peacetime production resulted in a temporary fall in output. There was, however, no fall in the demand for goods and services. At a time when consumers were using wartime savings to replenish their stocks of worn and obsolete durable goods, Congress was busy dismembering the system of wartime price and wage controls. The consequence was a terrific inflationary push during the immediate postwar years; this is clearly shown by the movement of the price index.

The behavior of the three series since 1950 is extremely interesting. Notice their behavior in the recessions of 1954 and 1958. While there was a fall in the level of real *GNP*, the price index increased. When output and employment fall, one would expect, as in the 1930s, an accompanying fall in the price level. The behavior of the series in 1954 and 1958 probably can be attributed to three factors. First, there is developing in the American economy strong resistance to wage and price declines in the face of falling demand. Such resistance would be impossible in a truly competitive environment. But the economy is characterized by large areas of imperfect competition in both labor and product markets. These market imperfections, coupled with public approval, make resistance to wage and price cuts possible and tend, in general, to make prices and wages flexible only in an upward direction. As will be shown in Chapter 21, this feature of our institutional structure is one of the factors that makes inflation such a serious long-run problem. Second, the government, by accepting the responsibility for maintaining the level of employment, is in a position where it must use its economic powers to maintain the level of money income in a period of falling output. Although the use of such powers has probably been effective in limiting the amount of unemployment, one of the effects has been to maintain the price level during periods of recession. Third, as we will show in Chapter 21, the consumer price index is not necessarily a good indicator of the degree of inflation in the economy.

1-4   The Program

This chapter has presented a picture of the United States economy since 1929 by using a simplified statistical framework. In Part I this framework will be analyzed more fully; in Part II the theory of the determination of net national product and its components will be studied. Part III is concerned with the determinants of the time path of both real and money net national product, and Part IV is devoted to some of the policy problems of attaining full employment, steady growth, and a stable price level.

The Measurement of Economic Activity

chapter 2

The gross national product account

2-1 Introduction

The national product account for the United States is presented by the Department of Commerce in a form very similar to the income statement of an individual business enterprise. This is not surprising because the two accounting statements are formulated for very similar reasons. In fact, much of the statistical material used in constructing the national product account is derived from business records. These business records are taken as our starting point.

2-2 Income and Production Statement for a Hypothetical Firm

At the end of an accounting period a firm will have a summary statement drawn up from its accumulated records showing its progress over the period. This summary statement, which condenses the multitude of daily transactions into manageable form, is called the "income statement." It is a record of the flows of product and income involving the firm over a period of time.

Table 2-1 presents an example of such an income statement for a hypothetical business firm which we shall call the X Corporation. The right side of the income statement shows the source of all the receipts of the firm during the year. In this example the X Corporation is assumed to have sold $2,000,000 worth of goods. Of this total, all but $125,000 was derived from the sale of goods to other business firms. The remaining $125,000 was derived from the sale of goods to other than business units, i.e., to nonbusiness sectors of the economy.

The left side of the income statement shows the allocation of these receipts among the various costs incurred in production and to profit. For the X Corporation these costs include, first, materials purchased from other firms of $780,000.[1] Second, they include the factor costs, wages and salaries of $800,000, social security contributions of the corporation of $25,000, and net interest payments by the corporation of $20,000.[2] The final element of cost is the nonfactor payments. The corporation charged $60,000 of its current receipts as an allowance for the depreciation or wear, tear, and obsolescence of its capital equipment. This depreciation allowance is the estimated reduction in the value of the capital equipment over the accounting period. Indirect taxes, such as excise and property taxes, added $30,000 to total cost.

Table 2-1   Simplified income statement for the X Corporation for the period January 1, 1961, to December 31, 1961   (thousands of dollars)

Expenditures		Receipts	
Purchases from other firms	$ 780	Sales to:	
Wages and salaries	800	Company A	$ 810
Social security contributions	25	Company B	240
Net interest	20	Company C	650
Depreciation	60	Company D	175
Indirect business taxes	30	Other sales	125
Corporate profits before tax	285		
Corporate profits tax.....$148			
Dividends paid......... 100			
Undistributed profits..... 37			
Total current expenses	$2,000	Total current receipts	$2,000

The deduction of these costs from current receipts leaves a profit residual, the return to the factor entrepreneurship, of $285,000. From this profit residual the corporation paid profits tax of $148,000 and $100,000 to stockholders in the form of dividends. The remaining $37,000 represents retained earnings which may be used for working capital, future expansion, and the like.

The two sides of the income statement for the firm must balance. The right side gives the total receipts, and the left side shows the way these receipts were allocated among the various items of cost and to profit. Profit is the

[1] This total will appear on the right side of the income statements of the other firms in the economy.

[2] This total is the net sum of interest paid minus interest received. Interest received is not treated as a current income receipt as is income derived from the sale of product.

balancing item, which may be positive, negative, or zero depending upon the relative magnitudes of receipts and costs.

Although the income statements of the individual producing units within the economy are the basis of the national accounts, they do not give all the information necessary to construct the accounts. This is because an income statement does not show total production, but only current sales. A firm may sell more than it produces by drawing down its inventory of finished products, or it may sell less than it produces. Only when the physical change in inventory is zero does the right side of the income statement equal the value of current production.[1] Consequently the net change in inventories must be known if current production, as opposed to current sales, is to be determined.

In Table 2-2 the income statement of Table 2-1 has been revised into a production statement. The differences between the two tables result from the fact that a different bundle of goods is under consideration. The right side of Table 2-2 includes the value of an inventory increase, while the factor costs on the left side have been adjusted to include the production costs of the goods added to inventory. Because in this example the net change in inventory is positive, the value of total production as shown in Table 2-2 is greater than the total receipts shown in Table 2-1. Had the corporation sold more than it produced during the accounting period, the opposite would have been the case. The right side of Table 2-2 would have shown a total value of production of less than $2,000,000. Costs and profit on the left side would also have been smaller, being only those amounts attributable to the actual current production.

Table 2-2 Production statement for the X Corporation for the period January 1, 1961, to December 31, 1961 (thousands of dollars)

Allocations		Receipts	
Purchases from other firms........	$ 820	Sales to:	
Wages and salaries..............	846	Company A...................	$ 810
Social security contributions.......	27	Company B...................	240
Net interest....................	20	Company C...................	650
Depreciation...................	60	Company D...................	175
Indirect business taxes...........	30	Other sales....................	125
Corporate profits before tax.......	297	Inventory increase..............	100
Corporate profits tax.....$155			
Dividends paid......... 100			
Undistributed profits..... 42			
Allocation of the total value of			
production...................	$2,100	Total value of production........	$2,100

Although the total value of production of the X Corporation was $2,100,000, the corporation's contribution to final output was somewhat less than this.

[1] Inventories of other than finished goods are ignored in the problem.

The X Corporation purchased raw materials and partly finished goods from other firms, increased their value by further processing, and either sold the finished product to others or added it to inventory. The amount by which the corporation increased the value of the materials received from other firms is shown by the difference between the total value of production and the cost of materials purchased (intermediate product). This difference is called the "net value added" or the "value of final product." It is this net value added that is the contribution of the X Corporation to the final national product. To include the total value of production for each productive unit would be to count the value of some goods over and over again as they moved through the economy.

A simplified illustration will help to make this point clear. Take for example a loaf of bread purchased by a consumer. Assume that four productive units contributed to making and distributing the bread. Suppose that the value of the grain produced by the farmer was 5 cents, that the total value of production (for the loaf of bread) for the miller was 12 cents and for the baker was 20 cents, and that the grocer sold the loaf of bread for 25 cents. To add together the total values of production shown in the several production statements gives a total value of 62 cents. But the final consumer paid only 25 cents for the loaf of bread. The correct answer of 25 cents is derived by adding together the net value added of each productive unit. The net value added by the farmer (assuming he purchased no goods or materials from others) is 5 cents. The net value added by the miller is 7 cents (12 − 5). Similarly, the net value added for the baker is 8 cents, and for the grocer 5 cents. The sum of the net-value-added figures is 25 cents, or the cost of the loaf to the ultimate consumer. The 62-cent figure resulted from counting the 5 cents of value added by the farmer four times, the 7 cents of value added by the miller three times, the 8 cents of value added by the baker twice, and the 5 cents of value added by the grocer once.

There would be no need to consider this problem if the economy were so integrated that some firms produced only final product, and the other firms produced none. In that case the sum of the output of the former firms would represent total final product. In fact, of course, most firms produce both final and intermediate goods, so that the two must be distinguished for each firm before total national product can be derived.

Returning to Table 2-2, note that the net value added of the X Corporation will be exactly equal to the costs other than for intermediate product incurred by the corporation in production. That is, if the value of intermediate product is deducted from both sides of the production statement, the balance is not altered. This illustrates the fact that the net value added can be estimated either by adding together the factor and nonfactor costs incurred by an enterprise or by deducting the value of intermediate product from the total value of production. The national income accountant adds the net-value-added figure of a business unit to the flow of product (right side of the national accounts) and the equivalent total of costs incurred to the flow of income (left side of the national accounts).

2-3 The National Accounts

The business sector.   In addition to corporate enterprises, the business sector, as defined by the Department of Commerce, includes all organizations producing goods and services sold at a price intended to cover at least the cost of production. This definition is broad enough to include such government business enterprises as the Tennessee Valley Authority. Also included are unincorporated business enterprises such as family businesses, farm operators, independent professional practitioners, and lessors of real property. Finally it includes financial intermediaries such as banks, insurance companies, and other financial institutions.

A consolidated income and product account for the business sector of the American economy based on figures for 1961 is shown in Table 2-3.[1] Most of the items are familiar from the discussion of the production statement of the X Corporation given in Table 2-2. The presentation of certain items is, however, somewhat different. For example, the right side of Table 2-3 gives the sales figures of final product of all business units broken down by the sector that purchased the goods or services. The item "sales to business on capital account" represents the sales of capital goods to other businesses.[2] Capital goods are interbusiness sales of final product, and hence must be included on the right side of Table 2-3. The item "net change in inventory" is the current value of the total physical change in all inventories held by the business sector. Although this represents goods not sold, it is part of current production, and is therefore included in the flow of product.

The left side of Table 2-3 shows the costs incurred by business in the production of the goods and services shown on the right side. The subtotal "income originating" of $354 billion is the total factor payments by business. This total includes wages and salaries, the rental income of persons (including imputed rent), the net interest payments by business (interest paid minus interest received), and the profit of incorporated and unincorporated business. In each case the profit item includes an inventory valuation adjustment to take out of profits any element of inventory "gain" or "loss" resulting from price changes.

---

[1] In 1958 the Department of Commerce revised its method of reporting the *GNP* accounts in two ways that affect this discussion. First, it stopped reporting an accounting of the production statement of the business sector. Second, it revised the method of reporting the account of the foreign sector. See U.S. Department of Commerce, *U.S. Income and Output*, Chap. 5, U.S. Government Printing Office, Washington, 1958. We have retained the older method of presentation because we feel it gives a better insight into the structure of the accounts.

[2] This item also includes residential houses.

This ensures that the two sides will balance because the net change in inventory on the right side is valued at current prices.

Table 2-3   Consolidated business income and product account, 1961 (billions of dollars)

1.	Wages and salaries.............	$230		Sales to:	
2.	Social security contributions.....	9	15.	Consumers....................	$317
3.	Unincorporated business net		16.	Government.................	54
	income and inventory valua-		17.	Abroad......................	4
	tion adjustment............	47	18.	Business on capital account......	67
4.	Rental income of persons.......	12	19.	Net change in inventory........	2
5.	Net interest...................	12			
	Corporate profits and inventory				
	valuation adjustment........	44			
6.	Corporate taxes........ $22				
7.	Dividends paid........ 14				
8.	Undistributed profits... 7				
9.	Inventory valuation				
	adjustment........ 1				
10.	Income originating.............	354			
11.	Indirect business taxes..........	46			
12.	Charges against business				
	net product..............	400			
13.	Depreciation.................	44			
14.	Charges against business				
	gross product..............	$444	20.	Business gross product..........	$444

Source: This table and subsequent tables in Part I are based upon the national accounts of the United States for 1961 published in U.S. Department of Commerce, *Survey of Current Business, July, 1962,* U.S. Government Printing Office, Washington, 1962.

The item "rental income of persons" did not appear in Tables 2-1 or 2-2 because this category includes only certain rent payments. The Department of Commerce considers the ownership of a residential house as a business activity. Thus the homeowner is assumed to own the house as a "business" and to rent it to himself. The difficulty is that the rent does not take a monetary form, so it cannot be estimated directly. This means that the Department of Commerce must make an estimate of what the rent would be if it did take a monetary form. This imputed rent is added to the flow of income side of the accounts as "rental income of persons," and the taxes and depreciation on the house are added to the appropriate items. An equivalent total is added to the flow of product side of the account. "Rental income of persons" also includes the earnings of those lessors of property who are not primarily engaged in the real estate business. Real estate businesses are treated as any other business and their rental income is treated as part of the income of the business sector.

The treatment of taxes is one of the most troublesome problems in separating factor from nonfactor income in the consolidated business income and product account. This income-originating figure of $354 billion shown in Table 2-3 includes personal and corporate income taxes and social security contributions by employers,[1] but excludes indirect business taxes. Social security contributions can be easily justified as a factor cost on the ground that they represent a cost to the employer in hiring labor. The inclusion of income taxes as a part of factor costs and the exclusion of indirect business taxes are more difficult to justify. If the factor cost component of business product is to be a useful one, it should change in magnitude only if there is a change in factor employment or prices. It is on this basis that the Department of Commerce excludes from the factor cost total indirect business taxes, which include excise taxes, real property taxes, etc. A change in such a tax would cause a change in the factor income total without any corresponding change in employment or factor prices. On the other hand, there are grounds for assuming that a change in income taxes will not change the factor income total. An increase in the profits tax rate, for example, would probably not change total profits, or therefore the factor income total.

The addition of indirect business taxes to income originating gives the total charges against business net product shown as $400 billion in Table 2-3. If to this total is added depreciation allowances, the resulting total of $444 billion represents all the charges against the business gross product total shown on the right side of the account. The depreciation allowance of $44 billion is the sum of the estimates by the various business firms of the loss in value of their capital equipment resulting from wear and tear and obsolescence.

Personal sector. Consider next the income and product originating in the personal sector of the economy.[2] The first problem encountered in estimating the income and product of the personal sector is that there is no twofold measurement of output, in terms of both product and cost, as there is for the business sector. Because there is no transaction representing the sale of the product of a domestic servant, for example, as distinct from the purchase of the servant's services, the factor cost of the servant must be used also as a measure of the product he or she produces.[3]

The only other element of factor cost or income originating in the personal sector in addition to wage payments is interest paid by households and institutions to nonpersonal lenders. Interest paid on installment purchases is an example.[4] Interest paid on a loan from one's parents is excluded because such

[1] Employee contributions are included with wages and salaries.

[2] The personal sector is defined to include institutions of nonbusiness character such as universities, charitable organizations, and the like, as well as households.

[3] To be strictly correct, supplies and materials used by the servant should be deducted as intermediate product. No attempt is made to do so, however; all such purchases are considered final product. The servant who "lives in" receives income in kind, and this is imputed as part of factor cost.

[4] Mortgage payments by households are considered part of the income and product originating in the business sector of the economy.

payments cancel out in the consolidation of all households. If inter-household interest payments are netted out of the national product total, why are wages of servants included? The Department of Commerce believes that the result of the labor of servants represents a product which should be included as a part of national output. Interhousehold interest payments are viewed as a simple transfer of income rather than as the creation of final product. Notice that, because the included purchases by households are considered final product, total, final, net, and gross output of the personal sector are all equal.

Table 2-4 shows the income and product account of the personal sector for the United States based on the figures for the year 1961. The wages and salary total of $13 billion includes, in addition to money payments to factors, employer contributions to social security and the imputed value of payments in kind. Interest payments of $7 billion include nonmortgage interest payments of various kinds such as interest on installment loans.

Table 2-4   Income and product account for the personal sector, 1961 (billions of dollars)

1. Wages and supplements........... $13		
2. Interest paid.................... 7		
3. Income originating.............. $20	4. Net and gross product originating...	$20

Source: See Table 2-3.

Government sector. The net and gross product originating in the government sector of the economy is measured, as in the personal sector, by the value of factor services purchased. In the case of government, however, interest payments on public debt are excluded on the ground that such payments are not for a currently used productive service, as are wage payments.

The alternative would be to value the output of the government sector by the taxes paid by the community. In this case taxes would be treated as analogous to the prices paid for the output of the business sector. However, the use of such an approach is open to criticism. In the first place, taxes are obligatory payments, unlike prices paid for goods and services on the market. In addition, what meaning does this approach have during a period of government deficits or surpluses? During a period of deficit financing by government the community would presumably be undervaluing the services of government, and during a period of surplus it would tend to overvalue these services. It was just such problems of interpretation that persuaded the Department of Commerce to value government output by the cost of the labor services hired.

Given the above decisions, the actual formulation of an account for the government sector is a simple matter. Table 2-5 presents the account for the United States based on the figures for 1961. The income-originating figure of $51 billion is the sum of wages and salaries paid to government employees including the armed forces, plus government contributions to social security. The total also includes an imputed value of food and personal issue of the armed forces, as well as wages and salary payments of government employees (including armed forces) in positions requiring them to live abroad, who nevertheless are considered American residents. The same total of $51 billion appears on the right side of the account as net and gross product originating in government.

Table 2-5 Income and product account for the government sector, 1961 (billions of dollars)

1. Wages and salaries............... $50		
2. Social security contributions....... 1		
3. Income originating.............. $51	4. Net and gross product originating.... $51

Source: See Table 2-3.

Rest-of-the-world sector. Some of the income and product originating in the United States accrues to foreigners who control factors of production situated in this country. On the other hand, some of the income originating in foreign countries accrues to American residents who own factors of production located abroad. Income and product originating in the rest-of-the-world sector is defined as the net movement of such factor payments to American residents. Thus the total can be negative if American residents pay more factor income to foreigners than vice versa. The use of factor income payments to measure output originating in the rest-of-the-world sector is identical to the procedure followed in estimating the product originating in the personal and government sectors. Table 2-6 presents the account for the rest-of-the-world. The left side itemizes the net factor payments under four headings, and the right side gives the same total as the measure of net and gross product.

Table 2-6 Income and product account for the rest-of-the world sector, 1961 (millions of dollars)

1. Wages and salaries (net)........ $ 20		
2. Interest (net)................. 700		
3. Dividends (net).............. 1,000		
4. Branch profits (net)........... 1,000		
5. Income originating............ $2,720	6. Net and gross product originating $2,720

Source: See Table 2-3.

There is no necessity for a rest-of-the-world sector at all. The profits of an American branch plant located abroad could be entered directly with the consolidated business income and product account. Similar consolidations could be made for the other items of net factor payments shown in Table 2-6.

But particular interest attaches to these net flows originating in the rest-of-the-world, and for this reason the Department of Commerce includes a separate account for such transactions.

National income and product account. Having derived the income and the net and gross product originating in the four sectors, it becomes a simple matter to combine them into a national total. Table 2-7 presents such a total using the income and product figures of Tables 2-3 through 2-6. The right side of Table 2-7 lists the product originating, and the left side gives the factor and nonfactor costs incurred in the production of that total output. Every item in the table is followed by numbers in parentheses. These numbers indicate where the item appears in the tables given previously. The item "indirect business taxes," for example, is shown in Table 2-7 with the code (3.11). This indicates that indirect business taxes appeared previously as item 11 in Table 2-3.

Table 2-7 National income and product account by sector or origin, 1961 (billions of dollars)

Income originating in:			Net and gross product originating in:		
Personal sector	$ 20	(4.3)	Personal sector	$ 20	(4.4)
Government sector	51	(5.3)	Government sector	51	(5.4)
Rest-of-the-world	3	(6.5)	Rest-of-the-world	3	(6.6)
Business sector	354	(3.10)	Gross product originating in		
National income	428		business sector	444	(3 20)
Indirect business taxes	46	(3.11)			
Total charges against net					
national product	474				
Depreciation	44	(3.13)			
Total charges against gross					
national product	$518		Gross national product	$518	

Source: Tables 2-3 to 2-6. The code numbers used in this table refer to entries in Tables 2-3 to 2-6. See text.

The sum of the factor costs, $428 billion, is known as national income—the total income of factors from participation in the current productive process. The addition of indirect business taxes to national income yields $474 billion, the total charges against net national product.

Finally, the addition of depreciation charges yields $518 billion, the total charges against gross national product.

Although Table 2-7 is a perfectly correct presentation of the gross national product account, considerably more light can be thrown on the anatomy of the total by a slightly different presentation. This alternative formulation is the one used by the Department of Commerce in its published accounts. This method presents the flow of product classified by the sector purchasing it rather than by the sector of origin. Also, the flow of income is classified by type of factor payment rather than by sector of origin.

Since we are interested in the sector purchasing the nation's output rather than the sector producing it, the rest-of-the-world account must be reformulated to show, in addition to net factor payments, the net exports of goods and services between American residents and the rest-of-the-world. Table 2-8 is such an extension of Table 2-6. Again, it is presented in net terms. Table 2-8 shows that American business sold $4 billion more goods and services to foreigners than they purchased. On the other hand, the personal and government sectors purchased more from foreigners than they sold.[1] The total of net factor payments from abroad and net sales (positive and negative) abroad represents net exports of goods and services from the United States to the rest-of-the-world. If positive, it means that the United States accumulated foreign credits; if negative, that foreigners accumulated credits in the United States. In 1961, the United States accumulated $4 billion in foreign credits by exporting $4 billion more goods and services than she imported. Table 2-8 shows that these credits (foreign debits) were covered by the transfer of United States Government funds to foreigners in the amount of $1 billion and by $3 billion made available to foreigners by American investment abroad.

Table 2-8   Foreign transactions account, 1961   (billions of dollars)

1. Wages and salaries (net).........	*	10. Transfer payments from United	
2. Interest (net)....................	$1	States Government...........	$1
3. Dividends (net).................	1	11. Net foreign investment...........	3
4. Branch profits (net)..............	1		
5. Income originating and net and gross product...............	3		
Net purchases from the United States:			
6. From business...................	4		
7. From government..............	−2		
8. From persons..................	−1		
9. Net exports of goods and services..	$4	12. Net payments to abroad...........	$4

* Less than $0.05 billion.
Source: See Table 2-3.

Table 2-9 presents the customary formulation of the gross national product account. All the figures used have been derived from Tables 2-3 to 2-5 and 2-8. Every item in Table 2-9, with the exception of wages and salaries, has the same two-part code used in previous tables.

[1] Government purchases do not include grants made to foreign countries.

Table 2-9 National income and product account, 1961   (billions of dollars)

Wages, salaries, and supplements		$303
Unincorporated business net income and inventory valuation adjustment		47 (3.3)
Rental income of persons		12 (3.4)
Net interest		20 (3.5, 4.2, 8.2)
Corporate profits and inventory valuation adjustment		46
Corporate tax	$22 (3.6)	
Domestic dividends	14 (3.7)	
Foreign dividends	1 (8.3)	
Undistributed profits (domestic)	7 (3.8)	
Foreign branch profits	1 (8.4)	
Inventory valuation adjustment	1 (3.9)	
National income		428
Indirect business taxes		46 (3.11)
Charges against net national product		
Depreciation		44 (3.13)
Charges against gross national product		$518

Personal consumption expenditures		$338
Direct services		$ 20 (4.4)
From business		317 (3.15)
From abroad		1 (8.8)
Gross private domestic investment		69
Business purchases on capital account		67 (3.18)
Net change in inventory		2 (3.19)
Net export of goods and services		4 (8.9)
Government expenditures		107
Direct services		51 (5.4)
From business		54 (3.16)
From abroad		2 (8.7)
Gross national product		$518

Source: Tables 2-3 to 2-5 and 2-8. The code numbers used in this table refer to entries in Tables 2-3 to 2-5 and 2-8.

The wages and salaries total of Table 2-9 does not carry a code number because it is made up of five items, which would be too clumsy to include in the table. The derivation of the total is shown below.

Derivation of wages, salaries, and supplements   (billions of dollars)

Wages, salaries, and supplements from:

Business..	$230	(3.1)
Business (Social Security)............................	9	(3.2)
Personal sector......................................	13	(4.1)
Government..	50	(5.1)
Government (Social Security)	1	(5.2)
Rest-of-the-world....................................	*	(6.1)
	$303	

* Less than $0.05 billion.

Gross national expenditure.   A final method of presenting the data appearing in the gross national product account is presented in Table 2-10. This statement, in which items are listed by type of expenditure, corresponds to the form used in Chapter 1. Only the product flow side of the account is presented; the income side is the same as shown in Table 2-9.

The Department of Commerce groups all consumer expenditures into three categories on the basis of durability. Goods consumed at the moment of purchase are classified as services; those consumed within a year are classed as nondurable commodities; and those lasting more than a year are considered durable commodities. Gross private domestic investment is divided into three categories: construction, producers' durables, and net changes in inventory. Finally, government expenditures are divided between Federal expenditures on the one hand and state and local expenditures on the other.

Table 2-10   Gross national expenditures by type of commodity, 1961 (billions of dollars)

Consumer expenditure...................................		$338
Durables..	$ 44	
Nondurables.......................................	155	
Services...	139	
Gross private domestic investment......................		69
Construction......................................	42	
Producers' durables................................	25	
Net change in inventory............................	2	
Net export of goods and services.......................		4
Government expenditure................................		107
Federal...	57	
State and local....................................	50	
Gross national product................................		$518

2-4   Summary

The gross national product total is a measure of the flow of final goods and services resulting from current production by Americans during a year. For each sector of the economy, an account is constructed showing the final, or unduplicated, output for all the units within the sector. Transactions between units within a sector are, in general, netted out in deriving final output. With the exception of business purchases of capital goods, which are clearly a part of final output, transactions between firms are netted out. Transactions between units in the personal sector, such as employment of domestic servants, are included as part of final product.

For the purpose of the accounts the consumer is considered to be at the center of the economic process. Anything which contributes to his present or future well-being is considered final product and is included in the account.

The actual structure of the accounts follows closely the accounting practices developed in business. Each transaction is recorded twice, representing the two sides of economic activity—a flow of product and a flow of income. The accounts therefore show who purchased the final output and how the income resulting from this productive activity was divided between the various elements of factor and nonfactor cost.

chapter 3

Conceptual problems in the estimation of gross national product

3-1 Introduction

Although the national product account for the economy as a whole is a combination of the consolidated current income and product accounts for the various sectors of the economy, the derivation of a national account is more than just a matter of simple addition. At every turn the income accountant is faced with fuzzy boundary areas that must be sharply delimited before he can proceed. At all such ambiguous points someone must make a decision about the procedure to be followed by the accountant. This chapter is concerned with these conceptual issues of national accounting.

As a general rule, we shall follow the conceptual judgments of the Department of Commerce accounts because these accounts are the most widely known, are the most up-to-date, and, because of the detail they present, have found the widest acceptance of any system of accounts. From time to time, however, alternative judgments will be presented for purposes of comparison.[1]

[1] The conceptual framework of the official national accounts is contained in U.S. Department of Commerce, *National Income Supplement, 1954*, U.S. Government Printing Office, Washington, 1954. See also Simon Kuznets, *National Income and Its Composition, 1919–1938*, Vol. I, Chap. 1, National Bureau of Economic Research, New York, 1941; Simon Kuznets, "National Income: A New Version," *Review of Economics and Statistics*, 30:151–179, 1948; G. Jaszi, E. F. Denison, M. Gilbert, and C. F. Schwartz, "Objectives of National Income

3-2   The Product to Be Included

The definition of economic activity. A gross national product account measures the value of the current output of economic activity. Economic activity involves the use of scarce resources (including time) in the provision of goods to satisfy unlimited wants. An economic good provides satisfaction, is relatively scarce, and is disposable. It may take the form of a tangible good such as an automobile or a loaf of bread, or it may take an intangible form such as the service furnished to a patient by his doctor or to a student by his teacher. But to include any activity providing a good or service meeting these three conditions is far too wide a task for the income accountant. To do so would mean that the national product total would include the activity of shaving oneself, because it does not differ from the same activity when carried on by a barber. It is obviously impossible to include the value of such personally rendered services in the national product accounts.

A line must therefore be drawn between goods that can be called "economic" because they result from economic activity and those goods and services which, although they provide satisfaction, result from the general activity of life. Fortunately, a convenient means of separating the two types of activity is readily available. Economic goods include goods appearing on markets, and economic activity includes only activities producing marketable goods.[1] All such goods or services will render satisfaction, will be scarce, and will be disposable. This general rule can be applied to any particular country at any point in time, but its usefulness is obviously restricted to highly developed countries at recent points in time. The farther one gets from a highly developed market economy, the less useful is the rule for distinguishing economic activity from the general activity of life.

It is important to realize the implications of this rule. For one thing, it means that many of the activities carried on within the household are excluded from the measurement of a nation's product. The most obvious example is the product of the activity of the housewife. The value of the meal cooked by the housewife and her effort in cooking it are excluded from economic activity, while the same activity carried on in a restaurant is considered to be economic activity. If, on the other hand, housewives cooked each other's meals and received payment for their efforts, cooking the meals would then be economic activity and the gross national product would be increased tremendously.[2]

Measurement: A Reply to Professor Kuznets," *Review of Economics and Statistics*, 30:179–195, 1948; and M. Gilbert and I. B. Kravis, *An International Comparison of National Products and the Purchasing Power of Currencies*, Chap. 6, Organization for European Economic Co-operation, Paris, 1954 (?).

[1] Some exceptions to the generality of this rule will be given later.

[2] The cost of intermediate product would have to be deducted from the selling price of the meals to arrive at the addition to national product.

The classification of activity carried on within the household as noneconomic is a generally accepted principle in income accounting. But it is accepted for practical rather than theoretical reasons. The difficulty of valuing the output of such activity is so great as to preclude its measurement entirely. Note that acceptance of the classification makes both intercountry comparisons and intertemporal comparisons within the same country of doubtful validity. Consider for a moment a comparison of national product estimates made for India and the United States. It is obvious that much activity considered economic in the United States because it takes place through markets is considered noneconomic in India because it takes place within the household. For example, when an Indian housewife bakes bread for her family, the value of the bread is excluded from Indian national product. The value of a loaf of bread purchased at a supermarket by an American housewife is included in American national product. Similarly, when comparing the national product of the United States in 1870 with that in 1958 there is the problem of an upward bias in the estimates due to the decrease in family activity.

There is no doubt that the degree of comparability between the national products of the United States and India, or of the United States at different times, is affected by the exclusion of some family activity. But there is a real question whether the value of such activity can be quantified, and whether or or not, even if quantifiable, it should be included in national product. If the concept of national product is to have any meaning at all, it must be restricted to the output of economic activity defined as the use of scarce resources which have alternative productive uses. It is not clear that the labor of the Indian housewife is a scarce resource; even if it is, there is the problem of valuing her output, which means assigning a value to the production lost because she decided to bake bread. Her time spent baking bread is quite possibly leisure time from an economic point of view because the labor service is not taken from the total supply of scarce factors of production. The bread is therefore no more a product than the coffee table produced in a home workshop by an American in his leisure time.

Excluded market transactions.   In the discussion thus far the assumption has been made that all market transactions involve goods or services that should be included in the national product total. But not all payments made represent exchanges of goods and services, and not all changes in the value of goods result from economic activity. The market transactions excluded from the national product total can be classified into three categories: transfer payments, capital gains, and illegal activities.

Transfer Payments.   Transfer payments are those payments of income that do not result from current productive activity. If a business firm distributes $100,000 in prize money for a contest held to publicize its product, the prize money, while representing a current expense to the firm, is a payment that differs fundamentally from a factor payment. The prize money is not a pay-

ment for a productive service currently used in producing a final good or
service.[1] A transfer payment, unlike a factor payment, constitutes a redistribution of income and is excluded from national product.[2]

The three levels of government are the largest source of transfer payments
in the American economy. The recent growth in nondefense expenditures of
American government has resulted from the increased duties imposed on
government involving the redistribution of income. This redistribution of
income by government takes a wide variety of forms, but in each case the
payments are transfers of income, and hence are excluded from the national
product total. Examples of government transfer payments include the great
variety of payments under the social insurance program, payments to veterans
under the GI bills, and direct relief payments.

One further type of government payment which is excluded from the
national product total is interest on the public debt. The rationale for exclusion
rests on the ground that the size of the debt is not closely related to the value
of the physical assets of government because it has arisen largely as a result of
deficit financing during wartime. If the debt were closely related to the value
of government physical assets, interest payments would be included as an
estimate of the current return on these assets. Some countries do indeed include
interest on the debt of the lower levels of government on the ground that this
debt was incurred to finance existing real assets. Other countries go further
and include an interest charge measured by applying the current rate of interest
on long-term government debt to the current value of the physical assets of all
levels of government as carried on the government's balance sheets.

Transfer payments of other kinds are excluded for similar reasons. Gifts, in-
heritances, and charity payments are examples of excluded income payments.[3]
Furthermore, a payment made for a tangible good is excluded if the good is not
produced currently. The purchase price of a medieval painting is excluded
from the accounts because the transaction represents a transfer of assets
rather than a payment for current productive activity. If, however, the art
dealer has restored the painting, the value of the restoration, estimated by its
cost (minus the cost of materials used), would be entered in the national total

[1] The cost to the firm of administering the contest represents an intermediate product and
is therefore excluded from national product.

[2] It should be noted in passing that no attempt is made by the Department of Commerce
to distinguish between wage payments on the basis of some definition of "productiveness."
Some countries exclude pay and allowances of armed forces personnel from their national
product total on the ground that these are not payments for a currently produced good or
service and hence are really transfer payments. The American accounts make no such
distinction. Wages include any compensation for current performance of work. Nonmoney
income payments will be discussed later.

[3] Net international gifts by persons and government are included in personal and government expenditure but are canceled out in the accounts by the inclusion of the same total with
opposite sign in the net foreign balance.

of productive activity. Thus the factor costs incurred by the art dealer, including profits on current activity, are entered on the income side of the account, and the corresponding value of the current activity of the art dealer is entered on the product side of the account. In the case of charitable institutions where there is no sale of product, factor payments must be used as the estimate of both income and product originating.

Capital Gains and Losses. Capital gains and losses are examples of changes in value resulting from market forces that nevertheless are excluded from the national product total. Suppose, for example, that the value of an existing capital asset, perhaps a house, increases as a result of monetary inflation. In this case the increase in market value is excluded from the national product total because the increase was not a result of current productive activity. It differs in this fundamental respect from the increase in the value of a house resulting from additions, say a new wing, made to it currently. The increase in the value of this second house (minus the cost of materials used in the addition) would be included in the measure of national productive activity. While it is true that realized capital gains are considered income by the tax authorities, these gains are excluded from national product because they do not result from current economic activity. Thus if a house is sold for a gain, all the net return would be taxed even if part of the appreciation in the value of the house resulted from monetary inflation. The same argument applies to capital gains on common stocks which are taxed by the Internal Revenue Service but which are excluded from the national product.

Another example of capital gains and losses is the change in asset valuation resulting from exogenous shifts in consumer demand. When consumers suddenly shift from 78-r.p.m. to LP records, it is obvious that gains and losses for various firms will result. But the gains and losses did not result from current economic activity, and hence they are excluded from national product. For similar reasons a sudden increase in the value of a tract of western grazing land because of the discovery of oil or of desolate land in Colorado because of the discovery of uranium are excluded. The increase in the value of the land over the previous investment in it is the result of an exogenous shift in demand.[1]

In general, those changes in the values of goods that result from ungovernable or unpredictable causes are treated as accidental shifts in the conditions of production outside economic activity proper. Those changes in value that can be anticipated and insured against, such as fire and flood, are also excluded because the adjustments for such shifts, i.e., insurance premiums, have been charged against the operations of previous years. Changes in asset valuation resulting from depreciation are subject to special treatment, which will be considered later.

[1] If discoveries of new natural resources are not included, the depletion (depreciation) of natural resources cannot be included as a charge against national product.

Illegal Activities. The final category of market transactions excluded from national product is illegal activities. This is a category of market activity excluded by all national income accountants. It is true that such transactions involve satisfactions for which a price is paid, and if this were the only basis for inclusion, such activities could not be omitted. But the national accounts attempt, as far as possible, to be a measure of socially useful economic activity. Although those who participate in illegal markets might be willing to defend their social usefulness, the fact that such activities are outlawed by society is taken to be sufficient ground for their exclusion.

This question of an individual versus a social judgment of productivity raises a wider issue. The implicit assumption behind a national product total is that the products of all economic activity, not excluded on other grounds, have a positive satisfaction for all members of society. The product of the distillery is included on the same basis as the product of the Bible publishing house. Longer and higher fins on automobiles are included as product, though they may be anathema to some. In general, it is not always true that the product of economic activity provides satisfaction to everybody. The old adage that "one man's meat is another man's poison" expresses the point adequately. But the problem goes deeper than that. Suppose a paper mill dumps its waste into a stream and pollutes the water. The product of the paper mill is included in national product, but so are the expenses of the communities that must purify the water before it can be used. There is a real question, therefore, whether the product of the paper mill should not be reduced by the expenses incurred by others as a result of its operation.

The best answer to the problem would be to devise a calculus by which the satisfaction to each individual, and to society as a whole, from possession of a good or service could be measured. The national product total would then measure the net additions to social satisfaction of the flow of output from current economic activity. An account constructed on this basis would be truly a social account.

Such a calculus is completely out of the question, and any approximation to it would involve unnecessary arbitrariness. For society has already indicated in the legal code the activities that are not considered socially productive, and the national accountant includes all legal activity without distinction. Note that the acceptance of this criterion by the Department of Commerce is a departure from the production concept that is the general basis for the inclusion of the output of economic activity. Furthermore, such a criterion is a changing one, for social mores differ between countries at any point in time and in the same country at different times. The prohibition era in the United States is a good example of the latter.

Nonmarket activities. We have already seen that not all money income flows are included in national product. At the other extreme, the national product total includes an imputed value of some goods and services that do not appear on markets. As a general rule, an imputed value is assigned to nonmarket activities if this makes the accounts internally comparable, if the nonmarket good is clearly separable from its source, and if an imputed value can be clearly and easily assigned.

Some workers receive part of their pay in the form of room and board rather than in the form of money wages.[1] To assure conformity with other workers who receive their total remuneration in the form of money wages, a value is imputed to the payment in kind received and added to money wages. This procedure is followed although the cost to the employer of the food used to provide the meals would under ordinary circumstances be excluded, as are other intermediate products.

Another example of imputed valuation arises in the case of output retained by a producer in order to consume it himself. This arises primarily in agriculture where the farmer frequently retains part of the produce of the farm for his own consumption. An imputed value is assigned to this retained production and included in total national output. This is a case where the nonmarket activity can be estimated with a fairly high degree of certainty and where the assignment of a value is relatively easy because there are market equivalents.

The third example of imputed valuation arises in the field of residential housing. If a family rents a house or an apartment, the rent payments (minus the cost of upkeep and repair) are a measure of the value of the output of the real estate industry. In the case of owner-occupied houses, however, no rent is paid explicitly, even though a house is a substantial source of satisfaction to the homeowner. It is also true that an automobile is a substantial source of satisfaction, although no imputed value is given to the services of the automobile owned by an individual. A house differs in that the service rendered is easily separable from the house itself, and an imputed value can be readily assigned by using rent payments as a guide.

The final example of imputation arises in the case of financial institutions such as commercial banks, insurance companies, and mutual trust funds. Such institutions provide a service and pay costs that cancel each other out. The example of an individual with a regular or checking account will illustrate this. The individual receives no interest on his deposit, although he could earn interest on the money were he to invest it. At the same time the bank makes only a nominal charge (perhaps with the requirement that a minimum balance be held) for safeguarding the money and processing the checks drawn against the account. Instead of paying interest on the money and then charging for services rendered, the bank cancels the one against the other. For the purposes of estimating national product, however, an imputed value must be given to these transactions if the total output of economic activity is to be evaluated. The other financial intermediaries have similar nonmonetary flows that must be allotted an imputed value.

[1] This category includes also food and personal issue of armed forces personnel.

3-3   Final and Intermediate Product

Final product. Thus far the discussion has been concerned with the distinction between economic and noneconomic activity. But as was pointed out in Chapter 2 with the example of a loaf ot bread, what is wanted is an unduplicated total that measures only the flow of goods to the ultimate consumer. The Department of Commerce defines such a final good as one produced and/or purchased but not resold during the current accounting period. Goods purchased for resale, with or without further processing in the physical sense, are termed "intermediate goods," and all such goods are excluded from the national product total.

Some additional examples will help to clarify the distinction. If a steel mill purchases a million tons of coal and uses nine-tenths of it during the accounting period, that much coal is considered intermediate product. The one-tenth that is not used currently is considered final product and is entered in the accounts as a net change in inventory. On the other hand, all coal purchased by a householder for home heating is final product. To take another example, suppose the steel mill purchases a machine. This machine is a final product, but that part of it used during the current accounting period is intermediate product and should be excluded from the accounts.[1]

The distinction between final and intermediate products obviously depends upon the definition of a productive enterprise. The example above of coal purchased for home heating would not hold if the household were considered a productive enterprise selling its labor services as its product. In this case the coal purchased by the householder would be considered intermediate product—product necessary for the further production of the firm. For the same reason the clothing, food, recreation, and shelter purchased by households would be considered intermediate product and therefore would be excluded from the national product total. Also, the cost of raising and educating children would be analogous to the costs of repair and maintenance of the capital stock of a business enterprise. To extend the definition of the productive enterprise to include the family unit is unthinkable, given the philosophies of most countries. Human beings are fundamentally different from machines. At the same time it means that the national product total is internally inconsistent when a distinction is made between the gross and net return on capital,[2] while no distinction is made between the gross and net return on wage earners.

Another result of treating households as final consumers is worth considering. A businessman traveling on an expense account can deduct such expenses from his income as a cost of operation, and the national income accountant will similarly deduct the expenses as intermediate product. The wage earner

---

[1] This intermediate product, the depreciation of capital equipment, is subject to particular difficulties, which will be discussed later.

[2] See the discussion on depreciation at the end of this chapter.

who must commute to his job cannot, however, treat such costs as an expense, and the national income investigator will count commuting costs as purchases of final product. Similarly, when a business buys water to use in its operations, the water is assumed to be intermediate product. When a householder buys water, it is assumed to be final product.

As the United States has become more and more an urbanized nation, the expenditures connected with urban living such as commuting, garbage collection, sewerage, and water supply have increased. Some investigators have contended that these expenditures by consumers should not be considered as expenditures for final products but rather as costs or offsets to urban living. Such products should, they contend, be treated as intermediate rather than as final. The argument is essentially that products should be counted as final if the consumer purchases them for the independent contribution they make to his welfare. Such investigators would exclude commuting costs, for example, because they are an expenditure resulting from urban living, i.e., an expense the consumer would not have if he did not live in the city. In other words, final product should be limited to those purchases the consumer would desire to make if he were not engaged in economic activity.

The answer given by the Department of Commerce is that this argument is fundamentally wrong and would lead to arbitrary measures of national product. Any attempt, for example, to divide the purchase price of a car by a wage earner into a production expense and a real consumption expense would of necessity be so arbitrary as to be worthless. In general, it is impossible to separate on any objective basis the ends and means involved in every consumer expenditure. Even if it were possible to make such a division, the Department of Commerce would contend that it was unnecessary. The wage earner who drives to work has a number of alternatives. He can walk, ride a bicycle, or take a bus. It is only reasonable to assume that if he drives his car he enjoys a product by so doing, and the value of the product he receives is equal to the expenses he incurs. All expenditure by the consumer is assumed by the Department of Commerce to be expenditure for final product.

In answer to the contention that the concept of intermediate product should be expanded to include substantial portions of consumer expenditure, the Department of Commerce argues that, even if it were possible to separate from each expenditure that amount representing real consumption, it would be a mistake to do so. Why should an increase in production resulting from increased urbanization be excluded if an increase in food production resulting from larger appetites is included? If Americans were not better off because of the existence of cities, they could always devote the resources to some other use. The fact that they do live in cities means that their product is greater, and the national product statistician must take account of this.

Net and gross investment. The distinction between net and gross national product hinges upon the fact that gross real capital formation includes the production of goods to replace elements of the capital stock worn out during the current period. Although the depreciation of a physical asset represents an intermediate product in the same way that coal used by a steel mill is intermediate product, the national product total given by the Department of Commerce includes depreciation. For that reason, the accounts are internally inconsistent; they include the net flow of goods and services to consumers, but the gross flow of capital goods. The inclusion of depreciation is necessary because it is almost impossible to estimate it on a basis comparable to that for other items in the product.[1]

Capital goods are divided into two general categories: the net change in inventory and the production of physical capital assets. Because depreciation does not enter into the net change in inventory, our concern in this section is only with real capital formation.

A real capital good is any good ordinarily consumed in a period greater than a year, generally as a result of its use in production. Real capital formation includes, in addition to producers' durables, construction activity of all kinds undertaken by business enterprises and residential construction.[2] The latter is considered capital formation rather than an ordinary consumption expenditure because home ownership is considered a business by the Department of Commerce.[3]

In calculating its depreciation allowance, a firm must take into account both the wear and tear of a piece of capital equipment and the decline in its relative efficiency as a result of obsolescence. The output attributable to the piece of equipment does not therefore represent a net addition to the flow of product.

Suppose, for example, that a lathe is used to produce a second exactly similar lathe; that this process takes the whole of the accounting period; and that the first lathe depreciates to zero in the process. Gross capital formation during the period is equal to one lathe. Net capital formation—the change in the stock of capital—is zero.[4] The number of lathes produced is exactly equal to the number of lathes consumed. If the original lathe is used to produce two of its kind during the accounting period, while itself depreciating to zero, gross capital formation will be equal to two lathes, while net capital formation will be equal to one. It is obvious that, while net real capital formation can be posi-

---

[1] The valuation of depreciation will be discussed later.

[2] Public construction (construction by government) is included by the Department of Commerce with other purchases of goods and services by government.

[3] Residential construction is the only expenditure by households that is not considered a consumption expenditure; any other good is assumed to be consumed by the household when purchased. This is obviously not the case with respect to automobiles and other durables. But because there is no practical way of estimating that part of the value of a durable consumed in any period of time, these goods are assumed to depreciate to zero within the accounting period.

[4] This assumes that prices do not change. Price changes will be discussed in the next section of this chapter.

tive, zero, or negative, it is never possible for gross real capital formation to be less than zero.

For the economy as a whole, if that part of the capital stock worn out during the process of production is exactly replaced by the current production of capital goods, then net real capital formation for the economy is zero. If current capital formation is greater than the depreciation of the existing capital stock, the capital stock has been increased and net capital formation is positive. On the other hand, if the capital stock is reduced during the accounting period, net capital formation is negative.

As has been suggested, the problem of estimating the depreciation of the capital stock is a difficult one. If a machine is used more intensively in one year than in another, the actual depreciation of the machine would differ between the two years. But the business firm, having chosen a particular method of depreciation, is obliged to adhere to that method, irrespective of the actual intensity of use.[1] Moreover, the actual depreciation of identical machines will differ between business firms. Whereas one firm may wear out a machine in two years, another firm may be able to utilize the same machine for six years. If both machines are depreciated by the firms over a two-year period, both net national product and the size of the capital stock will be underestimated over the six-year period. If, on the other hand, the machines are depreciated over a six-year period, the reverse will be the case.

An additional difficulty is that a large part of the annual depreciation charges recorded for the economy represent obsolescence rather than the physical wearing out of capital equipment. In the American economy, in which rapid technological advances are continually being made, no business enterprise could afford to depreciate its capital equipment at a rate measuring only physical wear and tear. To do so would mean a continual loss of competitive position in favor of those firms depreciating at a more rapid rate and replacing their capital equipment as more efficient ones come on the market. Depreciation allowances recorded by business firms may therefore differ considerably from the actual depreciation of capital equipment.

Considerations such as the above are almost impossible to allow for in constructing a net national product total. Consequently, the Department of Commerce presents a gross national product total which, as we have seen, involves the inclusion of some intermediate product. In other words, gross investment is entered on the product flow side of the account instead of the difficult-to-estimate net investment. As a consequence an estimate of depreciation must be added to the income flow side to ensure that the two sides balance. Notice that if a correct estimate of depreciation could be derived, there would be no change in the gross national product total; only the relative size of the depreciation and profit items would change.

In summary, the gross national product total as estimated by the Depart-

[1] The Internal Revenue Service sets maximum permissible depreciation rates.

ment of Commerce includes the final output of the business, government, and foreign sectors of the economy plus a small product originating in the household. Of those goods not appearing on markets, only the imputed value of payments in kind to employees, retained output of producers, rental values of owner-occupied houses, and the nonmonetary income and product flows of financial intermediaries are included. Excluded are the money payments representing transfers of income, capital gains and losses (whether realized or not), and gains resulting from illegal activities.

Up to this point the product to be included in the gross national product total has been decided. Still to be determined is the way this product is combined into a comprehensive total.

3-4 Valuation of the Product

The use of market prices. The diversity of the goods and services produced within the economy dictates that a common unit of measurement be used to combine them into a meaningful total. The only reasonable common unit is the dollar value of each good and service produced, although this does create certain problems. The Department of Commerce views its measure of national product as a measure of productivity and uses market prices to arrive at the total because no more convenient substitute is available.

There is, however, an alternative interpretation, which views the gross national product total as a measure of welfare. This interpretation is based on the contention that prices, as determined by the dollar votes of consumers, represent the social value of goods. In this view, an increase in national product per capita represents an increase in welfare, and intercountry welfare differences can be measured by differences in national product per capita.

But each consumer does not have the same number of dollar votes. The distribution of income is such that there are families at one end of the income scale that can do no more than provide for the necessities of life, while at the other end there are families that have no difficulty in living lavishly. Market prices therefore are an imperfect measure of the satisfaction derived from a good, when such prices reflect only those demands that can be backed by purchasing power.

Furthermore, consider a comparison of American gross national product between 1929 and 1958. Can it be stated that all the increase in gross national product measures an increase in welfare, when $40 billion was spent in 1958 for defense? Does air travel, which is a new addition to national product, represent a net addition when people are subjected to the noise associated with airports?

Finally, the welfare view is untenable in the case of intercountry comparisons. Canadian gross national product, for example, contains a large element of product associated with the relatively severe climate, but this item would not be included in the product of countries with more temperate climates. This does not mean, however, that Canadians are necessarily better off in a welfare sense. To appreciate this point, one has but to consider that in Elysium, where there is no economic activity, gross national product is zero.

Imputations.   The general problem of imputing value to nonmarket goods and services is solved by the Department of Commerce by assigning to them the value of identical or similar goods and services that do pass through markets. The trouble with this approach is that if the goods or services did appear on markets, market prices might change. A further problem arises from the fact that retained production or payments in kind may be of an inferior quality. To the extent that they are inferior, valuation by the prices of the nearest market equivalent will overstate the value of total production. A difficulty of a somewhat similar nature arises if those receiving payments in kind value such payments at less than market price. If such is the case, the factor cost as entered in the accounts overstates the true opportunity cost of the factors of production. Fortunately the actual magnitudes involved are relatively small, and erroneous imputations create only minor errors in the totals.

When the decision is made to include such goods at the value of their market equivalents, the adjustment of the accounts is a simple matter. In the case of retained farm production, the imputed gross value is added to consumption expenditure on the product side of the account, and an imputed net profit from farming is added on the income side. The difference between the gross and net figures is added to the appropriate expense items on the income flow side. In the case of payments in kind, the imputed value of these payments is added to consumption expenditure on the product side, and wages are increased by the same value on the income side.

The imputed rental value of owner-occupied houses is handled in a similar way. In effect, owning a house is conceptually separated into two transactions. The homeowner is assumed to own the house as a business and to rent the house to himself as a consumer. Thus the value of the output of the business sector of the economy is increased by the imputed gross rental payments, in the same way that rent payments to a real estate company are included in the value of output of the real estate industry. A net rental figure is entered on the income side of the account under net rent payments of persons. The difference between gross and net rent consists principally of depreciation and indirect business taxes that are included under the appropriate items on the income side. Materials purchased for the maintenance of an owner-occupied house are intermediate products of the business sector and hence do not enter the accounts.

Financial intermediaries such as commercial banks, investment funds, and life insurance companies raise another problem of imputation. A commercial bank, for example, holds customers' deposits in return for service charges collected on the number of checks drawn against the account. The value of the bank's final output is represented by the revenue received from the sale of its services minus its purchases from other firms. But the service charges actually assessed by the bank are such a small part of the value of the services rendered to depositors that the product of the bank will appear to be very small or even negative. The reason for this apparently nonsensical situation is that depositors pay for services received in a nonmonetary form. If a meaningful output figure for the bank is to be derived, a value must be imputed to these nonmonetary flows. The imputed money interest on checking accounts is assumed to be equal to the interest received by the bank from its loans minus the interest it actually pays on savings accounts. This total is entered on the income side of the gross national product account. The same total is entered on the product side of the account as the market value of the services provided by the bank. The imputed interest total is allocated between the three sectors on the basis of relative sizes of accounts held by each. Only the interest payments to individuals and to government actually enter the gross national product account; imputed interest to business representing an intermediate product is netted out of the total.

Inventory valuation. If the gross national product is to include a measure of the total output of the nation, it must take account of changes in inventories. Thus if a steel mill adds to its inventory of finished steel products during the year, it is clear that this increase represents current output and must be included in the gross national product. Also, if finished steel inventories are reduced during the year, total sales must have exceeded total production, and the inventory change will have to be deducted from the flow of product side of gross national product. At the same time, an increase in the inventory of iron ore held by the steel company represents current production not consumed as intermediate product; hence the increase must be included in the total of the nation's output.

It would appear to be a relatively simple matter to take figures of the net change in the physical volume of inventory (positive or negative), multiply by current prices, and add the resulting figure to total output. Not all business units, however, keep track of changing inventories, and those that do, keep records not in terms of physical units but in terms of value. This in itself is not a difficulty. The problem arises because items of inventory may be carried over more than one accounting period, because prices frequently change in the interim, and because the firm's record of inventory is generally kept in terms of original cost.

Suppose, for example, that over an accounting period the steel company sells some of its finished product inventory carried over from a previous period and adds to the inventory out of current production, so that there was a net increase in the physical volume of inventory. Suppose further that the whole period was one of rising steel prices. Because the units of inventory are carried on the books of the firm at their original cost, the units withdrawn will reduce the value of inventory held less than the added, currently produced units will increase it. The change in the book value of inventories will therefore overstate the actual physical change that occurred.

The similarity between this type of monetary gain (or loss) and capital gains and losses is obvious. Just as capital gains and losses are excluded from gross national product, so an inventory valuation adjustment is made to correct for gains and losses in inventory valuation resulting from price changes or other reasons. A negative inventory valuation adjustment means that "gains" were made in the book value of inventories as a result of rising prices. That is, the changes in the book value of inventories overstate the physical changes. A positive inventory valuation adjustment means that "losses" were made as a result of falling prices. The adjustment is added algebraically to the net change in inventories on the product side of the account and to business profits on the income side. The adjustment ensures that the actual physical change in inventories is measured in current prices—a necessary condition because all other current production is valued at current market prices.

Depreciation. The problem of valuing the depreciation of the capital stock is one of the most troublesome in the field of national income accounting. The problem is basically twofold. When the economist says that net investment is zero, he means that the nation's capital stock has been maintained unchanged. But what is the meaning of "keeping capital intact" in an economy in which the efficiency of capital equipment is constantly being improved? A further difficulty is that, as in the case of inventory, capital equipment is generally carried on a company's books at original cost rather than at current value or current replacement cost. In the case of inventory which has a relatively short life, the problem of estimating current value is not too difficult. But in the case of capital equipment, with a life of up to fifty years and more, the problem becomes in practice insurmountable.

The practical answer has been to accept business records as a measure of depreciation without attempting to rework the estimates in terms of current replacement cost. This means that depreciation is the only item in the accounts not on a current cost basis. For these reasons the Department of Commerce gives no estimate of net national product or net capital formation, but gives instead the gross total, even though it includes an admittedly intermediate product not valued at current prices.

3-5 Summary

The gross national product total published by the Department of Commerce is a measure, at current market prices, of the flow of final output resulting from the economic activity of American residents during a selected accounting period.

Economic activity is defined as the use of scarce resources to produce goods and services yielding satisfaction. The use of market prices to value the output produced is a practical matter and does not imply any concept of social welfare.

The total output includes some goods and services that do not appear on markets valued at their market equivalents. On the other hand, some market activities are excluded because they do not represent current socially productive activity or because they merely represent redistribution of income.

The national product total is generally an unduplicated one, including only additions to the flow of goods and services to consumers and the flow of capital goods. Any good purchased for resale in the current period is an intermediate good and is excluded from the final product total. The flow of capital goods raises serious problems for the accountant because of the difficulty of measuring the depreciation item. Here the Department of Commerce does include an intermediate product, depreciation, and moreover values it at other than current prices.

chapter 4

Sector accounts

4-1   Sector Accounts

As was shown in the last chapter, the national product estimates omit various flows, such as transfer payments, that have a useful economic meaning. Consequently the Department of Commerce supplements the national income and product accounts with complete current accounts for the personal and government sectors. We have then added current accounts for the business and foreign sectors. These accounts detail the interrelated transactions between sectors and thus provide a clearer picture of the economic structure of the nation than could be gained from the product account alone. In addition, the Department of Commerce publishes a consolidated savings and investment account for the economy as a whole. The purpose of this chapter is to examine these so-called "sector accounts."

The sectors discussed in this chapter are the same as those introduced previously—business, personal, government, and rest-of-the-world. It should be understood that there is nothing sacred about this particular sectoring of the economy. For some purposes it would be useful to sector the economy geographically; for others, to sector on an industrial basis. The sectoring used here has proved most useful for the type of analysis that follows in later chapters.

The business sector. The current account for the business sector is the same as that of Table 2-3. All current activity of the business sector is considered economic activity and is therefore included in gross national product. The account is shown here as Table 4-1.

Table 4-1 Consolidated business income and product account, 1961 (billions of dollars)

1. Wages and salaries	$230 (2.9)		Sales to:	
2. Social Security contributions	9 (3.16)		15. Consumers	$317 (2.4)
3. Unincorporated business net income and inventory valuation adjustment	47 (2.13)		16. Government	54 (3.4)
			17. Abroad	4 (4.6)
4. Rental income of persons	12 (2.14)		18. Business on capital account	67 (5.1)
5. Net interest	12 (2.17)			
Corporate profits and inventory valuation adjustment	44		19. Net change in inventory	2 (5.2)
6. Corporate taxes $22 (3.13)				
7. Dividends paid. 14 (2.15)				
8. Undistributed profits 7 (5.5)				
9. Inventory valuation adjustment 1 (5.6)				
10. Income originating	354			
11. Indirect business taxes	46 (3.14)			
12. Charges against business net product	400			
13. Depreciation	44 (5.8)			
14. Charges against business gross product	$444		20. Business gross product	$444

Source: See Table 2-3. The code numbers used in this table refer to entries in Tables 4-2 to 4-5.

The procedure used in Chapter 2, in which each item in some tables carries a two-part code, is followed here. Thus item 1 of Table 4-1, "wages and salaries," is followed by the code (2.9) to indicate that it appears as item 9 of Table 4-2. Similarly, when the item appears in Table 4-2, it carries the code (1.1).

The personal sector. The income and expenditure account of the personal sector is shown in Table 4-2. This table shows the total expenses and receipts between the personal sector and the other sectors of the economy.[1] The account includes the income and net (and gross) product originating (see Table 2-4) as well as other items not included in gross national product, such as transfer payments.

[1] Wages, supplements, and imputed income of personal servants are considered both an expense and a receipt of the personal sector.

The largest source of receipts of the personal sector is wages and salaries, which appear with the sector of origin. As can be seen from the table, the business sector is the major source of labor income. Income of unincorporated business enterprises (plus the inventory valuation adjustment) is also included as part of the receipts of the personal sector. These receipts include income of professional practitioners, income from farm operations, and the like. Rental income and dividends (domestic and foreign) are expenses of the business sector, but are receipts of the personal sector. All unincorporated business income is treated as a receipt of the personal sector because no satisfactory method has been found to break this total down into its component parts, as is possible with corporate income. In the case of corporate income, only dividends accrue to persons, and therefore they are the only part of corporate profits included among the receipts of the personal sector.

Table 4-2 Personal income and expenditures, 1961   (billions of dollars)

Purchases of direct services:		Wages and supplements from:	
1. Wages and supplements.	$ 13 (2.11)	9. Business.................	$230 (1.1)
2. Interest paid..........	7 (2.18)	10. Government..............	50 (3.1)
3. Income originating and		11. Households..............	13 (2.1)
net and gross		12. Abroad..................	* (4.1)
product..........	20	13. Unincorporated business net	
4. Purchases from business	317 (1.15)	income and inventory	
5. Purchases from abroad..	1 (4.8)	valuation adjustment...	47 (1.3)
6. Personal taxes........	53 (3.12)	14. Rental income of persons...	12 (1.4)
7. Saving................	25 (5.9)	Dividends...............	15
		15. Domestic... $14 (1.7)	
		16. Foreign.... 1 (4.3)	
		Personal interest income....	27
		17. Business.... 12 (1.5)	
		18. Persons.... 7 (2.2)	
		19. Abroad.... 1 (4.2)	
		20. Government 7 (3.9)	
		21. Transfer payments......	32 (3.7)
		22. Minus, personal Social	
		Security payments.....	−10 (3.15)
8. Personal outlay and			
saving...........	$416	23. Personal income.........	$416

* Less than $0.05 billion.
Source: See Table 2-3. The code numbers used in this table refer to entries in Tables 4-1 to 4-5.

Personal interest income represents total interest receipts of persons from business, from other persons (shown also as an expense of persons[1]), from

[1] This item would ordinarily be netted out in the consolidation of the personal sector. Because it is included as part of income originating in the personal sector, it must also appear on the expense side of the account.

abroad, and from government. The interest figure of $27 billion is $7 billion greater than the interest figure that appears as part of the income flow in the gross national product account. This $7 billion is the amount of government interest payments to persons; although a part of the receipts of persons, it is considered a transfer payment and is therefore excluded from gross national product. The remaining item of personal receipts includes all other government transfer payments including those made to foreigners. Personal Social Security contributions, which are a personal expense, are nevertheless shown on the receipts side of the sector account but with a negative sign. This procedure is followed because these contributions represent a deduction from wage and salary receipts as far as the personal sector is concerned.

The expenses of the personal sector include the purchases of direct services (income originating and net and gross product) already included on the receipts side of the sector account. In addition, the payments to business for goods and services purchased by the personal sector are included, along with the net purchases by households from abroad. The final expense of the personal sector is the personal taxes paid to all levels of government. This total therefore includes, in addition to income taxes, all forms of state and local taxes.

The savings of the personal sector are shown as $25 billion. This is a balancing item, the difference between receipts and expenditures. Thus savings are the total left over after the personal sector has covered its expenses; this can, like the balancing items in other accounts, be positive, negative, or zero.

The government sector.   The government receipts and expenditure account shown in Table 4-3, like the personal sector account, records total receipts and expenditures including those transactions that do not appear as part of gross national product. In addition to the flows resulting from general government activity, Table 4-3 includes receipts and disbursements of social insurance funds administered by all levels of government.

The receipts side of the government sector includes three major tax items that account for the largest part of total government receipts. The personal taxes of $53 billion are expenses of the personal sector; an additional $68 billion is derived from the business sector; the remaining receipt items are those of the various social insurance funds administered by all levels of government. These funds are shown in Table 4-3 with the sector of origin.

The first entry on the expenditure side of the account shows the costs of the purchases of direct services by government. This total of $51 billion is also the amount of income originating and the net and gross product of government. In the personal sector, income originating and net and gross product appear as both an expense and a receipt. This does not occur in the case of the government sector, where only social security contributions by government to employees appear on both sides of the account. Wages and salaries paid by government are an expense of government and a receipt of households.

In addition to direct services, government purchases goods and services from business and from abroad. Both totals are shown as net purchases of goods and services. The meaning of the word "net," as used here, is not the same as in the phrase "net value added," for government is considered a final consumer and purchases no intermediate product. It is net in the sense that sales to business and foreigners are deducted from government purchases from these sectors to derive the net flow of product.[1]

Table 4-3   Government receipts and expenditures account, 1961   (billions of dollars)

Purchases of direct services:		Receipts from:	
1. Wages............... $ 50 (2.10)		12. Personal taxes.......... $ 53 (2.6)	
2. Social Security payments. 1 (3.17)		13. Corporate taxes........ 22 (1.6)	
3. Income originating and net		14. Indirect business taxes.... 46 (1.11)	
and gross product... 51		Social Security receipts... 20	
4. Purchases from business.. 54 (1.16)		15. Persons. $10 (2.22)	
5. Purchases from abroad... 2 (4.7)		16. Business 9 (1.2)	
6. Transfer payments...... 33		17. Govern-	
7. To per-		ment . 1 (3.2)	
sons.. $32 (2.21)		18. House-	
8. To for-		holds . *(2.1)	
eigners 1 (4.10)			
9. Net interest paid........ 7 (2.20)			
10. Minus, surplus or deficit. −6 (5.10)			
11. Government expenditures			
and surplus........ $141		19. Government receipts.... $141	

* Less than 0.05 billion.

Source: See Table 283. The code numbers used in this table refer to entries in Tables 4-1 to 4-5.

The final two expenditures items are transfer payments and net interest paid by government. The government makes interest payments on public debt to sectors other than the personal sector; but because it is impossible to segregate government interest payments by the sector that receives them, the Department of Commerce considers that any interest payment to other than the personal sector eventually arrives at the personal sector anyway. Thus interest payments to business will increase business profits and will be distributed to the personal sector in the form of dividends. Therefore the whole net interest figure of $7 billion appears as a receipt of the personal sector. The final item— the balancing item—is the deficit or surplus on current government activity. In 1961 there was a deficit of $6 billion.

The rest-of-the-world sector. The account for the rest-of-the-world shown in Table 4-4 is identical with that of Table 2-8. As explained there, the

[1] These are sales resulting from general government activity. Sales by government business enterprises are included in the business sector. Sales of surplus materials would be an example of general government sales to business.

account is entirely in net terms, recording on the left side the net residual of the flow of goods and services across the boundaries of the continental United States. If the net flow is into the United States, it is recorded with a positive sign. The total of $4 billion shown in Table 4-4 means that Americans received $4 billion more from foreigners than they paid to foreigners. The $4 billion Americans received for their net output of goods and services sold to foreigners represents part of American output and is included as part of American *GNP*. Foreigners met this debt through their earnings of American dollars from American investments of $3 billion in foreign countries and by a grant of $1 billion from the United States Government.

Table 4-4   Rest-of-the-world account, 1961   (billions of dollars)

1. Wages and salaries (net)...	* (2.12)	10. Transfer payments from
2. Interest (net).............	$1 (2.19)	United States government $1 (3.8)
3. Dividends (net)...........	1 (2.16)	11. Net foreign investment...... 3 (5.3)
4. Branch profits (net).......	1 (5.7)	
5. Income originating and net		
and gross product.....	3	
Net purchases from the		
United States:		
6. From business.........	4 (1.17)	
7. From government.......	−2 (3.5)	
8. From persons..........	−1 (2.5)	
9. Net exports of goods and		
services.............	$4	12. Net payments to abroad..... $4

* Less than $0.05 billion.

Source: See Table 2-3. The code numbers used in this table refer to entries in Tables 4-1 to 4-3 and 4-5.

The gross saving and investment account.   This final account, shown in Table 4-5, does not record the transactions of a separate sector. However, the account is of particular importance and is therefore included. Each of the sector accounts given above includes a residual item, representing some form of saving, which appears only once in the sector accounts, while every other item has appeared twice—once as a receipt and once as an expenditure. The savings items appear only once because they represent transactions with capital rather than transactions with current accounts. Thus personal savings do not represent the purchase of a currently produced good or service. They show that $25 billion of personal receipts was not spent. The purpose of the gross savings and investment account shown in Table 4-5 is to draw together all these capital items into one account.

Much will be said in later chapters about the equality of savings and investment. It should be made clear at this point that the equality shown by the fact that the two sides of Table 4-5 balance results because only realized, or actual, savings and investments are recorded. The account must of necessity balance.

The right side of the account lists personal savings, the government surplus or deficit, and corporate savings which include undistributed earnings of domestic corporations and foreign branch profits (net). Because unincorporated business profits cannot be distinguished from unincorporated business net income, no unincorporated profit or inventory valuation adjustment can be included.

Table 4-5   Gross saving and investment account, 1961   (billions of dollars)

1. Business purchases on capital account.. $67 (1.18)	Corporate saving.............. $53	
2. Net change in inventory.......... 2 (1.19)	5. Undistributed profit........ $ 7 (1.8)	
3. Net foreign investment.......... 3 (4.11)	6. Inventory valuation adjustment 1 (1.9)	
	7. Foreign branch profits....... 1 (4.4)	
	8. Depreciation.... 44 (1.13)	
	9. Personal saving............... 25 (2.7)	
	10. Minus, government surplus or deficit................... −6 (3.10)	
4. Gross investment... $72	11. Gross saving.................. $72	

Source: See Table 2-3. The code numbers used in this table refer to entries in Tables 4-1 to 4-4.

It will be noted that the saving-investment account is given in gross terms. As explained in Chapter 3, the Department of Commerce has not been successful in deriving a net investment total because it has proved impossible to derive an adequate current price estimate of depreciation. For this reason the depreciation item of $44 billion must be added to the right side to balance the gross business purchases on capital account shown on the left side. The other investment items are net changes in business inventories and net investment by the United States in the rest of the world.

A full understanding of the interrelated structure of the economy is facilitated by an examination of the five accounts given here in conjunction with the gross national product account discussed in Chapter 2. The *GNP* account taken by itself leaves out many transactions that do not result from current economic activity. Moreover, the consolidation of the data into one account hides many flows between sectors. The sector accounts presented in this chapter supplement the gross national product account by including flows that would otherwise be ignored and by making explicit other transactions that are important in economic analysis.[1]

[1] Gains resulting from illegal activities and capital gains and losses are excluded from both the gross national product and the sector accounts.

4-2   A Simplified System of Accounts

The sector accounts presented above are devised to present the maximum amount of statistical information in such a way that they can be used readily for a number of different purposes. For the purposes of this book, further consolidation, to reduce the complexity of the accounts, will facilitate subsequent analysis.

The basis of this further consolidation is to divide the economy into the same number of sectors, but to assume that all income and product originate in the business sector. Thus the incomes originating in the personal and government sectors shown in Tables 4-2 and 4-3 are now assumed to be purchases from the business sector, with the factor payments then being paid by the business sector to persons. Finally, the business sector is assumed to handle all foreign transactions. Under these assumptions the receipt and expenditure account of the business sector will be the same as the gross national product account shown in Table 1-9.

In the business sector account of Table 4-6 the item "payments to the personal sector" of $387 billion is made up of the income originating in the personal sector ($13 billion) and wages and salaries paid by the government sector ($50 billion) plus income originating in the business sector. This latter item is composed of wages and salaries ($230 billion), unincorporated net income and inventory valuation adjustment ($47 billion), rental income of persons ($12 billion), net interest payments ($19 billion domestic, $1 billion foreign), dividends ($14 billion domestic and $1 billion foreign). Direct taxes are composed of the corporate income tax ($22 billion) plus the social security payments by business, government, and households ($10 billion), all of which are now assumed to be paid by business. Business saving of $9 billion is the algebraic sum of undistributed earnings ($7 billion), inventory valuation adjustment ($1 billion), and foreign branch profits ($1 billion).

Table 4-6   Business sector and gross national product, 1961   (billions of dollars)

Payments to the personal sector	$387	Sales to consumers	$338
Direct taxes	32	Net exports of goods and services.	4
Corporate profits tax $22		Government expenditure	107
Business and government Social		Gross private domestic investment	69
Security payments 10			
Corporate saving	9		
National income	428		
Indirect business taxes	46		
Capital consumption allowances	44		
Gross national product	$518	Gross national product	$518

Source: See text.

The subtotal of $428 billion shown in Table 4-6 is therefore national income at factor cost — the direct factor cost of producing the nation's output. The addition of the nonfactor costs, indirect business taxes and depreciation, gives the total charges against gross national product.

Table 4-7   Personal sector account, 1961   (billions of dollars)

Payments to business..............	$338	Receipts from business.............	$387
Payments to government...........	63	Receipts from government..........	39
Personal tax.............. $53		Interest................. $ 7	
Personal Social Security		Transfers 32	
payments.............. 10			
Personal saving...................	25		
Personal payments and saving.......	$426	Personal receipts.................	$426

Source: See text.

The right side of Table 4-6 shows the receipts from the sale of all goods and services in the economy as receipts of the business sector. The sales-to-consumers figure of $338 billion is the sum of business sales to consumers ($317 billion), purchases of direct services by persons ($20 billion), and purchases by persons from abroad ($1 billion). Similarly, government expenditures of $107 billion are made up of business sales to government ($54 billion), purchases of direct services by government ($51 billion), and government purchases from abroad ($2 billion). Finally, the net change in inventory ($2 billion) has been added to business purchases on capital account to derive a gross private domestic investment total of $69 billion. The net export of goods and services has been left as a separate item.

Table 4-8   Government sector account, 1961   (billions of dollars)

Payments to business..............	$107	Receipts from persons.............	$ 63
Transfer payments................	40	Receipts from business............	78
Interest................. $ 7		Direct taxes.............. $32	
Domestic................ 32		Indirect taxes............ 46	
Foreign................. 1			
Minus, surplus or deficit...........	−6		
Government payments and deficit....	$141	Government receipts..............	$141

Source: See text.

Table 4-7 presents the summary account for the personal sector. The transactions between this sector and the business sector have already been explained in connection with Table 4-6, but the transactions with the government sector require explanation. Payments to government are shown as $63 billion, although in Table 4-2 they are shown as $53 billion. The $10 billion difference results from transferring personal Social Security contributions from the receipts side of the personal sector account, where the Department of Commerce places it, to the expense side and including it with personal taxes. This changes the balance of the personal sector account from $416 billion (Table 4-2) to $426 billion. On the right side of Table 4-7, the receipts of the personal sector from government are the sum of transfer payments ($32 billion) and net interest paid by government ($7 billion). Finally, the personal sector shows an excess of receipts over expenditures, personal saving, of $25 billion.

All the items of the government sector account shown in Table 4-8 have already been explained in connection with Tables 4-6 and 4-7.

The rest-of-the-world account shown in Table 4-9 requires no explanation.

Table 4-9 Rest-of-the-world sector, 1961   (billions of dollars)

	Transfer payments from United States Government...................... $1
	Net foreign investment............... 3
Net exports of goods and services..... $4	Net payments to abroad.............. $4

Source: See text.

The capital account shown in Table 4-10 is presented in a different form from that in Table 4-2. The depreciation item has been separated from business purchases on capital account to show a net investment figure. This is done in spite of the warnings given above about the practical difficulties faced in estimating the current value of depreciation. The concept of net investment is such an important one in subsequent analysis that even though it has no operational equivalent, we will nevertheless assume that it is equal to gross investment minus depreciation.

Table 4-10 Saving and investment account, 1961   (billions of dollars)

Net investment....................	$25	Business saving....................	$ 9
Depreciation.....................	44	Personal saving....................	25
Net foreign investment............	3	Government deficit.................	−6
		Depreciation......................	44
Gross investment.................	$72	Gross saving......................	$72

Source: See text.

4-3 Income Identities

The fact that each transaction between the sectors of the economy appears twice in the sector accounts makes the form of a matrix a convenient way to present an over-all picture of the economy. Table 4-11 presents a matrix based on the accounts shown in Tables 4-6 to 4-10. Although the sector accounts have a total of 30 items, the matrix shows only 18 items. In fact, the matrix would have shown only 16 items if indirect business taxes and depreciation had not been separated out for special purposes. In Table 4-11 each row represents a payment, the left side of a sector account, while each column shows the corresponding receipt entered on the right side of another sector account. For example, consumption expenditure of $338 billion is shown, reading across the table, as an expense of the personal sector and also, reading down the table, as a business receipt.

Some basic income identities can be readily derived from Table 4-11. The following notation is used for ease of presentation:

Gross national product = GNP
Net national product = Y
National income = NI
Disposable income = Y_d
Consumption expenditure = C
Government expenditure = G
Net exports = $X - M$
Net foreign investment = I_f
Net domestic investment = I_r
Personal receipts = R_p
Transfer payments (domestic) = T_r
Transfers to foreigners = T_f
Personal saving = S_p
Government saving = S_g
Business saving = S_b
Direct taxes (persons) = T_p
Direct taxes (business) = T_b
Indirect taxes = T_i
Depreciation = D

From column 1 of Table 4-11,

$$GNP \equiv C + G + (X - M) + I_r + D \qquad (4\text{-}1)$$
$$518 \equiv 338 + 107 + 4 + 25 + 44$$

Gross national product is the sum of the expenditures by all sectors in the economy. Again, from column 1,

$$Y \equiv GNP - D$$
or
$$Y \equiv C + G + (X - M) + I_r \qquad (4\text{-}2)$$
$$474 \equiv 338 + 107 + 4 + 25$$

The net national product total represents the net additions to the flow of goods and services to individuals, either directly from business (domestic and foreign) or through government, and to the capital stock. That is, net national

Table 4-11 Income and product flow matrix (billions of dollars)

	Receipts								
Payments	*Business*	*Persons*	*Government*	*Net foreign payments*	*Net saving*	*National income*	*Indirect business taxes*	*Depreciation*	*Total*
Business............		$387(R_p)$	$32(T_b)$		$9(S_b)$	$428(NI)$	$46(T_i)$	$44(D)$	518
Persons.............	$338(C)$		$63(T_p)$	$1(T_f)$	$25(S_p)$				426
Government.........	$107(G)$	$39(T_r)$			$-6(S_g)$				141
Net exports........	$4(X - M)$								4
Net investment.....	$25(I_r)$			$3(I_f)$					28
Net national product..	$474(Y)$								
Indirect business taxes....			$46(T_i)$						
Depreciation........	$44(D)$								
Total............	518	426	141	4	28				

Source: See text.

product is gross national product less depreciation or, alternatively, the expenditures by the personal and government sectors and the net additions to the capital stock.[1]

From row 1

$$GNP \equiv R_p + T_b + S_b + T_i + D \qquad (4\text{-}3)$$

but from column 2 and row 2,

$$R_p + T_r \equiv C + T_p + S_p$$

or
$$R_p \equiv C + T_p + S_p - T_r \qquad (4\text{-}4)$$

and from column 3 and row 3,

$$T_b + T_p + T_i \equiv G + T_r + T_f + S_g$$

or
$$T_b + T_i \equiv G + T_r + T_f + S_g - T_p \qquad (4\text{-}5)$$

Substituting (4-4) and (4-5) into (4-3), we have

$$GNP \equiv C + T_p + S_p - T_r + G + T_r + T_f + S_g - T_p + S_b + D$$

or
$$GNP \equiv C + S_p + G + T_f + S_g + S_b + D \qquad (4\text{-}6)$$

Equating (4-1) and (4-6), we have

$$(X - M) + I_r + D \equiv S_p + S_g + T_f + S_b + D$$

Remembering that $(X - M) - T_f \equiv I_f$, we have

$$I_f + I_r + D \equiv S_p + S_g + S_b + D \qquad (4\text{-}7)$$
$$3 + 25 + 44 \equiv 25 - 6 + 9 + 44$$
$$72 \equiv 72$$

This identity represents both sides of the gross saving and investment account (Table 4-10).

Netting depreciation out of identity (4-7), we have

$$I_f + I_r \equiv S_p + S_g + S_b$$
$$3 + 25 \equiv 25 - 6 + 9$$
$$28 \equiv 28$$

which represents the equality of net saving and net investment.

The identity of saving and investment plays a large part in the subsequent analysis. In the accounts it is clear that saving and investment have been defined as equal. That part of final output not purchased by consumers and government has been called "investment" and must by definition be equal to that amount of receipts not paid out for final goods or services by persons, government, or business.

---

[1] Both the change in inventory and the net exports are given in net terms.

National income may also be obtained by subtracting indirect taxes from Y.

$$Y - T_i \equiv NI$$
$$474 - 46 \equiv 428$$

National income may also be obtained by adding total personal income payments to direct business taxes and net business savings. Accordingly, from row 1,

$$NI \equiv R_p + T_b + S_b$$
$$428 \equiv 387 + 32 + 9$$

Further, from column 2 and row 2,

$$R_p + T_r \equiv C + T_p + S_p \qquad\qquad (4\text{-}8)$$
$$387 + 39 \equiv 338 + 63 + 25$$

The left side of identity (4-8) lists personal income (factor payments plus transfers to persons from government); the right side shows the way persons dispose of their income: consumption expenditures for goods and services, direct taxes, and saving.

If personal taxes are transposed in identity (4-8), the left side becomes personal disposable income, i.e., total income receipts of persons minus their tax payments.

$$R_p + T_r - T_p \equiv C + S_p \equiv Y_d$$
$$387 + 39 - 63 \equiv 338 + 25 \equiv 363$$

Disposable income, as shown by this identity, can be either spent (C) or saved (S_p).

Disposable income can be derived from the net national product total subtracting from Y that part which does not accrue to persons and adding government transfer payments to persons. Thus

$$Y_d \equiv Y - (T_i + T_p + T_b) + T_r - S_b$$
$$363 \equiv 474 - (46 + 63 + 32) + 39 - 9$$

Finally, let

$$T_i + T_p + T_b - T_r \equiv T$$
$$46 + 63 + 32 - 39 \equiv 102$$

where T is defined as net taxes, so that

$$Y_d \equiv Y - T - S_b$$
$$363 \equiv 474 - 102 - 9$$

Notice, moreover, that the government surplus can be calculated by subtracting government expenditures and transfers to foreigners from net taxes. Thus

$$S_g \equiv T - (G + T_f)$$
$$-6 \equiv 102 - (107 + 1)$$

4-4 Summary

In this first part of the book we have presented a fairly detailed picture of the national income and product accounts as developed by the Department of Commerce. At various stages in the discussion we pointed out that in some details the accounts are, for practical reasons, not always consistent. At the same time, there is an underlying rationale to the accounts that overrides the practical difficulties of estimation. The underlying rationale derives from the attempt to measure the annual flows of income and final product in the economy as a basis for evaluating the economy's utilization of its economic resources. In presenting figures the Department of Commerce tries at the same time to give those that will fit into the body of economic theory from which evaluation and predictions can arise.

As the discussion in Chapter 1 indicated, the annual volume of output is determined by the expenditures for final goods and services, which, in turn, are related in part to the incomes received by the units making expenditure decisions. Therefore, the *GNP* account is broken down by the Department of Commerce in terms of income receipts by economic units and expenditures by the same units.

In Part II we shall examine the factors underlying the expenditure decisions of the economic units and the effects of these decisions upon the volume of final output. From such a study, and with the picture of the economy derived from the national accounts in mind, we shall be in a position to understand what determines the level of national output and to suggest measures that may be employed to affect that level.

part II

The Level of Economic Activity

chapter 5

Consumption, savings, and the simple
theory of income determination

5-1 The Consumption Function

In Chapter 1 we observed that there is a close relationship between aggregate consumption expenditures and the level of disposable income. This relationship leads to one of the central propositions of the theory of income determination: The consumption expenditures of the community are determined principally by the community's level of disposable income. The schedule that relates consumption to disposable income is called the "propensity to consume" or "the consumption function," or sometimes also the schedule of "intended consumption."

A consumption function for a hypothetical economy is shown in Figure 5-1. Disposable income is measured on the horizontal axis. Consumption is measured on the vertical axis. The 45-degree line is a guideline which denotes that any point on the line is equidistant from the two axes. This means that the distance from the origin to some point on the horizontal axis will be the same as the vertical distance from that point on the horizontal axis to the 45-degree line. The level of disposable income can therefore be measured either vertically to the 45-degree line or along the horizontal axis.

The consumption function is drawn as a straight line with a slope of less than one. Although no one would seriously argue that the straight-line assumption is not an oversimplification, it is not enough of a distortion to justify the added complication of introducing a nonlinear schedule. The slope of the consumption function, or "marginal propensity to consume," indicates the percentage of each additional dollar of disposable income that will be consumed. The value of the marginal propensity to consume is less than unity because it is assumed that out of each additional dollar of disposable income received the community will increase its consumption by some percentage of the dollar and save the remainder.

An additional assumption is that there is some level of disposable income ($100 billion in Figure 5-1) at which all disposable income is consumed. Below this disposable income level (often called the "point of zero savings") consumers will make expenditures in excess of their disposable income even though this means dissaving, i.e., dipping into past savings or going into debt.

The marginal propensity to consume is, in the example of Figure 5-1, assumed to be 0.75. The point of zero saving is assumed to occur when disposable income is $100 billion. But as disposable income rises to $200 billion, consumption rises by only 0.75×100, which means that savings must rise by

Figure 5-1   The consumption and savings functions   (all values in real terms).

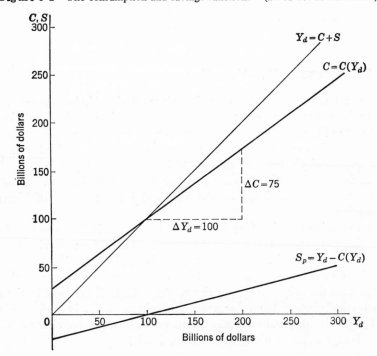

0.25 × 100. When disposable income is $200 billion, consumption expenditures must therefore be $175 billion, and savings must be $25 billion. At disposable income levels below $100 billion the community is so poor that it prefers to go into debt rather than spend only its current disposable income on consumption. If it were possible to reduce disposable income to zero dollars, consumption would fall to $25 billion. Personal savings would therefore be −$25 billion.

In addition to the consumption function, Figure 5-1 also includes the schedule of intended personal savings, S_p. This schedule is simply the difference between the consumption function and the 45-degree line. The slope of the savings schedule, called the "marginal propensity to save," is always one minus the marginal propensity to consume. In the present example, the marginal propensity to consume is 0.75. The marginal propensity to save is therefore 0.25 because any addition to disposable income that is not spent must, by definition, be saved.[1]

5-2   Simple Income Determination

As a means of getting the analysis off the ground in an uncomplicated manner, let us visualize an economy in which there is no government, in which corpora-

---

[1] Algebraically we may summarize what has been said thus far as follows: The hypothesis that consumption is a function of disposable income can be written

$$C = C(Y_d)$$

where C stands for aggregate real consumption and Y_d represents aggregate real disposable income. In the event that the consumption function is linear,

$$C = C_0 + \mathbf{b}Y_d$$

where $\mathbf{b}$ is the marginal propensity to consume and C_0 is the level of consumption at zero disposable income. In the present example $\mathbf{b} = 0.75$. Therefore

$$C = C_0 + 0.75Y_d$$

From Figure 5-1 it is evident that at an income level of $100 billion savings are zero. Consumption is therefore equal to disposable income at this point. Accordingly,

$$100 = C_0 + 0.75 \times 100$$

so that

$$C_0 = 25$$

The equation for the schedule of intended consumption therefore becomes

$$C = 25 + 0.75Y_d$$

Because personal savings are simply the difference between consumption and disposable income,

$$S_p = Y_d - C = Y_d - 25 - 0.75Y_d = -25 + 0.25Y_d$$

is the equation for the savings function.

tions retain no earnings, in which there is no foreign trade, and in which the level of net intended investment is geared to long-term expectations and is therefore independent of the level of current income. Without any government or retained earnings, disposable income and real *NNP* (*Y*) are identical. The national income accountant's framework in this economy is

$$Y = C + I_r \qquad (5\text{-}1)$$

where *C* is real consumption and I_r is net realized investment. By "realized investment" we mean all net investment regardless of whether it is intentional or unintentional. All income becomes disposable income under present assumptions, so that

$$Y = C + S_p \qquad (5\text{-}2)$$

Since there are no corporate savings, net private savings *S* becomes identical with net personal savings S_p. By equating (5-1) with (5-2) and substituting *S* for S_p, we note that

$$I_r = S \qquad (5\text{-}3)$$

which becomes the fundamental accounting identity in this simplified economy.

Now suppose that the community's consumption function is that of Figure 5-1 and that producers desire to spend $20 billion on investment goods (net of depreciation) at all levels of income.[1] Under these conditions, what will the equilibrium level of income be?

One way to determine the equilibrium level of income is to add the schedule of intended investment to the consumption schedule and to observe at what point this "aggregate demand" function (*C* + *I*) intersects the 45-degree line.[2] Another way of finding equilibrium is to find the point where the schedule of intended investment cuts the savings schedule. In both cases equilibrium is at $180 billion.

What is the logic behind the equilibrium solution? Suppose that producers believe they will be able to sell $220 billion worth of goods. With production at $220 billion, disposable income will be $220 billion. The consumption function indicates that at an income level of $220 billion, consumers will spend $190 billion on consumption goods and save $30 billion. (Observe the situation at an income of $220 billion in Figure 5-2.) The intended investment schedule shows that businessmen wish to purchase $20 billion worth of investment goods. The total demand for goods and services (aggregate demand) at an income level of $220 billion is therefore $210 billion. But since production is greater than sales by $10 billion, the extra $10 billion worth of goods will be

[1] Note that we now have *Y* instead of Y_d on the horizontal axis.
[2] Algebraically, if $C = 0.75Y + 25$ and if $I = 20$, then by substituting into $Y = C + I$ we have

$$Y = \frac{25 + 20}{1 - 0.75} = 180$$

accumulated by businesses in the form of unintended investment in inventories (I_u). If businessmen continue to produce $220 billion worth of goods, inventories will continue to pile up at the rate of $10 billion per year. There will thus be a tendency for business to cut back production.

At the $220 billion income level savings are $30 billion, intended investment (I) is $20 billion, and unintended investment (I_u) is $10 billion. Consequently the national income accountant will note that realized investment (I_r = intended + unintended investment) is exactly equal to realized savings. It must always be true that

$$I + I_u = I_r = S$$

but only in equilibrium will it be true that intended investment equals savings, or

$$I = S$$

because the existence of unintended inventory investment or disinvestment indicates that production and sales are not synchronized.

Again, consider the situation that would arise if businessmen underestimated the demand for goods and services and therefore produced only $140 billion worth of goods while intended investment remains unchanged at $20 billion

Figure 5-2 Simple income determination   (all values in real terms).

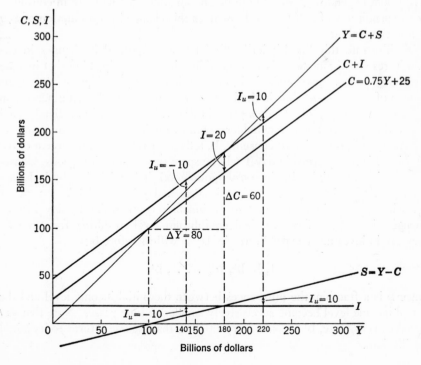

(see Figure 5-2 again at $Y = 140$). When $Y = 140$, $C = 130$, with the consequence that aggregate demand $(C + I) = 150$; thus there will be a $10 billion reduction in inventories not anticipated by businessmen. Since savings are $10 billion and unintended investment is $-$10 billion,

$$I + I_u = 10 = S$$

There will now be a tendency for production and income to increase to a level of $180 billion where $C = 160$, $S = 20$, $I = 20$, and $I_u = 0$. The equilibrium level of income, it appears, necessarily requires equality between intended investment and savings.

5-3 The Multiplier

Suppose that intended investment expenditures are zero. The equilibrium level of income would, in this case, be $100 billion (see Figure 5-2 again). Next pretend that businessmen suddenly decide to spend $20 billion each year on new plants and equipment. The aggregate demand schedule $(C + I)$ would therefore shift up by $20 billion. Notice, however, that the level of income rises not by $20 billion but by $80 billion. Observe, finally, that the over-all change in income of $80 billion consists of two components—the change in investment expenditures of $20 billion and an additional increase in consumption expenditures of $60 billion. How does this change in consumption of $60 billion come about?

To illustrate this "multiplier" effect let us suppose that changes in expenditures are instantaneously translated into income receipts, but that income recipients do not spend today's income until tomorrow. Suppose next that, instead of a permanent shift in the investment demand schedule, an increase in investment spending of $1 takes place in day 1. This $1 is immediately paid out to the wage earners, stockholders, etc., of the investment goods industry. The marginal propensity to consume, **b**, tells us that on day 2, **b** percent of the additional income earned in day 1 will be spent on consumption goods. Consequently, income originating in consumption goods industries rises by **b** dollars on day 2, of which **b** percent, or $\mathbf{b}^2$, is spent in day 3, of which **b** percent, or $\mathbf{b}^3$, will be spent in day 4, and so on indefinitely. The day-by-day income changes, in excess of the original equilibrium level, resulting from the $1 increase in investment expenditures in day 1 will therefore be

$$1, \mathbf{b}, \mathbf{b}^2, \mathbf{b}^3, \ldots, \mathbf{b}^t$$

Since **b** is a fraction, the differences between the initial income level and the actual income level become successively smaller as time passes. Note that as t becomes very large, $\mathbf{b}^t$ becomes very small so that income returns to its initial equilibrium.

The time path of income for a value of **b** = 0.75 is traced in Figure 5-3. In day 1 the $1 increase in spending raises the income level by $1 over the initial value of Y_0. In day 2 the amount of $0.75 \times \$1$, or 75 cents, is respent on consumption goods. Income in day 2 is therefore $Y_0 + 75$ cents. In day 3 income will be 0.75×0.75, or $(0.75)^2 \times \$1$, in excess of the initial level, and in day t it will be $(0.75)^{t-1} \times \$1$ in excess of the initial level. As t grows very large, the difference between the initial level and the actual level of income approaches zero.

Figure 5-3 The multiplier with a single expenditure (all values in real terms).

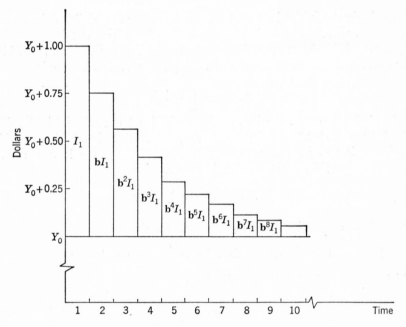

The case just considered may be visualized most easily by imagining an automobile cruising down a level road at a constant speed of 40 miles per hour with the accelerator held steady exactly half way from the floor of the car. Imagine that the driver pushes the accelerator to the floor but that he then releases it and holds it steady in its original position. The car will first lurch forward, picking up speed, but will immediately begin to decelerate and gradually approach its previous 40 mile per hour speed.

What will happen if the driver pushes the accelerator to the floor and keeps it there? The car will pick up speed and continue to accelerate, but at a decreasing rate, until gradually the speed of the car approaches a new constant velocity. This latter case, in which the accelerator is pressed to the floor and held there, is exactly the kind of thing that happens when investment expenditures are increased by some amount and are maintained at the new higher level permanently. In other words, an upward shift of the investment demand schedule of $1 implies that there will be a $1 increase in investment spending in period 1; another dollar will be spent in period 2, another dollar in period 3, and so on indefinitely.

How will the level of income change over time under this new set of assumptions? In day 1 the investment schedule shifts up so that on this first day the level of income rises by $1. The level of income in day 1 is therefore

$$Y_1 = Y_0 + 1$$

where Y_0 is the initial income level. In day 2 another dollar of investment expenditures is added to the income stream. But in addition to this extra dollar, b percent of the dollar of the investment expenditures of the first day will be spent on consumption. Consequently on day 2 the level of income is

$$Y_2 = Y_0 + 1 + b$$

In day 3, b percent of the income change in day 2 over the initial level, or $b(1 + b) = b + b^2$, will be respent on consumption, in addition to which another dollar of investment expenditures is added to the income stream. Consequently on day 3 the level of income rises to

$$Y_3 = Y_0 + 1 + b + b^2$$

The process repeats itself indefinitely so that in day t

$$Y_t = Y_0 + 1 + b + b^2 + b^3 + \cdots + b^{t-1}$$

which, as can easily be shown,[1] simplifies to

$$Y_t = Y_0 + \frac{1 - b^t}{1 - b}$$

[1] Note that

$$Y_t = Y_0 + 1 + b + b^2 + b^3 + \cdots + b^{t-1}$$

is a geometric series. In order to sum such a series we need merely multiply each term by b:

$$bY_t = bY_0 + b + b^2 + b^3 + \cdots + b^{t-1} + b^t$$

and observe that when the second series is subtracted from the first series, all but the first two terms from the right-hand side of the first series drop out, while only the first and last terms of the right-hand side of the second series remain, i.e.,

$$Y_t - bY_t = Y_0 - bY_0 + 1 - b^t$$

which simplifies to

$$Y_t = Y_0 + \frac{1 - b^t}{1 - b}$$

As t grows very large, b^t becomes very small so that in the limit the new equilibrium value of income Y_t, is

$$Y_t = Y_0 + \frac{1}{1 - b}$$

The change in income, $Y_t - Y_0$, due to a \$1 per day increase in investment spending therefore is $1/(1 - b)$, which is known as the "multiplier." Remembering that b is the marginal propensity to consume, it becomes a simple matter to calculate the value of the multiplier by simply measuring the slope of the consumption function. If $b = 0.75$, the multiplier is 4, i.e., a \$1 increase in investment spending raises the level of income by \$4. If $b = 0.50$, the multiplier is 2. If $b = 0$, the multiplier is 1. In this last case, all additional income through the increase in investment will be saved, so that there is no respending on consumption, and consequently the level of income rises only by the amount of the increase in investment expenditure.

A diagram similar to Figure 5-3 may help to illustrate the process of adjustment to the new equilibrium level. Assume that $b = 0.50$ and that each day \$1 of new investment expenditures materializes. In the first day the level of income rises by \$1. In the second day 0.50 of this is respent, in addition to which another dollar of investment expenditures takes place. In the third day 0.50 of the \$1.50 is respent on consumption and added to the \$1 of investment spending which materialized on day 3. This gives an increase in income, over the initial level, of 1.75. The successive day-to-day increases over the previous day become smaller and smaller and gradually the level of income approaches its new equilibrium level of $Y_0 + 2$.

One of the most useful ways to visualize the multiplier is as follows: We know from our previous discussion that income cannot be in equilibrium unless intended investment and savings are equal. If, therefore, we begin in a position of equilibrium and if intended investment now rises permanently by \$1, we know from the equilibrium condition that unless savings also rise by \$1, equilibrium will not have been restored. Thus all we need to do is to ask: By how much must income rise in order that one more dollar of savings be generated? And this question is identical to asking what the value of the multiplier is. If the marginal propensity to consume is 0.75, the marginal propensity to save is 0.25. This means that each time income rises by \$1, savings will rise by 25 cents. But since we require savings to rise by \$1, and since a \$1 rise in income generates only a 25 cent increase in savings, the necessary income increase must be $(1/0.25)$ or \$4. Had the marginal propensity to save been 0.5, an additional dollar of income would generate an additional 50 cents of savings so that the multiplier would be $1/0.50 = 2$. In general, if the marginal propensity to save is $1 - b$, an additional dollar of income creates added savings in an amount $1 - b$ so that a \$1 increase in savings would be generated by an income increase of $1/(1 - b)$.

Figure 5-4 The multiplier with a continuous injection (all values in real terms).

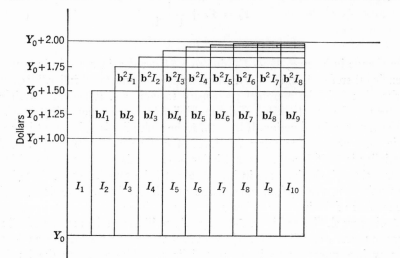

5-4 Factors Affecting Consumption Expenditure

The proposition that aggregate consumption is a function of aggregate disposable income stems from the revolutionary work of J. M. Keynes.[1] Keynes's theory of the consumption function held out hope that a firm basis for forecasting consumption expenditure had at last been found. However, forecasts of post-World War II consumption were quite far off the mark. The forecasts failed because they did not take into account the fact that the consumption behavior of the community depends on a good deal more than the current level of disposable income. This section is devoted to a survey of some of the hypotheses that have been formulated to explain the level of consumption expenditure.[2]

Some of the variables that may be relevant are ignored in this discussion. It has long been supposed, for example, that an increase in the rate of interest would lead to an increase in savings and therefore a reduction in consumption.

[1] J. M. Keynes, *The General Theory of Employment Interest and Money*, Harcourt, Brace and Company, Inc., New York, 1936.

[2] For a careful and comprehensive survey of the material discussed in this section see R. Ferber, "Research on Household Behavior," *American Economic Review*, 52:19–63, 1962.

Since this will be treated at some length in Chapter 13, we shall ignore the effects of interest-rate changes on consumption. Similarly, it has been argued that a fall in the general level of prices will cause the real value of the accumulated liquid assets of the public to rise, and this increase in "wealth" will serve to stimulate consumption. This subject is considered in Chapter 11 and may be passed over here.

It was Keynes's belief that the marginal propensity to consume of low-income groups would be higher than the marginal propensity to consume of high-income groups. This belief suggested that aggregate demand might be raised by a policy of income redistribution. If the marginal propensity to consume of a rich man is 0.60 while the marginal propensity to consume of a poor man is 0.90, a redistribution of income of $1 from the rich to the poor man would raise aggregate consumption by 30 cents. If a redistribution of a given level of disposable income will change the level of consumption, the consumption function for the community as a whole would have to be considered a function of both the level of disposable income and the way in which disposable income is distributed.

In a study of German time-series data, Staehle[1] found that the distribution of income was an important factor in determining aggregate consumption. However, investigations using American "cross-section" data failed to find any significant relationship between income distribution and aggregate consumption.[2] As a result of these studies, many economists no longer feel that an income-leveling policy will significantly help to raise total consumption.

Statistical studies have shown that the shape of the consumption function differs radically depending upon the type of data used to plot the function. When aggregate consumption expenditures are plotted against disposable income for different years, the consumption function appears as a line (C_L in Figure 5-5) emanating from the origin with a slope of approximately 0.9. But when consumption expenditures are plotted for a cross section of family-income groups at one point in time, the shape is more in line with the consumption function plotted in Figure 5-1 and corresponds to the functions C_{S_0}, C_{S_1}, and C_{S_2} of Figure 5-5. The poorest families do, indeed, dissave in the short run, and, as became evident in 1932, the community as a whole may dissave for a time under the pressure of a drastic income shrinkage.

How can these differently shaped consumption schedules be reconciled? One possible approach is to suppose that the observed community consumption level for a period of time is but one point on an existing schedule of intentions and that the short-run schedules drift upward over time. In Figure 5-5 points

---

[1] H. Staehle, "Short Period Variations in the Distribution of Incomes," *Review of Economic Statistics*, 19:133–143, 1937.

[2] H. Lubell, "Effects of Income Redistribution on Consumers' Expenditures," *American Economic Review*, 37:157–170, 1947. See also J. Marschak's classic paper, "Personal and Collective Budget Functions," *Review of Economic Statistics*, 21:161–170, 1939.

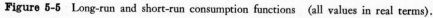

Figure 5-5   Long-run and short-run consumption functions   (all values in real terms).

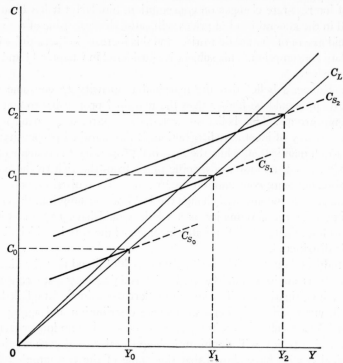

(C_0, Y_0), (C_1, Y_1), and (C_2, Y_2) are observed points in the years 0, 1, and 2. The schedules C_{S_0}, C_{S_1}, and C_{S_2} are the schedules that reflect the true propensity to consume in years 0, 1, and 2. If a hypothesis can be introduced that explains why the short-run consumption function drifts upward over time, the cross section and time-series observations can be reconciled.

One possible explanation for the secular upward drift of the consumption function is Duesenberry's "relative income" hypothesis.[1] Duesenberry observed that a negro family with an income of $5,000 saves more than a white family with a comparable level of income. Since the negro family is likely to reside in a lower rent district than the white family and since a negro with a $5,000 income is likely to be on a higher point in the distribution of income in his neighborhood, Duesenberry concluded that the difference in consumption behavior could be explained by differences in the level of relative income, i.e., income in relation to what one is accustomed. These observations then led Duesenberry to formulate the following hypothesis with respect to aggregate

[1] J. S. Duesenberry, *Income, Saving, and the Theory of Consumer Behavior*, Harvard University Press, Cambridge, Mass., 1952. F. Modigliani, "Fluctuations in the Savings–Income Ratio: A Problem in Economic Forecasting," in *Studies in Income and Wealth*, Vol. 11, National Bureau of Economic Research, New York, 1949.

consumption behavior. Suppose that in Figure 5-5 the community's level of income is Y_0. Having become accustomed to this standard of living, a fall in income from Y_0 causes consumers to defend their living standards by maintaining their consumption expenditures. They therefore move backward along the function C_{S_0}, reducing savings drastically while maintaining consumption. Should income rise back toward Y_0, consumption rises by only a little because consumers attempt to recover the preceding peak level of savings. This implies that as income rises the community moves upward along the C_{S_0} schedule. But when Y_0 is reached, the previous highest standard of consumption and savings to which the community is accustomed is restored. Further increases in income therefore cause a sharp rise in the marginal propensity to consume. Additions to income are then split so as to maintain a constant consumption-income ratio. When income is above the highest past peak, the community moves along C_L. If income reaches Y_1 but subsequently falls, the community repeats its attempt to preserve its newly acquired higher living standard and moves backward along C_{S_1}.

While Duesenberry's hypothesis explains the secular upward drift of the consumption function, his "relative income" hypothesis is by no means the only explanation. Tobin,[1] for example, showed that the difference in the savings habits between negroes and whites could be explained by the fact that although a negro and a white family might have the same current income, the white family is likely to be wealthier and more secure and will therefore tend to save less.

Another factor that helps to explain the upward drift of the consumption function is the introduction of new products. New products may so change consumer preferences that consumers are willing to revise their expenditure plans and purchase the new commodity at the expense of savings. A comparison, by one of the authors,[2] of the buyers of television in 1950 with groups of non-buyers confirmed the suspicion that this particular new product was purchased primarily at the expense of savings rather than at the expense of alternative consumption expenditures.

Dissatisfaction with the hypothesis that consumption is primarily a function of current income arises from a number of additional sources. One difficulty is that if we plot consumption against income over a six-month period, we shall obtain a substantially less steeply sloped consumption function than if we choose one year as our time period. Indeed, the longer the time period that we

[1] J. Tobin, "Relative Income, Absolute Income, and Savings," in *Money, Trade and Economic Growth, Essays in Honor of John H. Williams,* The Macmillan Company, New York, 1951.

[2] T. F. Dernburg, "The Consumption–Income Ratio and Product Innovation," Purdue University, Institute for Quantitative Research in Economics and Management, Institute Paper No. 9, 1960. See also T. F. Dernburg, "Consumer Response to Innovation," in *Studies in Household Economic Behavior,* Yale University Press, New Haven, Conn., 1958.

choose, the steeper the observed consumption function becomes. The presumption is that lengthening the period over which the flow of income and consumption are measured tends to eliminate the effects of short-run variations in income and of lags in the adjustment of consumption to changes in income. Mrs. Mack[1] has shown that if we divide families according to income class, the higher income groups will contain a larger proportion of people whose incomes have recently risen, while the lower income groups will contain a larger proportion of families whose incomes have recently fallen. Since some of these income changes may be temporary, and since it takes time to adjust consumption expenditures even to income changes that are permanent, the measured consumption level of the higher income groups will be lower than would be true in the long run, while the measured consumption levels of the lower income groups will be higher than would be true in the long run. Therefore, a cross-section consumption function of consumption plotted against income over some fairly short period of time will tend to make the observed consumption function a good deal flatter than the "true" propensity to consume.

Difficulties of the sort outlined above have led some economists to take the view that consumption is primarily related not to current income but to some measure of long-run income or wealth. Short-run fluctuations in income are then regarded as affecting primarily the level of savings. The best known such hypothesis is the "permanent income" hypothesis of Friedman.[2] He argues that the relevant variable explaining a family's consumption is its permanent income, by which he means the present value of its expected future receipts. Short-run variations in savings are then explained as resulting from windfall or "transitory" income changes. Since consumption expenditures are geared to permanent income, a windfall will produce only a small rise in consumption expenditures. Should permanent income change, however, the effect on consumer spending would be substantially larger.

Watts[3] proposes the hypothesis that the relevant variable that explains the level of consumption spending is expected income. He defines E, expected income, as that annual income which, if paid as an annuity, would just equal the present value of the sum of all expected future incomes up to retirement. A high E implies a high level of current consumption, while a low E implies the opposite. Among the factors affecting E, Watts finds age, education, occu-

[1] R. P. Mack, "The Direction of Change in Income and the Consumption Function," *Review of Economics and Statistics*, 30:239–258, 1948.

[2] M. Friedman, *A Theory of the Consumption Function*, National Bureau of Economic Research, New York, 1955. A hypothesis similar to that of Friedman is advanced in F. Modigliani and R. Brumberg, "Utility Analysis and the Consumption Function–An Interpretation of Cross-Section Data," in K. K. Kurihara, ed., *Post-Keynesian Economics*, Rutgers University Press, New Brunswick, N.J., 1954. See also R. Brumberg, "An Approximation to the Aggregate Savings Function," *Economic Journal*, 66:66–72, 1956.

[3] H. Watts, "Long-run Income Expectations and Consumer Savings," *Studies in Household Economic Behavior*, Yale University Press, New Haven, Conn., 1958.

pation, race, and location to be significant. For spending units with younger heads, those that have had a college education save the least because their expected income is greatest. Professional and business people have a higher expected income and therefore save less than do unskilled workers. Opportunities for high future income are presumably greater in urban areas, and in areas of high population density there are likely to be stronger imitative effects. Urban households therefore generally save less than do rural households. Spending units close to retirement save more than do younger units because their expected income and their current income are tending to equality. However, the age group that is currently putting its children through college saves less than other older age groups.

In order to put together the foundation stones of macro-economic theory in as simple a manner as possible, we shall return, throughout the next few chapters, to the simple hypothesis that consumption is a function of current disposable income. But it should be borne in mind, as the foregoing discussion has suggested, that the determination of aggregate consumption expenditure is no simple matter.

chapter 6

Government and the level of income

6-1 Government Expenditures, Taxation, and the Equilibrium Level of Income

In this chapter we turn our attention to the effect of government expenditures and taxation on the level of income. The assumptions that corporate savings are negligible and that the economy does not engage in foreign trade are retained. Under these conditions real net national product (Y) is the sum of personal consumption expenditures, net private domestic investment, and government expenditures, or

$$Y = C + I_r + G$$

The income pie is split up between the government (taxes) and the public (disposable income). Hence

$$Y = Y_d + T$$

and, since the public is free either to spend its disposable income on consumption or to save it,

$$Y = C + S + T$$

What is the condition for equilibrium? Previously it was argued that intended investment must equal savings. When government expenditures and taxation are added to the model, the equilibrium condition is that intended investment plus government expenditures must equal savings plus taxes. That this must be true can easily be seen by introducing the notion of an income leakage and a compensating expenditure. In the simplified model of Chapter 5 where government did not enter into the picture, a portion of the current income pie was spent on consumption and therefore reentered the spending stream. However, a portion also "leaked" into savings. It was noted, moreover, that if an amount of intended investment just sufficient to balance the savings took place, the level of income would remain unchanged because production and sales plus intended changes in inventories would then be synchronized. But this is the same as saying that investment expenditures are just sufficient to make up for the leakages, due to savings, from the expenditure stream. If savings are greater than intended investment, more will leak out of the expenditure stream than is pumped in via consumption and intended investment. Taxes, like savings, are income leakages, while government expenditures, like intended investment, are compensating expenditures. If the sum of taxes and savings is greater than the sum of government expenditures and intended investment, more will have been produced than sold or intentionally accumulated because insufficient expenditures have been made to compensate for the leakages.

Taxes present an interesting problem. Not only do they constitute leakages from the expenditure stream; they also determine to what extent savings will constitute leakages. A tax of $50 billion reduces disposable income by $50 billion. But if the marginal propensity to consume is less than unity, say 0.75, consumption falls by only $0.75 \times 50 = \$37.5$ billion, the remaining $12.5 billion coming from a reduction in savings. Total leakages resulting from the tax therefore do not increase by the full amount of the tax but by the tax minus the fall in savings which the tax causes.

Bearing the new equilibrium condition in mind, let us return to the conditions of the simple economy depicted in Chapter 5. Figure 6-1 is based upon Figure 5-2. C_1, S_1, and I_1 are the same consumption, savings, and investment demand schedules as in Figure 5-2. With intended investment of $20 billion, the equilibrium level of income is $180 billion. At this level of income consumption is $160 billion, and savings are $20 billion. Now let us introduce government expenditures of $20 billion. These expenditures are legislated by Congress and are independent of the level of income. Since it makes no difference where a dollar of expenditure originates, the government expenditures may simply be added to the $C_1 + I_1$ schedule to yield the new aggregate demand schedule $C_1 + I_1 + G_1$, and to the investment demand schedule I_1 to yield $I_1 + G_1$. Since government expenditures have increased by $20 billion, the multiplier may be applied to this change, and the new equilibrium level of income can be calculated. Since the multiplier is 4, the equilibrium level of income must rise by $80 billion to a new level of $260 billion. To check whether this answer is correct, we note that at the computed equilibrium level consumption expenditures are $220 billion. Thus $40 billion leaks into savings, but since this $40 billion is compensated for by $20 billion of investment expenditures and $20 billion of government expenditures, unintended investment is zero and thus equilibrium is established.

Next consider the imposition of a $20 billion tax. Assume, moreover, that Congress somehow manages to collect $20 billion in taxes regardless of the level of income. The immediate effect of the tax is to reduce the level of disposable income by $20 billion. But if disposable income falls by $20 billion, the marginal propensity to consume indicates that consumption will fall by 0.75×20, or $15 billion, and the marginal propensity to save indicates that savings will fall by $5 billion. Thus, whereas at an income level of $100 billion consumption was $100 billion, consumption will now be $85 billion. Similarly, at an income level of $200 billion, consumption, which was previously $175 billion, is now $160 billion. In fact, consumption will be $15 billion less than before at all levels of income. This means that the $20 billion tax lowers the consumption schedule by $15 billion to C_2, and thus the aggregate demand schedule falls by $15 billion to $C_2 + I_1 + G_1$. Since aggregate demand falls by

Figure 6-1 Government expenditures, taxes, and the level of income (all values in real terms).

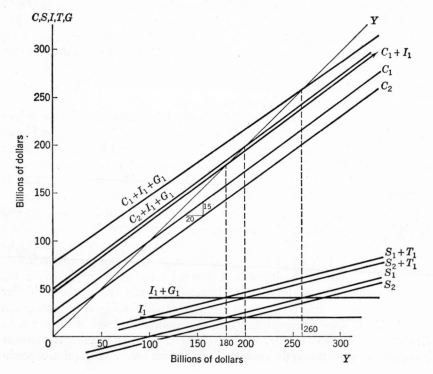

$15 billion, the equilibrium level of income falls by $60 billion (the multiplier times 15) to a new level of $200 billion.

Notice that although the amount spent by the government equals the amount withdrawn in the form of taxes, the new equilibrium level of income has nevertheless increased by $20 billion. This is so because the net change in leakages resulting from the $20 billion tax is not $20 billion but $15 billion. The imposition of the tax, as shown by the savings schedule S_2, has reduced the leakages due to savings by $5 billion. The $20 billion tax, by reducing disposable income by $20 billion, reduces savings at all levels of income by $5 billion. The savings schedule therefore shifts down by $5 billion at all levels of income. The sum total of leakages can then be found by adding the tax schedule to the savings schedule to obtain $S_2 + T_1$, which is not $20 billion (the amount of the tax) but $15 billion greater than S_1 at all levels of income. Since only $15 billion of compensating government expenditure is required to maintain the equilibrium level of income after the imposition of the tax, and since G has actually risen by $20 billion, the net effect of the tax should be an increase in income of the $5 billion government expenditure in excess of required compensating expenditures times the multiplier. This value is $20 billion, which is the change in the equilibrium level of income, taking both taxes and government expenditures into account.

At the new equilibrium income level of $200 billion, disposable income is $180 billion. Savings are therefore $20 billion, and since taxes are also $20 billion, total leakages are $40 billion. Government expenditures are $20 billion and intended investment is $20 billion, so that total compensating expenditures are $40 billion. Since savings plus taxes also equal $40 billion, total leakages equal total compensating expenditures.

6-2   Algebraic Analysis of Taxation and Expenditures

Through most of this book mathematical manipulations will be restricted to footnotes and appendixes. In this section, however, we shall deviate from this plan and work through some simple fiscal policy models. Despite the frightening number of symbols, the analysis is simple and intelligible. As will be indicated from time to time, these models demonstrate a number of conclusions to practical policy problems. In addition, they will serve as an introduction to the method of analysis frequently employed in more advanced literature.

Consider the simple model of the last section. Intended investment, government expenditures, and taxes were all assumed fixed. Thus

$$I = \bar{I} \qquad G = \bar{G} \qquad T = \bar{T} \tag{6-1}$$

where the bars denote that these quantities are constants. The definition of equilibrium net national product is

$$Y = C + I + G \tag{6-2}$$

and the consumption function is

$$C = \mathbf{b}(Y - T) + C_0 \tag{6-3}$$

where $(Y - T)$ is disposable income. Substituting Eqs. (6-1) and (6-3) in Eq. (6-2) and solving for Y gives

$$Y = \frac{-\mathbf{b}\bar{T} + C_0 + \bar{I} + \bar{G}}{1 - \mathbf{b}} \tag{6-4}$$

as an algebraic expression for the equilibrium level of income. In the previous example, $\mathbf{b} = 0.75$, $\bar{T} = 20$, $\bar{I} = 20$, $C_0 = 25$, and $\bar{G} = 20$. Thus

$$Y = \frac{-0.75 \times 20 + 25 + 20 + 20}{1 - 0.75} = 200$$

which checks with our diagrammatic results.

How much will changes in G, I, C_0, and T affect the level of income? In the last chapter the multiplier was calculated by summing the chain of increments to income resulting from respending on consumption over successive periods. Rather than go through this cumbersome procedure again, let us utilize an alternative. Let investment change by some amount ΔI, and let us add this ΔI into the right-hand side of the equation. This change in investment will lead to some change in income ΔY. Adding this change to the left-hand side, we obtain

$$Y + \Delta Y = \frac{-\mathbf{b}\bar{T} + C_0 + \bar{I} + \bar{G} + \Delta I}{1 - \mathbf{b}}$$

which can be rewritten

$$Y + \Delta Y = \frac{-\mathbf{b}\bar{T} + C_0 + \bar{I} + \bar{G}}{1 - \mathbf{b}} + \frac{\Delta I}{1 - \mathbf{b}}$$

If Y is subtracted from both sides,

$$\Delta Y = \frac{\Delta I}{1 - \mathbf{b}}$$

which states that an increase in investment expenditures of \$1 will raise the level of income by \$4, if the marginal propensity to consume is 0.75.

Following the same procedure, we find that the change in income for equal changes in consumption, investment, and government expenditures will be identical. Symbolically,

$$\Delta Y = \frac{\Delta I}{1 - \mathbf{b}} = \frac{\Delta C_0}{1 - \mathbf{b}} = \frac{\Delta G}{1 - \mathbf{b}} \tag{6-5}$$

where $\Delta I = \Delta C_0 = \Delta G$. But for an increase in taxes,

$$\Delta Y = \frac{-b\Delta T}{1 - b} \qquad (6\text{-}6)$$

which indicates, as was shown previously, that taxes have a less high-powered effect on the level of income than do government expenditures. In case this is not yet clear, let us look at it in the following way: Taxes affect the level of income through their effect on consumption. The change in income which results from a change in consumption is, from Eq. (6-5),

$$\Delta Y = \frac{\Delta C_0}{1 - b}$$

i.e., the change in consumption times the multiplier $1/(1 - b)$. The change in consumption resulting from a tax increase of ΔT is not equal to ΔT but is equal to the marginal propensity to consume times ΔT. Thus, if the marginal propensity to consume is 0.75, a tax increase of \$1, by lowering disposable income by \$1, reduces consumption by 0.75 times \$1. We may therefore write

$$\Delta C_0 = -b\Delta T$$

and substitute this in Eq. (6-5) to obtain

$$\Delta Y = \frac{-b\Delta T}{1 - b} \qquad (6\text{-}6)$$

Using the numerical values of Section 6-1, an increase in government expenditures of \$20 billion raises aggregate demand by \$20 billion and raises the level of income by

$$\Delta Y = \frac{20}{1 - 0.75} = 80$$

On the other hand, an increase in taxes of \$20 billion reduces consumption, and therefore aggregate demand, by $0.75 \times 20 = 15$, and thus lowers the level of income by

$$\Delta Y = \frac{-0.75 \times 20}{1 - 0.75} = -60$$

The combined effect of the \$20 billion increase in both taxes and government expenditures is therefore $80 - 60 = \$20$ billion, a value which is just exactly equal to the change in G and T. This last result is known as the "balanced budget" or "unit" multiplier theorem. Notice that the value of the marginal propensity to consume is irrelevant to the result because the multiplier for government expenditures is always one greater than the multiplier for taxes. Adding the two multipliers together yields

$$\frac{\Delta Y}{\Delta G} + \frac{\Delta Y}{\Delta T} = \frac{1}{1 - b} + \frac{-b}{1 - b} = \frac{1 - b}{1 - b} = 1$$

Of what interest is this result to governmental finance and budgeting? It is sometimes crudely assumed that if the budget is balanced, the government must be fiscally neutral. It is apparent from the above, however, that the level at which the budget is balanced is also important. If the budget is balanced at a level of $20 billion, the level of income, as was noted previously, will be $20 billion higher than if the budget were balanced at a zero level of taxes and expenditures.

One of the weaknesses of the fiscal policy model just studied is the assumption that the amount of the tax collected is independent of the level of income. This would be possible if Congress were to legislate a poll tax under which each individual would be liable for a fixed sum irrespective of his income. In practice, however, Congress legislates income brackets and imposes tax rates on these brackets. Therefore total tax receipts will depend on the level of income. A step in the right direction can be taken by assuming that taxes are a linear function of the level of income. Let the tax function be given by

$$T = \mathbf{u} + \mathbf{t}Y \tag{6-7}$$

where $\mathbf{t}$ may be defined as the marginal tax rate. Disposable income is

$$Y_d = Y - T = Y - \mathbf{u} - \mathbf{t}Y = (1 - \mathbf{t})Y - \mathbf{u} \tag{6-8}$$

Substituting this expression into Eq. (6-3) gives the consumption function

$$C = \mathbf{b}(1 - \mathbf{t})Y - \mathbf{b}\mathbf{u} + C_0 \tag{6-9}$$

Substituting this expression in Eq. (6-2) and again assuming investment and government expenditures to be constant, we have

$$Y = \frac{-\mathbf{b}\mathbf{u} + C_0 + \bar{I} - \bar{G}}{1 - \mathbf{b}(1 - \mathbf{t})} \tag{6-10}$$

as the expression for the equilibrium level of income. The multiplier for a change in government expenditure as derived from Eq. (6-4) is $1/(1 - \mathbf{b})$, while from Eq. (6-10) it is $1/[1 - \mathbf{b}(1 - \mathbf{t})]$. Since $\mathbf{t}$ is positive (say 10 percent), the multiplier obtained from this present model is less than for the previous model; that is,

$$\frac{1}{1 - \mathbf{b}} > \frac{1}{1 - \mathbf{b}(1 - \mathbf{t})}$$

What accounts for this change? In the original model taxes are fixed and independent of the level of income. Thus, if government expenditures rise by $1, disposable income rises by $1, of which $\mathbf{b}$ percent is then respent on consumption. As we know, this respending chain can be summed up to yield $1/(1 - \mathbf{b})$. But under the conditions of the new model, in which taxes depend on the level of income, an increase in government expenditures, while raising the level of income by $1, raises the level of disposable income by only $(1 - \mathbf{t})$

times $1 because **t** percent of the increase in income flows right back to the Treasury in the form of taxes. Since disposable income rises by only $(1 - t)$ percent, and since **b** percent of the change in disposable income is respent on consumption, $b(1 - t)$ percent of the dollar, instead of **b** percent, will be respent on consumption. This means that the effective marginal propensity to consume is reduced by the imposition of the tax.

These considerations serve to point up what is often forgotten in policy discussions: that an increase in government expenditures of X dollars will not necessarily create a budgetary deficit of X dollars because part of the increase in income resulting from the expenditure flows right back to the Treasury. It also suggests that efforts to balance the budget via tax-rate increases may, to some extent, defeat themselves because the tax-rate increase lowers the level of disposable income, and therefore collections may not increase by as much as anticipated.

The model illustrates a concept we met briefly before—the notion of built-in or automatic stability. By reducing the effective marginal propensity to consume out of *NNP*, the income tax reduces the value of the multiplier and therefore makes the economy less subject to violent fluctuations. In the American economy there is a further stabilizing effect resulting from the fact that tax rates are progressively graduated. This means that as personal incomes rise, taxpayers shift into higher brackets, and a higher proportion of their income is taken by taxes. Similarly, when personal incomes fall, taxpayers shift into lower brackets. The net effect is that disposable income and consumption are stabilized even more than they would have been in the case of a proportional tax.

As a final problem, consider the effect of a change in the tax rate of Δt. Although the derivation requires some knowledge of differential calculus, the final result is simple enough to understand.[1] The change in income will be approximately

$$\Delta Y = \frac{-bY \, \Delta t}{1 - b(1 - t)}$$

from which it appears that the change in income that results from a change in tax rates will itself depend upon the level of income that prevails before the

[1] We have

$$Y = \frac{-bu + C_0 + I + \bar{G}}{1 - b(1 - t)}$$

Taking the derivative of Y with respect to **t** yields

$$\frac{dY}{dt} = \frac{-(-bu + C_0 + I + \bar{G})b}{[1 - b(1 - t)]^2}$$

which simplifies to

$$\frac{dY}{dt} = \frac{-bY}{1 - b(1 - t)}$$

change. The higher the level of income, the greater the increase in tax collections will be, and this means that the fall in disposable income and consumption, and therefore also income, will be greater. In the extreme case of a zero level of income, an increase in the marginal tax rate will result in the collection of no additional taxes. The rate change cannot therefore affect the level of income.

This last result helps to account for a number of policy dilemmas. If the economy enters a slump, many minds turn to the thought of a tax cut. But standing in the way of such a cut is the fact that when income drops, tax collections automatically fall. Since many public officials are wedded to the notion that a time of budgetary deficit is a poor time to cut taxes, there is danger that tax cuts will arouse opposition just at the time when they are most needed. During the late 1950s, moreover, the theory was advanced that if Congress were to cut taxes, it would never have the fortitude to raise them again. Finally the fear is often expressed that a tax cut, after only a mild business downturn, may lead to excessive stimulation of consumption and therefore create inflationary pressures.

There is considerable danger in these attitudes. If the business slump is allowed to become aggravated, the ultimate tax cut that will be required to bring the economy back to full employment will be much greater than would have been needed had immediate action been taken. Moreover, an additional fall in income, due to the reluctance to cut taxes, may cause a greater budgetary imbalance and even greater reluctance to cut taxes. Finally, the more taxes are cut, the more they have to be raised once full employment is restored.

Political capital can unfortunately be made of our failure to understand the ABC's of fiscal policy. It is common for politicians to attract votes during a period of recession by informing the public that the opposition party not only cannot maintain prosperity but also runs a slovenly fiscal system. The logic of the argument is impeccable because a recession is always accompanied by a budgetary deficit. If we would realize that government revenues fall as a recession develops and that a budgetary deficit is therefore practically inevitable, we would soon learn to discount such political skulduggery.

chapter 7

The level of investment

7-1 Introduction

Thus far we have examined two of the components of aggregate expenditure—consumption and government expenditure. Consumption depends primarily on the level of disposable income, which in turn depends principally on the level of *NNP* and the tax structure. About government expenditures we have, at the moment, little to say because these must be considered "autonomous," i.e., determined by Congress, and they are not directly related to the internal structure of the economic system.[1] Investment, like government expenditures, has so far been treated as autonomous. In this chapter we abandon the simple notion that the level of investment is fixed.

In deciding how to arrange his portfolio, a holder of wealth must decide how, given the fact that different assets yield different returns and have different risks attached to them, he can best arrange his portfolio so as to give him maximum satisfaction. He must, for example, decide whether the disutility of the risk of holding an equity as opposed to a bond is balanced by the utility of the higher earnings on the equity. The wealth holder must decide whether,

---

[1] It is, of course, true that government expenditures may be raised in response to a fall in income. But since there is nothing automatic about most such expenditure increases, government expenditures must be treated as an "autonomous" or "exogenous" variable.

and in what proportion, to hold long-term bonds, short-term bonds, equities, or other types of asset. A businessman must decide whether it is more profitable to use his funds for capital expansion or for the purchase of some existing asset, say an equity in another company. Similarly, he must decide whether the cost of borrowing for purposes of capital expansion is more than compensated for by the expected return on the new investment. The problem of determining the demand for new investment goods may therefore be looked at as a problem in portfolio management, because the decision to invest depends on the profitability of the new investment as opposed to the profitability of holding existing earning assets. If, for example, an investor is able to earn 5 percent on a government bond and can expect to earn only 4 percent on the purchase of a new machine, he will certainly not buy the machine, unless the bond is a far more risky venture than the machine. If, furthermore, the monetary authority would like to see him purchase the machine because that will raise the level of income, it must somehow contrive to change his asset preference in such a way that the machine becomes a more appealing alternative than other earning assets. The first step that needs to be taken if we are to understand this relationship between different types of assets is to inquire into the relationship between the market value of an asset and the rate of return, or yield, of the asset.

7-2 Discounting and the Present Value of an Asset

Suppose that the rate of interest is 5 percent. If today an individual lends $100, he will at the end of one year get back the original $100 plus the original sum multiplied by the rate of interest. Arithmetically,

$$100 + 100 \times 0.05 = 100(1 + 0.05) = \$105$$

In general, if the interest rate is denoted by i and the sum lent is denoted by P_0, the individual will get back at the end of one year

$$P_1 = P_0(1 + i) \tag{7-1}$$

If he lends the whole sum P_1 for a second year, he will receive

$$P_2 = P_1(1 + i)$$

But since $P_1 = P_0(1 + i)$,

$$P_2 = P_0(1 + i)(1 + i) = P_0(1 + i)^2$$

If he lends P_0 for three years, he will get back

$$P_3 = P_0(1 + i)^3$$

from which we may infer that a sum P_0 lent at interest for t years will pay back at the end of t years[1]

$$P_t = P_0(1 + i)^t \qquad\qquad (7\text{-}2)$$

The next step is to turn the original question around and ask: If an individual gets back P_1 dollars in one year, what is today's value of that claim? The answer can be found by solving for P_0 in Eq. (7-1). This yields

$$P_0 = \frac{P_1}{1 + i}$$

which indicates that a claim worth \$105 in one year, with the current market rate of interest at 5 percent, has a value today of \$100. If the owner tried to sell this future claim for anything more than \$100 he would not be able to find

---

[1] In Eq. 7-2 it is assumed that interest is compounded once a year. Often, however, interest is compounded semiannually. In the latter case interest for the first six months is figured on P_0. But since only a half year's interest is earned, the effective rate on P_0 is not i but $i/2$. This means that the value of the claim at the end of six months is $P_0(1 + i/2)$, which becomes the principal on which interest for the next six months is figured. At the end of the year

$$P_1 = P_0\left(1 + \frac{i}{2}\right)\left(1 + \frac{i}{2}\right) = P_0\left(1 + \frac{i}{2}\right)^2$$

from which we may infer that

$$P_t = P_0\left(1 + \frac{i}{2}\right)^{2t}$$

If interest is compounded g times a year we have

$$P_t = P_0\left(1 + \frac{i}{g}\right)^{gt}$$

For some purposes it is useful to know P_t if compounding takes place instantaneously. Rewrite the last equation as

$$P_t = P_0\left[\left(1 + \frac{i}{g}\right)^{g/i}\right]^{it}$$

The term $\left(1 + \frac{i}{g}\right)^{g/i}$ approaches the number 2.7183 when g grows very large. This number is often referred to as e and forms the base of the natural logarithmic system just as 10 forms the base of the common logarithmic system. Hence we have

$$P_t = P_0 e^{it}$$

Notice that

$$\log_e P_t = \log_e P_0 + it \log_e e$$

But since $\log_e e = 1$, we have the straight-line function,

$$\log_e P_t = \log_e P_0 + it$$

a buyer because with an outlay of $100 today the potential buyer can get back $105 in a year and therefore would be foolish to give him more than $100 for this claim. Similarly, the owner would be unwise to sell his future claim for anything less than $100. If he sells the claim for less than $100 and reinvests the proceeds, he would end up with less than $105 at the end of the year, assuming a market rate of 5 percent. The only possible value that the $105 future claim can therefore have is $100. Notice that if the market rate of interest falls to 2 percent, the present value of the claim which pays $105 would increase to $102.94 because this is the amount that would have to be lent at the new rate of interest in order to get back $105 at the end of one year.

A sum P_0 lent today will be worth $P_2 = P_0(1 + i)^2$ at the end of two years. Such a claim could today be sold for P_0. Anyone foolish enough to give more than P_0 for the claim would, at the market rate, have been able to earn more than P_2 in two years with the sum he has paid. On the other hand, if the owner were foolish enough to sell the claim for less than P_0, he could not get back as much as P_2 in two years by lending the amount he sold the claim for. In general, if in t years a claim of P_t is collectible, the present value of that claim is

$$P_0 = \frac{P_t}{(1 + i)^t} \tag{7-3}$$

A claim that is not collectible until far in the future must have very little present value, as compared with the collection sum. Although the Indians who sold Manhattan Island for $24 in wampum in 1624 are now derided for having made a foolish bargain, they could theoretically, by lending the $24 out at interest and waiting 339 years, have earned a sum which might compare favorably with what Manhattan Island could be sold for in 1963.

Consider next the determination of the present value of a bond. Instead of one claim collectible at a certain future date, a bond represents a series of claims collectible at different times in the future. Suppose that each year a coupon can be clipped from the bond and cashed in for a fixed sum R. When there are no more coupons left, the bond reaches maturity and is cashed in for its par value P. Today's value of the bond must be the present value of the sum of all the discounted future returns plus the discounted value of the maturity value. The coupon that is to be clipped in one year and that will have a value of R could be sold today for $R/(1 + i)$; the coupon which is to be clipped in two years from now could be sold today for $R/(1 + i)^2$; the last coupon to be clipped could be sold for $R/(1 + i)^n$, where n is the number of years from the present to maturity; and the claim over the maturity value can be sold for $P/(1 + i)^n$. Consequently the present value of the bond is

$$V = \frac{R}{(1 + i)} + \frac{R}{(1 + i)^2} + \cdots + \frac{R}{(1 + i)^n} + \frac{P}{(1 + i)^n}$$

which, by applying the simple technique used to sum a geometric series, reduces to[1]

$$V = \frac{R}{i}\left[1 - \frac{1}{(1+i)^n}\right] + \frac{P}{(1+i)^n} \qquad (7\text{-}4)$$

Notice that when the maturity date is far off in the future (when a bond has no maturity date it is called a "consol"), n becomes very large so that

$$V = \frac{R}{i} \qquad (7\text{-}5)$$

Equation (7-5) says that if a consol earns $50 each year and if the market rate of interest is 5 percent, the value of the bond must be $1,000. Even if the owner is not familiar with the mathematics of compound interest, he will soon find through painful experience that there can be only one price for the bond. If he tries to sell the bond for more than $1,000, prospective buyers will scoff because they could earn $50 by lending $1,000 on the market; since that is all the bond will yield, it would be quite senseless to pay more than $1,000 for it. If he were foolish enough to accept $900 for the bond, he would discover to his dismay that when he lent the $900 for one year, he would get only $45 in return; if he had kept the bond, he would have received $50 at the end of the year.

Equations (7-4) and (7-5) indicate that there is a definite inverse relationship between bond prices and interest rates. Suppose that the interest rate falls to 2 percent. The value of the consol that previously sold for $1,000, to yield 5 percent or $50 per year, now increases in value to $2,500. The reason for this is that with an interest rate of 2 percent a potential buyer would have to put up $2,500 to earn $50 per year, whereas at the 5 percent rate he has to put up only $1,000. Again the owner would be foolish to sell the bond for $2,000 because if he lent this sum he would earn only $40 in interest, whereas if he keeps the bond he can earn $50.

7-3   The Decision to Invest

The decision to invest in new machinery or equipment depends on whether the expected rate of return on the machine is greater than the cost of borrowing the necessary funds or, if the funds are already available, the cost of the earnings lost by purchasing the machine rather than by lending out the funds. But what is the expected rate of return on a machine which may not yield any

---

[1] Note that when the market rate of interest just equals the rate earned on the par value of the bond, $R = iP$ so that

$$V = \frac{iP}{i}\left[1 - \frac{1}{(1+i)^n}\right] + \frac{P}{(1+i)^n} = P$$

return at all for n years and which yields a return of x dollars in year $n + 1$, a return of y dollars in $n + 2$, a return of z dollars in $n + j$—in short, a return in any given year which may not be the same as the return in any other year? One way of finding out is to ask the question: What rate of interest would make the discounted value of all expected future earnings exactly equal to the cost of the machine? If this rate is r and is the same as the rate at which money can be borrowed, then it is a matter of indifference whether funds are used to purchase a machine or to lend at interest. On the other hand, if $r > i$, the present value of the future earnings of the machine is greater than the present value of a bond (the bond is simply the I.O.U. given in return for the loan of funds), so that it will be more profitable to buy the machine than to lend funds to someone else. Similarly, if $r > i$ and if the prospective purchaser does not have the funds with which to buy the machine, it will pay to borrow in order to purchase the machine.

The rate of return over cost, r, is called the "marginal efficiency of capital." It may be calculated as follows: Let $R_1, R_2, \ldots, R_n$ be the expected earnings of a new capital asset in year $1, 2, \ldots, n$, respectively; let J be the scrap value of the machine at the time of replacement; Q the initial cost of the machine; and r the rate of return over cost. Then

$$Q = \frac{R_1}{(1 + r)} + \frac{R_2}{(1 + r)^2} + \cdots + \frac{R_n}{(1 + r)^n} + \frac{J}{(1 + r)^n}$$

Therefore if Q, J, and the R's are known, r can be calculated.

Consider the simplest case of a machine with an indefinite expected lifetime which yields an identical return R each year. In this case, $Q = R/r$ so that if the machine costs \$1,000 and R is \$100, the expected rate of return over cost of the machine is 10 percent. If the market rate of interest is 5 percent, the \$1,000 would bring a return of \$50 if lent on the market. But if the \$1,000 is invested in the new machine, the annual return is \$100. Consequently it pays to invest in the machine rather than in the bond. Similarly, if the \$1,000 is not available, it would pay to borrow at 5 percent in order to purchase the machine on which 10 percent can be earned.

It is evident that the number of new machines that will be bought in any period of time will depend on the market rate of interest. It is for this reason that economists frequently write the investment demand function as

$$I = I(i) \tag{7-6}$$

A ranking of prospective investment projects in order of decreasing profitability permits us to define an investment demand schedule of the type presented in Figure 7-1. The rate of interest and the marginal efficiency of capital are measured on the vertical axis, while the level of investment in some arbitrary period of time is measured horizontally. At i_0 the level of investment will be I_0.

Figure 7-1   The investment demand function   (all values in real terms).

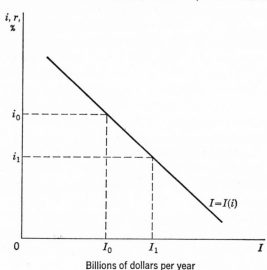

Billions of dollars per year

Additional projects will not be undertaken because the rate of return on those projects is less than the cost of borrowing or the return from lending funds at interest. If the interest rate falls to i_1, it pays to increase the level of investment by $I_1 - I_0$ to I_1 until the return on the marginal project again equals the cost of borrowing.

7-4 Factors Affecting Investment Spending

There has been a great deal of discussion about the relationship between the rate of interest and the volume of investment spending per unit of time. Traditionally economists have been inclined to the view that investment was highly sensitive to interest-rate changes. Skepticism of this view, however, developed during the 1930s. Subsequent statistical investigations, though inconclusive, seem to corroborate the view that the interest rate is an unimportant determinant of the level of investment.[1]

The empirical investigations were conducted by asking businessmen to list the factors that determine their decision to invest. The replies placed very little

[1] J. E. Meade and P. W. S. Andrews, "Summary of Replies to Questions on the Effects of Interest Rates," *Oxford Economic Papers*, 1:14–31, 1938; R. S. Sayers, "Businessmen and the Terms of Borrowing," *Oxford Economic Papers*, 3:23–31, 1940; P. W. S. Andrews, "A Further Inquiry into the Effects of Rates of Interest," *Oxford Economic Papers*, 3:32–73, 1940; J. F. Ebersole, "The Influence of Interest Rates upon Entrepreneurial Decisions in Business—A Case Study," *Harvard Business Review*, 17:35–43, 1938. For a critical survey of these studies, see W. H. White, "Interest Inelasticity of Investment Demand," *American Economic Review*, 46:565–587, 1956.

emphasis upon the cost (the interest rate) of borrowing funds. Such a conclusion, obtained by means of questionnaires, is not very startling. First of all, the supply of funds to an individual firm may be quite interest-inelastic, i.e., the rate of interest may be irrelevant to the firm because it cannot get additional funds at that rate of interest. Secondly, we do not really expect most firms to regard the cost of borrowing as important since most of their prospective investment projects have expected returns substantially in excess of that cost. In Figure 7-1 if a firm has an investment project that promises to yield a rate of return equivalent to i_0, and if the rate of interest at the time the questionnaire is answered is i_1, the firm will undoubtedly regard the cost of borrowing as a trivial consideration. The rate of interest is important only to the firms with marginal investment projects, namely, those whose yields are in the neighborhood of i_1. The questionnaire approach may, therefore, be misleading. It lumps all firms and all investment projects together when we should be attempting instead to observe the effect of interest-rate changes on marginal projects.

It is our belief that the effect of the interest rate on the level of investment will vary with the stage of the business cycle and the rate of technical change. As we shall show in Chapter 12, the interest rate will be irrelevant as an economic calculator during depressions since such periods will be marked by the existence of excess capacity. If we have 100 machines available for use, and if the present level of demand is depressed so that we only need 60 machines, a fall in the rate of interest is certainly not going to induce us to invest.

What then determines the position of the investment demand schedule? It is clear that expectations play a large role.[1] A firm with optimistic views of future sales prospects will be more willing to invest than one with pessimistic views of the future. Because past experience is the only basis upon which projections can be made, a firm's expectations about the future course of events will be a function of its past experience. Thus a firm that has recently experienced increases in the demand for its product is likely to be more optimistic about the future than a firm with a stagnant demand. However, even though a firm is optimistic about the expected demand for its product, it may not increase its capital equipment if it has sufficient excess capacity today to handle the expected future demand. Finally, technical progress will affect the current level of investment. A firm's whole view of the future and its ability to compete effectively will be shifted if an invention occurs that renders part of its capital stock obsolete.

All these factors taken together determine the position of the investment demand schedule for a firm. Thus if falling interest rates coincide with a down-

---

[1] J. S. Duesenberry, *Business Cycles and Economic Growth*, Chaps. 4 and 5, McGraw-Hill Book Company, Inc., New York, 1958, and M. Kalecki, *Theory of Economic Dynamics*, Chaps. 6–10, George Allen & Unwin, Ltd., London, 1954, are useful supplements to the following discussion.

ward shift of the investment demand schedule, the net effect may well be a decrease in the annual volume of investment expenditure. The importance of expectations in investment decisions is a large part of the explanation of the cyclical variations in the volume of investment. Changes in current economic conditions induce cumulative movements in business expectations, causing sharp changes in the aggregate investment demand schedule.

It does not necessarily follow that a firm will borrow even if it has productive outlets for funds (its own or somebody else's) at the going rate of interest. If a firm sells bonds and if the investment for which the funds are used proves unprofitable, then the future earnings on the equity issue of the firm are reduced because of the increased obligatory fixed interest payments. This would be a real cost to the firm in the future; although it is in part a function of the cost of borrowing, it is also a function of past financing decisions and therefore is independent of the current cost of borrowing. There is, of course, the alternative of increasing the ordinary stock issue. Again, if the proceeds of the new issue are not used so that they increase profits proportionately as much as the increase in share capital, the project is not likely to be attractive to management. Furthermore, there are definite limits to any firm's ability to increase its equity issue. There is finally the alternative that the firm can "plough back" its accumulated reserves. Although this protects the firm from the necessity of going to the market, internally financed investment, if unprofitable, is no more likely to be undertaken than the same investment with borrowed funds.[1] These possible future costs of present borrowing are factors influencing a firm's decision to invest and have little, if anything, to do with the current cost of borrowing. Thus, while the supply of funds for the economy as a whole may be interest-elastic, for any one firm the risks involved when it increases its debt may preclude further investment, even though the investment demand schedule for the firm shifts outward.

Taking these various factors into account, what can be done in the way of formal amendment of Eq. (7-6)? Empirical studies have shown that the level of investment is highly correlated with the level of profits. This may be because profits are only partly paid out in the form of dividends; an increase in profits therefore provides the firm with a larger pool of internal finance. A rise in profits, moreover, indicates improvement in business conditions which call for expansion of capacity and improve the state of business "confidence." Because profits and the level of income are highly correlated, economists often rewrite the investment demand equation as

$$I = I(i,Y) \qquad (7\text{-}7)$$

It is assumed in this formulation that investment is inversely associated

[1] See J. Meyer and E. Kuh, *The Investment Decision*, Harvard University Press, Cambridge, Mass., 1957, for a comprehensive analysis of the role played by internal sources of funds in the investment decision of firms.

Figure 7-2 Investment as a function of the interest rate and the level of income (all values in real terms).

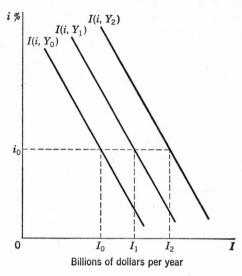

with the rate of interest and directly associated with the level of income. If we now redraw Figure 7-1 (see Figure 7-2), we will have a whole family of investment demand schedules. Each schedule is associated with a particular level of income. At interest rate i_0 the level of investment will be I_0 when the level of income is Y_0. If income rises to Y_1, investment rises to I_1, and when income rises to Y_2, investment rises to I_2.

An alternative formulation of the investment demand equation is

$$I = I(i, \Delta Y) \tag{7-8}$$

where the change in income, ΔY, replaces the level of income. This formulation is based on the notion that business will need to expand its productive capacity only if output *increases*, whereas a constant level of output requires no additional capacity. This hypothesis is called the "acceleration principle." It is often said that in the present case investment is "change-induced," whereas in Eq. (7-7) investment is said to be "level-induced."

Throughout the analysis of Part II we shall retain Eq. (7-6) as our investment demand hypothesis. The level- and change-induced hypotheses become relevant and interesting when we take up the dynamic problems of Part III.

chapter 8

Interest and money

8-1 Introduction

In the previous chapter attention was called to the fact that there is a definite relationship between the rate of interest or yield on an asset and the market value of the asset. From this it follows that determination of the rate of interest is a matter of determining the supply of and the demand for different earning assets. The problem can also be looked at in another way. The supply of and the demand for different types of earning assets will not be in equilibrium unless the supply of and the demand for money (non-interest-bearing assets) are in equilibrium. A wealth holder who has deposits in his bank and cash in his pocket in excess of what he wishes to hold for various purposes will try to trade these deposits and cash in return for earning assets. An excess supply of money, other things being equal, therefore implies that interest rates must fall. The question of determining interest rates may accordingly be looked at in terms of the supply of and demand for bonds, and it may also be looked at as a problem of determining the supply of and demand for money. The latter approach has found favor in recent years and is the approach taken here.

To begin, assume that the economy is entirely riskless, i.e., a bank takes no risk of default when it makes a loan; a bondholder encounters no risk of capital loss; and the expected future returns on new investment projects are, in fact, certain returns. Under these conditions it must be the case that the bank lending rate i_l, the bond rate i_b, and the rate of return on the least profitable (marginal) investment projects undertaken, r, must all be equal. If the bond rate is 5 percent, the rate of return on new investment is 7 percent, and banks try to charge 10 percent on their loans, the banks will be unable to find borrowers, while bondholders will attempt to sell their bonds and use the proceeds to make loans for current investment projects, i.e., they will try to trade existing securities for new securities. The effect of these arbitrage operations will be to force bond prices down and bond rates up. Meanwhile the banks in order not to lose business, would be obliged to lower their loan rate. The bond rate and the loan rate must therefore tend to equality. Alternatively, if the bond rate and loan rate are less than the rate of return on the least profitable investment project, businessmen will be tempted to purchase additional new machines with borrowed funds and to sell their bondholdings in order to buy machines. The effect of this operation will be to lower the rate of return on the marginal investment project, and at the same time raise the bond and bank rates.

In reality there are many different bond rates, none of which is likely to correspond to the bank lending rate or to the rate of return on the marginal investment project. This simply follows from the fact that there are different degrees of risk attached to different types of assets; that imperfect knowledge as to the most profitable opportunity for the investment of funds prevails; and that funds, once committed, may be recovered only on pain of capital loss if more profitable opportunities arise in the future. A bank takes a greater risk when it makes a business loan than it does when it buys a government bond. Similarly, the bank takes a greater risk by buying a long-term bond than a 60-day Treasury bill. If bond prices fall, a holder of a short-term bond need merely hold the bond to its maturity date (say 60 days) in order to collect the face value. However, if he holds a 20-year bond he may not be so lucky. The price of the bond may not, within the near future, rise to what he paid for it. He may therefore be "pinned in" in the sense that if he wants to recover the par value of the bond, he must hold it for 20 years, meanwhile foregoing the possibility of more profitable ways to use his funds. In order to get bondholders to take the risk of capital loss on a long-term bond when they do not take such a risk with a short-term security, the yield on long-term bonds must be greater than on short-term bonds.[1] Similarly, since the future returns on a new machine can only be guessed at, investment in a new machine involves a considerable risk. Some wealth holders therefore prefer a fairly safe bond on which they earn 3 percent to an equity on which they are likely, but less certain, to earn 6 percent. Similarly, entrepreneurs may be unwilling to risk

[1] This is not always true. A large increase in the supply of short-term bonds may force the short rate above the long rate. Because of imperfections in the capital market, this relationship between short and long rates may persist for considerable periods of time.

investment in a new machine unless the expected rate of return over cost is 15 percent, when in fact the cost of borrowing is only 7 percent.

The upshot is that if account is taken of differences in risk and of ignorance and immobility, the rates of return on all types of assets will tend to be equalized at the margin. Under such conditions the structure of interest rates may be thought of as one common rate, and we may suppose that there is no difference between a long-term and a short-term bond and no difference between the I.O.U. which a bank gets in return for the loan of funds and the bond which you or I might get from the U.S. Treasury or from a corporation in return for the loan of our funds. Since the yield i on this typical I.O.U. is simply the amount required to induce the public and the banks to part with funds—i.e., the cost of borrowing—and since excess supply of money implies excess demand for earning assets, the problem of interest-rate determination may provisionally be viewed as a problem of determining the supply of and the demand for money.

Before proceeding to an analysis of the determinants of the demand for and supply of money, we need to be certain that we are agreed on a definition of money. The conventional definition is the following: Money is the sum total of currency and bank deposits, but not savings (time) deposits held by the nonbank public. This means in effect that money amounts to the stock of non-interest-bearing liquid assets held by the nonbank public.

8-2 The Demand for Money

A simple and extremely useful way to look at the demand for money to hold is to divide it into three "motives"—a transactions motive, a precautionary motive, and a speculative motive. Let us consider these motives and the factors on which they depend.

The transactions motive. Money balances are held for the purpose of making transactions. If receipts and expenditures were always perfectly synchronized, there would be no need for such balances. Since, however, the typical person is paid once a month or once a week and makes disbursements throughout the period, he must maintain some idle balance for transactions. A person who is paid y dollars at the beginning of the month and who makes consumption expenditures of c dollars at a uniform rate throughout the month will usually maintain a bank balance which averages one-half of his monthly expenditures, or $c/2$ dollars. If his income rises by Δy dollars, then his consumption expenditures will rise by $b\Delta y$ dollars (assuming that his marginal propensity to consume is b) so that the average balance he must keep in his account will be $(c + b\Delta y)/2$. On the other hand, if the price level doubles, the amount he must maintain in his account will double. As a first approximation, the transactions demand for money may be taken to depend on the level of money income.

Aside from the level of money income, what factors affect the transactions demand for money? Institutional arrangements obviously play an important role. If an individual begins to receive his pay check each week instead of each month, he would have to maintain only one-fourth of the average balance he had previously maintained. Since payment practices tend to change slowly, such institutional effects on the demand for money may be ignored in our present short-run analysis.

It is quite possible that the transactions demand for money may depend not only on the level of income but also, to some extent, on the rate of interest. Suppose that an individual plans to spend all his income at a uniform rate throughout the month. Of the y dollars he receives at the beginning of the month, three-quarters will be idle for the first week (assume that each month has exactly four weeks); one-half of the balance will be idle for the first two weeks; and one-quarter of the balance will be idle for the first three weeks. He may therefore take these idle funds and purchase an earning asset. At the beginning of the month he may take three-quarters of his income and purchase bonds. At the end of the first week he requires some additional transactions cash so he cashes in one-third of his bond holdings (one-quarter of his income) to spend during the second week. At the end of the second week he cashes in another one-third of the original bond purchases to spend during the third week; at the end of the third week he cashes in the remainder. Instead of going into the bond market four times as in the present example, he may go in only two times, or he may go in n times. It is important to note that the more often he goes into the bond market, the less his average idle bank balance will be.

What governs the decision as to how many times to go into the market during the month? Since there is some cost of making each transaction, there is a definite drawback to going into the market which must be balanced off against the desirability of holding earning assets as opposed to idle funds. If n is the number of transactions, c is the beginning-of-the-month transactions balance, i is the rate of interest, and $\mathbf{a}$ is the cost per transaction, the optimum number of transactions is[1]

$$n = \sqrt{\frac{ci}{2\mathbf{a}}}$$

[1] Let i be the rate of interest, n the number of transactions per income expenditure period, B the value of bond holdings, $\mathbf{a}$ the cost per transaction, c the beginning-of-the-month transaction balance, and P the profit. Assuming that the cost of transactions depends only on the number of transactions and not on the size of the transactions, we have the transactions cost C given by

$$C = n\mathbf{a}$$

At the beginning of the month, an individual will buy $[(n - 1)c]/n$ bonds. Each $1/n$ days he sells c/n bonds so that average bondholdings are which depends on the rate of interest, the transactions cost, and the size of the beginning balance. Notice that when the rate of interest rises, the optimum number of transactions rises. This means that the quantity of money demanded for transactions purposes decreases as the interest rate rises.

The precautionary motive. A salesman planning a business trip from Chicago to New Orleans will require a certain amount of cash to pay for travel expenses. However, if he is prudent, he will take along more money than the average amount he usually requires to make transactions during such a trip. If, for example, his car breaks down and he is unable to pay for the repairs, he may never get to New Orleans to conduct his business. Because of this failure he may miss out on a promotion or he may even lose his job. Once having been fired, his reputation is damaged, and he may have difficulty finding a new job. All this may happen because his failure to maintain some precautionary balance of money has made him a victim of the "linkage of risks."

The precautionary demand, like the transactions demand, is probably quite closely related to the level of money income. If the cost of automobile repairs rises or if the number of business trips taken each year increases, the salesman's precautionary requirements will probably rise in proportion. However, as in the case of transactions demand, there may be some relationship between the precautionary demand and the rate of interest. An increase in interest rates may make the purchase of earning assets so tempting that the salesman may be willing to assume a slightly greater risk in the form of a lower precautionary balance in return for the added interest earnings.

The speculative motive. Despite the fact that the holding of idle balances seems at first glance to be unwise (since these balances could be put to

---

$$\bar{B} = \frac{(n-1)c}{2n}$$

Since the interest earnings on this average balance are $[(n-1)ci]/2n$, total profits must be

$$P = \frac{(n-1)ci}{2n} - n\mathbf{a}$$

The optimum number of transactions is the value of n which makes P maximum. Accordingly,

$$\frac{dP}{dn} = \frac{2ci}{4n^2} - \mathbf{a} = 0$$

so that

$$n = \sqrt{\frac{ci}{2\mathbf{a}}}$$

This analysis follows J. Tobin, "The Interest Elasticity of the Transactions Demand for Cash," *Review of Economics and Statistics*, 38:241–247, 1956. Tobin also considers a model in which transactions costs are made a function of the size of the transactions. See also W. J. Baumol, "The Transactions Demand for Cash: An Inventory Theoretic Approach," *Quarterly Journal of Economics*, 66:545–556, 1952.

work by trading them for earning assets), there is a large group of economists, usually denoted as "Keynesians," who believe that wealth holders will wish to maintain a pool of cash and deposits in excess of transactions and precautionary needs. The size of this pool of funds varies inversely with the rate of interest. At a high rate of interest the speculative demand for money will be low, whereas at a low rate of interest it will be large. What is the logic behind this notion?

When the rate of interest is very low, security prices are very high. Consequently a small yield can be earned only at the expense of a relatively large outlay. In such a situation a bond purchase does not look like a very attractive bargain. Moreover, if in the past the rate of interest was high but has since fallen to a lower level below which it is not expected to go, the balance of expectations will be in favor of a future rise in the rate. Anyone owning a bond at a time when the rate rises will suffer a capital loss. Consequently, if there is a general expectation that the rate of interest will rise, there will be a preference for liquidity. Since a capital loss cannot be taken on cash (except through a rise in the price level),[1] a situation may arise in which individuals will prefer to hold onto their cash rather than invest in earning assets. They do this in the expectation that interest rates in the future will be higher than at present and that they will therefore be able to strike a better bargain at a subsequent date.

This argument, first presented by Lord Keynes,[2] has been criticized on the ground that it implies an all-or-none kind of behavior. If the interest earnings of a bond are in excess of the expected capital loss, it will pay to invest all one's funds in bonds. If the expected capital loss is greater than the interest earnings, no bonds will be held. Consequently, the minute the critical point is reached where the scales tip in favor of bonds, we would expect a mass exodus from cash into bonds. Keynes's explanation for the fact that this mass exodus does not occur was based on the assumption that different people have different expectations with regard to the future. This view, however, is open to the criticism that if the low rate of interest persists long enough, it will begin to be viewed as permanent so that expectations will converge, the fear of capital loss will disappear, and the speculative demand for money will fade out.

If the above theory is open to criticism, is there anything to the notion that there is a speculative demand for money which is inversely related to the interest rate? Data for the United States economy certainly suggest that there is, for when short-term-paper rates are plotted against average idle deposits, a

---

[1] The expectation of a fall in the price level will make money a relatively more attractive way to hold wealth than physical assets. But this is true of any kind of liquid asset whose money value does not vary with the price level. Price expectations help to explain relative preferences between physical and liquid assets, but do not explain relative preferences among different types of liquid assets.

[2] J. M. Keynes, *The General Theory of Employment Interest and Money*, Chap. 13, Macmillan & Co., Ltd., London, 1936.

strong inverse relationship emerges.[1] Is there then an alternative explanation? To illustrate the argument of the economists who hold that there is, we must prepare the ground by abandoning the notion that there is only one kind of security, and recognize instead that there is in fact a wide range of securities varying in diverse ways with regard to risk, return, and date of maturity. Since investors are not likely to want to keep all their eggs in one basket, they will instead diversify their portfolios and hold some of several different kinds of assets.[2] Included in this portfolio will be some money which, although it earns no interest, has the advantage of a high liquidity premium. In other words, there is a definite value attached to holding money as opposed to other assets because of its maneuverability (the fact that it is easier, at a moment's notice, to convert money into other assets than other assets into money).

To simplify the discussion, suppose that there are only two kinds of bonds— long-term and short-term—and assume that an individual's portfolio consists of some long-term bonds, some short-term bonds, and some cash. The investor would prefer to hold only long-term bonds because of their greater yield, but is dissuaded from this by their greater risk. Only part of his portfolio will therefore consist of long-term bonds. If interest rates rise, the interest that is lost by holding cash becomes greater. Some of the investor's risk aversion will be overcome, and he will therefore substitute some long-term bonds for short-term bonds and some short-term bonds for cash. If interest rates fall, the return on long-term bonds no longer compensates for the risk, while the loss of interest due to the holding of cash and short-term bonds becomes relatively smaller. Consequently, as interest rates fall, investors will have a tendency to adjust their portfolios in the direction of increased liquidity.

This present form of the liquidity preference argument is free from dependence on a one-sided expectation of the future and a difficult-to-justify assumption that expectations will not ultimately converge. It rests on the simple principle of not putting all one's eggs in one basket and thus appeals to common sense and everyday experience.

8-3 Alternative Theories of the Demand for Money

The analysis of the demand for money has thus far been presented in fairly general terms. Because the nature of the demand for money is crucial from the standpoint of the theory of income and employment and also from the standpoint of monetary as opposed to fiscal policy, it is useful to spend some

---

[1] See the evidence presented by J. Tobin, "Liquidity Preference and Monetary Policy," *Review of Economics and Statistics*, 29:124–131, 1947.

[2] This discussion follows the line of J. Tobin, "Liquidity Preference as Behavior towards Risk," *Review of Economic Studies*, 25(2):65–86, 1958. The current view seems to have been quite clearly foreshadowed by J. R. Hicks, "A Suggestion for Simplifying the Theory of Money," *Economica*, New Series, 5:1–19, 1935.

time in segregating the assumptions made about the demand for money by different groups of economists.

One of the most familiar equations in economics is the "quantity equation"

$$MV = pY$$

The equation is a simple truism which states that the quantity of money M times the velocity of turnover of money V must equal the value of money income pY, where p is an index of prices and Y is the level of real income measured in base-period prices.

In some interpretations it is assumed that V is a constant. Velocity may change because institutional payments practices change, because a change in the rate of interest causes a change in the quantity of money demanded for various purposes, or because of many other factors. In any case, the assumption that V is a constant constitutes denial of the existence of the speculative demand for money. This denial follows from the assumption that no wealth holder will be irrational enough to hold money balances in excess of transactions and precautionary needs when he could use the balances to purchase earning assets. Under these "classical" assumptions, the quantity equation becomes more than a mere truism and becomes instead the well-known quantity theory, according to which an increase in the money supply must lead either to an increase in real income Y or to an increase in the price level p, or to some combination of the two. An increase in the supply of money, the velocity of turnover being fixed, implies that wealth holders will attempt to rid themselves of the idle balances by purchasing earning assets. This means that the prices of earning assets will be bid up, interest rates will fall, and investment and income will increase. If idle resources are available, Y may rise. If, instead, the economy is already at full employment, competition for the available supply of physical output will raise prices. Since competition for earning assets will continue until all the excess money balances are absorbed into transactions demands, we may infer that V being fixed, the level of money income will always be proportional to the money supply.

The quantity equation can be rewritten as

$$m = M/p = \mathbf{k}Y$$

where M/p is the real value of the money supply and $\mathbf{k}$ is the reciprocal of V, the average length of time that money is held between transactions. In this form the equation has been called the "Cambridge quantity equation" and $\mathbf{k}$ has been denoted as the "Marshallian $\mathbf{k}$ ratio."

By introducing the speculative demand for money, Keynes specifically denied the constant velocity assumption. Like his predecessors, however, Keynes believed that the transactions and precautionary demands were dependent on the level of money income and not specifically associated with the rate of interest. The Keynesian variant of the demand for money may therefore be written as

$$m = M/p = \mathbf{k}Y + L(i)$$

where $L(i)$ is the speculative demand for money which varies inversely with the rate of interest and where $\mathbf{k}$ must now be interpreted to mean the ratio of transactions money balances to the volume of transactions.[1]

An interesting feature of the Keynesian variant is that once a critically low rate of interest is reached, increases in the supply of money will not achieve any further reduction in the rate of interest. Such a situation may arise from the fact that at very low rates of interest the yield on earning assets is so low and the risk of holding earning assets is so high that, given the liquidity premium of holding money, wealth holders will be willing to substitute money for earning assets in their portfolios without requiring an inducement in the form of higher bond prices.

Alternatively, consider the following situation: Suppose that the Federal Reserve System attempts to increase the money supply by purchasing government bonds from the public. Under normal circumstances such an increase in the demand for bonds would raise bond prices and lower interest rates. However, if interest rates are so low that wealth holders are undecided whether the cost of not investing compensates for the risk of capital loss, they may be willing to sell their bondholdings at existing prices. The fact that the Federal Reserve is supporting the market and may not continue to do so in the future may be taken as a golden opportunity to unload bondholdings. In the type of "liquidity trap" situation here described, the public's supply of bonds is infinitely elastic, which implies that the demand for speculative money balances will also be infinitely elastic with respect to the rate of interest.

Another monetary variant, which for lack of a better name we shall arbitrarily call the "modified Keynesian" variant, would include in the transactions and precautionary demands the assumption that these demands are inversely related to the rate of interest. Therefore, this variant may be written

$$m = L_1(i,Y) + L_2(i)$$

where L_1 refers to the transactions and precautionary demands and L_2 to the speculative demand. Since all the motives for holding money appear to depend on the rate of interest, the modified Keynesian variant implies that the distinc-

[1] This way of writing the demand for money assumes that the speculative demand, as well as the transactions and precautionary demands, is, given a constant rate of interest, proportional to the price level. Although Keynes made no such assumption, we shall follow Patinkin, "Keynesian Economics and the Quantity Theory," in K. K. Kurihara, ed., *Post-Keynesian Economics*, Rutgers University Press, New Brunswick, N.J., 1954, and assume that an increase in the price level will lead to a proportional increase in the demand for speculative balances.

Figure 8-1   Demand and supply for money balances   (all values in real terms).

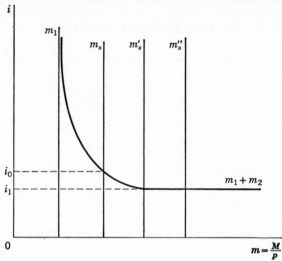

tion between the various motives is somewhat artificial, so that the above expression may just as well be compressed to

$$m = L(i,Y)$$

Recent developments in monetary theory place emphasis on the importance of wealth in determining the demand for money. Tobin's[1] theory of portfolio balance suggests that an increase in the quantity of money demanded will occur not only if income rises and/or the rate of interest falls, but also if wealth holders become richer. An increment to wealth, in other words, causes wealth holders to attempt to distribute this increment over additional holdings of not one, but several forms of wealth. Thus Tobin[2] specifies the demand for money as

$$m = L(i,Y,K)$$

where K, the capital stock, represents the earning power, or productive wealth, of society.[3] Let us denote this final form of the demand for money the "modern Keynesian" variant.

---

[1] Tobin, "Liquidity Preference as Behavior towards Risk," *op. cit.*

[2] J. Tobin, "A Dynamic Aggregative Model," *Journal of Political Economy*, 63:103–115, 1955.

[3] Emphasis on wealth as an important determinant of the demand for money is carried farthest by the so-called "modern quantity" theorists. The modern quantity theorist as exemplified by Milton Friedman differs from the modern Keynesian in that he regards the rate of interest and the level of current income as of only minor importance in determining the demand for money. See Milton Friedman, "The Quantity Theory of Money: A Restatement," *Studies in the Quantity Theory of Money*, Chap. 1, University of Chicago Press, Chicago, 1956, and "The Demand for Money: Some Theoretical and Empirical Results," *Journal of Political Economy*, 67:327–351, 1959.

The Keynesian variant is diagramed in Figure 8-1. The rate of interest is measured on the vertical axis. The transactions and precautionary demand for money m_1 is assumed to be inelastic with respect to the rate of interest. When the speculative demand for money m_2 is added, the total demand for money, $m_1 + m_2$, is obtained. If the supply of money balances is m_s, the demand and supply schedules intersect at interest rate i_0. If the money supply increases to m_s', wealth holders will be induced to hold the added balances only if the interest rate falls to i_1. At i_1 the liquidity trap, where the demand for money is infinitely elastic, is reached. An increase in the supply of money from m_s' to m_s'' yields no fall in the rate of interest.

8-4 The Supply of Money

Recall the definition of money as the sum total of currency and bank deposits, but not savings deposits, held by the nonbank public. In the past there was a direct link between a country's gold stock and its stock, or supply, of money. But with the growth of fractional-reserve-deposit banking, the abandonment of specie as a medium of exchange, and the separation of the currency from specie backing, the connection between the gold stock and the domestic supply of money has become very faint.

While it is not vital for present purposes to ask how the money supply got where it is, it is nevertheless crucial to know how the money supply can be changed. In order to do this, we draw up four balance sheets (Table 8-1) of financial assets and liabilities—a balance sheet for the U.S. Treasury, a balance sheet for the Federal Reserve System, a consolidated balance sheet for the commercial banking system, and a balance sheet for the general public. The balance sheets are hypothetical statements in which we are going to post only changes in various accounts, since it is only the changes that interest us.

Suppose that a gold miner, by dint of his own hard labor, digs $1,000 worth of gold out of the ground. This $1,000 is an asset to the gold miner which means that the assets of the public increase by $1,000, and so also does the public's net worth. The increase in assets and net worth due to the creation of the new wealth in the form of gold is labeled a in the public's balance sheet.

By law, the gold miner must take the gold to the U.S. Treasury. The Treasury accepts the gold, which becomes an asset in its balance sheet, and in return writes a check to the gold miner. This check will ultimately reduce the Treasury's bank account, which it keeps with the Federal Reserve System. The miner then takes the check and deposits it in his commercial bank. He therefore trades one asset (gold) in favor of another asset (bank deposits). The commercial bank receives the check and credits the gold miner with a deposit. This is entered on the right-hand side of the bank's balance sheet because the deposit is a debt which the bank must pay the depositor on demand. But while the bank incurs a liability, it also receives a new asset of $1,000 which it deposits in its own bank account (called "reserves") with the Federal Reserve

System. The Federal Reserve[1] upon receipt of the check credits the account of the commercial bank and thus increases its deposit liability to the banking system (Member Bank Deposits), but at the same time makes a deduction from the Treasury's account of $1,000. All these transactions, starting with the receipt of the gold by the Treasury are labeled b in the various balance sheets.

Table 8-1

U.S. Treasury		Federal Reserve banks	
Deposits with Federal Reserve −1,000 b +1,000 c	Gold certificates +1,000 c	Gold certificates +1,000 c	Treasury deposits −1,000 b +1,000 c
Gold +1,000 b			Member bank deposits +1,000 b

Commercial banks		Public	
Loans and securities +800 d +640 f	Deposits +1,000 b + 800 e + 640 g	Deposits +1,000 b + 800 e + 640 g	Net worth +1,000 a
Reserves +1,000 b − 800 d + 800 e − 640 f + 640 g		Securities − 800 d − 640 f Other assets +1,000 a −1,000 b	

Notice that the Treasury has traded a portion of its bank account in return for the gold, while the gold miner has done the opposite. The net effect therefore is to increase the money supply (measured by the demand deposits and currency held by the public) by $1,000.

How can the Treasury replenish its account? The usual procedure is for the Treasury to print gold certificates which it sells to the Federal Reserve System for deposit credit. When this operation (labeled c) has been accomplished, the Treasury's account is back where it was previously. The net effect, so far as the Treasury is concerned, is an increase in its assets (gold) and an increase in liabilities (gold certificates) of $1,000. The net effect as far as the Federal

[1] The easiest way to think of the Federal Reserve System is as a bank for bankers and for the U.S. Treasury.

Reserve is concerned is a $1,000 increase in its deposit liabilities, in return for which it has gained an asset in the form of a gold certificate. The commercial banks have an increase in deposit liabilities, in return for which they have an added deposit of $1,000 with the Federal Reserve System. The public, finally, has traded $1,000 of gold in return for a bank deposit.

Is the $1,000 change in deposits the net effect on the money supply? Not necessarily: Suppose that the legal minimum reserve requirement is 20 percent. This means that the commercial banks must hold 20 percent of demand deposits (0.20 × $1,000) idle in their Federal Reserve accounts but that the remaining $800, known as "excess reserves," may be used to purchase earning assets. Suppose the bank receiving the $1,000 purchases an $800 bond from a member of the public. The bank writes a check which is received in payment for the bond (d), but the check is redeposited somewhere in the commercial banking system (e). This means that the added reserves due to the Treasury gold sale are still $1,000. But with deposits of $1,800 there are now excess reserves of $640 ($1,000 − 0.20 × $1,800), which may be used to purchase additional securities (f).   But since the proceeds will be redeposited (g), deposits rise to $2,440 ($1,000 + $800 + $640).

Notice that each time excess reserves are used to buy earning assets, the proceeds are redeposited somewhere in the commercial banking system. This means that, after the original $1,000 increase in reserves, which came from outside the commercial banking system, the purchase of earning assets does not change total reserves. But the purchase of earning assets does change *required* reserves because these purchases cause deposits to increase. Thus we may infer from the fact that the net change in reserves is $1,000 and from the fact that required reserves are 20 percent of demand deposits that excess reserves will be exhausted when deposits have risen by $5,000. A 5:1 expansion of deposits will therefore be possible on the basis of the original increase in reserves of $1,000. The final situation is shown in Table 8-2, where it can be seen that after the initial $1,000 increase in deposits and net worth due to the gold production and sale (a), the public has traded the banking system $4,000 worth of earning assets in return for $4,000 of deposits (b). The net effect of the gold purchase on the supply of money is therefore $5,000.

Table 8-2

	Commercial Banks			Public		
Securities		Deposits		Deposits		Net worth
	+4,000 *b*		+1,000 *a*		+1,000 *a*	+1,000 *a*
			+4,000 *b*		+4,000 *b*	
Reserves						
	+1,000 *a*			Securities		
					−4,000 *b*	

It is not necessary for gold to be discovered in order for the money supply to be increased. Whenever additional reserves are placed in the commercial banking system, deposit expansion may proceed. The identical result could, for example, be achieved by a Federal Reserve open-market purchase of government bonds. In this case, the Federal Reserve trades the public a deposit of $1,000 in return for the bond. This, in turn, creates added reserves of $1,000 (see Table 8-1) and leaves the way open for the same kind of multiple expansion as before. The Federal Reserve could also neutralize the monetary effect of the Treasury gold purchase. If the Federal Reserve had sold a government bond of $1,000, this would have reduced deposits and reserves by $1,000 and therefore would have canceled the effect of the gold purchase.

An expansion of the money supply could also result from a net export of goods and services from the economy. The monetary effects of the gold flows received in return are identical to those that result when the gold is dug out of the ground. The expansion could also result from commercial-bank borrowing from the Federal Reserve. In this event, the commercial bank incurs a liability with the Federal Reserve in return for additional reserves. It is important to note that in all cases monetary expansion can take place only if some additional reserves appear from outside the commercial banking system, for if an individual bank wishes to replenish its reserves by selling a security to a member of the public, it does so at the expense of the deposits and reserves of some other commercial bank.

We noted above that with a legal minimum reserve requirement of 20 percent, a $1,000 increase in reserves could lead to a $5,000 expansion of the money supply. The $5,000 is a theoretical maximum that will be realized only as long as there is no hoarding either by the banks or by the public. If, for example, the banks simply hold the added reserves instead of converting them into earning assets, the money supply increases by only $1,000. Similarly, if one of the sellers of the bonds purchased by the banks converts his additional deposits into cash which he hides in a cookie jar, the process of expansion will be arrested at that point.

The foregoing possibilities suggest that although the monetary authority (Federal Reserve) can make the level of member bank reserves whatever it wants, it cannot always be sure that the money supply will rise in a constant proportion to a rise in reserves. Indeed, the ratio of deposits to reserves can be expected to fluctuate considerably. Banks are not likely to utilize all their excess reserves to purchase earning assets. The typical bank operates under conditions of uncertainty. Whether new deposits in any period will exceed withdrawals is never known for certain. Even if the bank regards the chances that deposits will match withdrawals as even, the penalty attached to being caught short is enough to make it hold excess reserves.[1] There is little reason

[1] For an analysis of the effect of uncertainty on credit expansion see D. Orr and W. J. Mellon, "Stochastic Reserve Losses and Expansion of Bank Credit," *American Economic Review*, 51:614–23, 1961.

to suppose, moreover, that banks differ fundamentally from other wealth holders. Assuming that their portfolio balance behavior is similar to that of individuals, banks will be likely to hold larger quantities of excess reserves during periods of low interest rates. A rise in bond yields and loan rates will make banks less reluctant to lend and will therefore increase the ratio of earning assets to reserves and also the supply of money. Thus the supply of money, as well as the demand for money, appears to be partially determined by the rate of interest.

In summary, the potential size of the money supply depends in the final analysis on the volume of bank reserves. Since the volume of these reserves is almost entirely dependent on Federal Reserve–Treasury action, the money supply is often treated as a "policy variable," i.e., fixed unless changed by central direction. As we have seen, the ratio between the actual and the potential money supply may fluctuate under the impact of changing interest rates and varying degrees of uncertainty. Consequently, to treat the supply of money as a policy variable is not entirely satisfactory. The main purpose of the following chapter, however, can very well be achieved by assuming that the supply of money is fixed unless changed by central direction. But in Chapter 10 we shall try to become a bit more sophisticated and shall, therefore, drop this simplifying assumption.

8-5   Monetary Effects of a Fiscal Operation

If we are to gain an understanding of the workings and the effectiveness of monetary and fiscal policies, it is extremely important that we understand the monetary effects of a fiscal operation. A "pure" fiscal policy can be defined as a Treasury operation that changes the size of the current income stream while leaving the money supply unaffected. A "pure" monetary policy is defined as an operation that affects the money supply without directly altering the current income stream. A Federal Reserve purchase of government bonds from a member of the public alters the money supply but has no direct effect on the level of current income.[1] On the other hand, an increase in government expenditures directly increases income, while an increase in taxes has the opposite effect.

Insofar as the payment of taxes to the Treasury reduces demand deposits, the fiscal operation will not be "pure" in the sense that there is no effect on the money supply. If we are able to talk about "pure" fiscal policy, we must assume that the tax revenues are utilized to retire debt held by the public, or that government expenditures in an equal amount are made at the same time. In both cases, the monetary effects of the fiscal operation(s) just cancel. Although it may be difficult at the moment to grasp the purpose of these

---

[1] The Federal Reserve purchase may, through its effect on interest rates, raise the level of investment and income. We regard such an effect as indirect.

subtleties of definition and segregation, it will subsequently become apparent why the distinction must be held firmly in mind.

Consider the monetary effects of an increase in government expenditures. Suppose that the Treasury makes a payment of $100 to a mail carrier. The $100 is an income payment and therefore constitutes a fiscal operation. But the $100 payment is also an addition to the money supply; if it is not offset by a corresponding reduction, it must be considered a combined monetary-fiscal change. Whether or not such an offset occurs depends on the method of financing the $100 expenditure.

1. If the Treasury increases tax collections by $100, there will be a reduction in demand deposits of $100. The monetary effects of the expenditure and the tax cancel each other. A tax-financed expenditure can therefore be regarded as a "pure" fiscal policy.

2. If the Treasury replenishes its account by selling bonds to the public, the public will make payment from its deposits in return for bonds. Again, the monetary effects of the fiscal operation cancel out. A deficit financed by a sale of bonds to the public may therefore be considered a "pure" fiscal policy. When reference is made to fiscal policy, it should always be assumed that deficits are financed by borrowing from the public and that surpluses are used to retire debt held by the public.

3. It is possible for the Treasury to replenish its account by selling bonds to the Federal Reserve System. In this case, the $100 payment to the mail carrier remains as a net increase in the reserves of the banking system. The government expenditure in this case is a combined monetary-fiscal operation since it both increases income and changes the money supply.

8-6   The Program

In the next chapter the building blocks of Chapters 5 through 8 are put together into a general equilibrium model of the economic system. The necessity for this stems from the following consideration: Referring again to Figure 8-1, if the rate of interest is i_0, a certain level of investment is thereby implied. This level of investment in turn implies a certain equilibrium level of income. Suppose, however, that the supply of money is increased to m_s'. This increase in the money supply lowers the rate of interest and stimulates the level of investment. But this means that income will rise; if income rises, the transactions demand for money rises, and this in turn will affect the rate of interest. An endless chain of action and reaction can therefore be set off—a chain that cannot be properly analyzed with our existing apparatus. The purpose of the next chapter is to develop a more effective model that will (1) help to avoid the pitfalls of partial equilibrium analysis and (2) provide a framework within which to consider the effectiveness of alternative stabilization policies.

chapter 9

General equilibrium of the product and money markets

9-1 Introduction

In the last chapter it was suggested that a change in the money supply would affect the rate of interest both directly through the initial change and indirectly through changes induced by the effect of interest-rate changes on the level of investment and the level of income. The same kind of reaction can be set off in the market for final goods. An innovation, for example, will shift the investment demand schedule to the right and bring about a change in the level of income. But an increase in investment, by increasing the level of income, leads to an increase in the transactions and precautionary demands for money balances. If wealth holders (including banks) are to be induced to release the necessary balances from speculative hoards, interest rates must rise. But this in turn means that investment will fall, income will fall, and the process will go through another round of action and reaction. Evidently it will help to introduce a model that will give the final equilibrium solution even if it does not trace the process whereby equilibrium is reached.[1]

To simplify matters at the outset, let us again pretend that the government does not exist and that foreign trade does not take place. Under these condi-

[1] The model used here was first presented by J. R. Hicks, "Mr. Keynes and the 'Classics': A Suggested Interpretation," *Econometrica*, New Series, 5:147–159, 1937.

tions equilibrium of the market for final goods (product market) requires equality between intended savings and investment. The general form of the savings function can be written

$$S = Y - C(Y) \tag{9-1}$$

which, together with the investment demand schedule,

$$I = I(i) \tag{9-2}$$

gives the product market equilibrium condition

$$I(i) = Y - C(Y) \tag{9-3}$$

The condition states that for any arbitrary rate of interest there is some level (or levels) of income that will make intended investment and savings equal. This relationship between the rate of interest and the level of income is referred to as the "*IS* function."

Assuming a Keynesian-type demand for money function (i.e., the real speculative demand for money is a function of the rate of interest, and the real transactions and precautionary demands[1] are proportional to the level of real income), monetary equilibrium will be given by

$$m_s = kY + L(i) \tag{9-4}$$

where m_s, the supply of real money balances, is assumed to be constant. Given the supply of real money balances, there will be some level (or levels) of real income that is (are) associated with a particular rate of interest. This relationship is called the "*LM* function."

Notice that the equilibrium condition in the two markets is a function of two variables—the rate of interest and the level of income. It would therefore be possible to solve the two equations and obtain the final equilibrium solution for the rate of interest and the level of income. Our understanding will be facilitated, however, if we trace the process of solution in a set of simple diagrams.

9-2 Graphic Derivation of the *IS* and *LM* Functions

The investment demand schedule $I = I(i)$ is plotted as a straight line in the first quadrant of Figure 9-1. The rate of interest is posted on the vertical axis, and the level of investment on the horizontal axis.[2] In quadrant 2 the intended investment-savings equilibrium condition is posted. This curve must be a straight line rising from the origin at a 45-degree angle because intended investment must equal savings at equilibrium. The familiar savings schedule

---

[1] From now on the combined transactions and precautionary demands will be referred to simply as the "transactions demand."

[2] The equation for the investment demand schedule is assumed to be $i = 0.05 - 0.0004I$ or, rearranging terms to make I the dependent variable, $I = (i - 0.05)/-0.0004$.

Figure 9-1   Product market equilibrium   (all values in real terms).

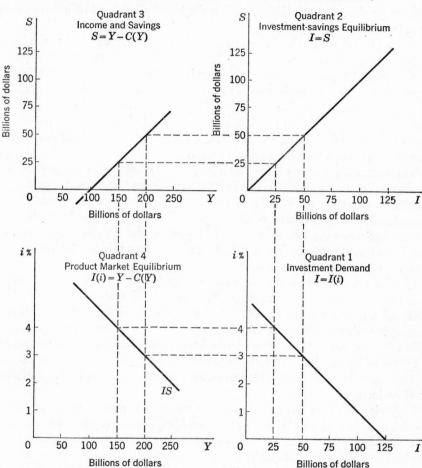

is plotted in quadrant 3. We assume in this case that savings are zero[1] at an income level of $100 billion and that the marginal propensity to save is 0.5.

Starting with an interest rate of 3 percent, we note in quadrant 1 that investment of $50 billion will be undertaken. Moving to quadrant 2, we observe that savings must also be $50 billion. In quadrant 3 the savings function indicates that $50 billion will be saved at an income level of $200 billion. Finally, in quadrant 4 we obtain one point of product market equilibrium, i.e., when the rate of interest is 3 percent, the level of income that will just make intended investment equal savings is $200 billion.

If the rate of interest is raised to 4 percent, the level of investment drops to $25 billion. This means that savings must be $25 billion, and therefore that

[1] The equation for the savings function is given by $S = -50 + 0.5Y$.

the level of income must be \$150 billion. If the rate of interest falls to 1 percent, investment rises to \$100 billion, so that the equilibrium level of income must be \$300 billion.

If this procedure of selecting arbitrary rates of interest and finding the level of income that is consistent with each rate of interest is continued, a curve known as the "*IS* curve" will be traced out in quadrant 4. This curve is a simple graphic representation of the product market equilibrium condition of Eq. (9-3) and shows the level of income that will yield equality of intended savings and investment at different possible interest rates.[1] Evidently we may also interpret the *IS* schedule as the schedule of aggregate demand for goods and services with respect to the rate of interest.

The identical procedure used above may now be applied to the problem of finding monetary equilibrium. In quadrant 1 of Figure 9-2 the real speculative demand for money, $m_2 = L(i)$, is plotted against the rate of interest. It is assumed that the inhabitants of the economy balance their portfolios in such a way that when the rate of interest is 3 percent, the speculative demand is \$25 billion. At 2 percent it is \$50 billion, at 1 percent it is \$75 billion, and at 0 percent it is \$100 billion or more.

Quadrant 2 shows how the given money supply of \$125 billion can be split between transactions and speculative balances. If the transactions demand is \$100 billion, then \$25 billion will be left over for speculative purposes. If the transactions demand is \$75 billion, \$50 billion will be left over for speculative balances. In quadrant 3 the transactions demand, assumed to be proportional to the level of income in a 1:2 ratio, is posted. Finally, in quadrant 4 the rate of interest that is consistent with monetary equilibrium is posted against the level of income.

Beginning with an interest rate of 3 percent, we note in quadrant 1 that wealth holders desire to hold \$25 billion of idle cash and deposits for speculative purposes. In quadrant 2 we observe that \$100 billion will be released for transactions purposes. But quadrant 3 indicates that \$100 billion of transactions money is consistent with a level of income of \$200 billion. Moving to quadrant 4, we observe that the level of income that yields monetary equilibrium with a money supply of \$125 billion and an interest rate of 3 percent is \$200 billion.

Now start with an interest rate of 2 percent. At this rate of interest wealth holders will wish to hold idle speculative balances of \$50 billion. This means that the amount released for transactions purposes will be \$75 billion, which is consistent with a level of income of \$150 billion (quadrant 3). Accordingly, we note in quadrant 4 that the level of income that will yield monetary equilibrium at a 2 percent rate of interest is \$150 billion.

---

[1] The equation for intended investment is $i = 0.05 - 0.0004I$, which may be rewritten $I = (i - 0.05)/-0.0004$. The savings function is $S = -50 + 0.5Y$; If intended investment is equated with savings, we have $(i - 0.05)/-0.0004 = -50 + 0.5Y$, which simplifies to $i = 0.07 - 0.0002Y$; this is the equation for the *IS* function and should correspond with the points plotted in Fig. 9-1.

Figure 9-2 Monetary equilibrium (all values in real terms).

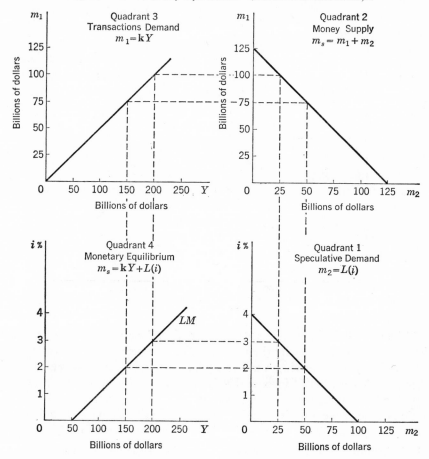

If this process of selecting arbitrary rates of interest and finding the level of income that is consistent with monetary equilibrium at each rate of interest is continued, a curve known as the "LM curve" will be traced out in quadrant 4.[1] This curve is a simple diagrammatic representation of the monetary equilibrium condition of Eq. (9-4).

[1] Inspection of quadrant 1 of Fig. 9-2 indicates that the speculative demand is a straight line with the equation $i = 0.04 - 0.0004m_2$, which may be rewritten as

$$m_2 = (i - 0.04)/-0.0004$$

The transactions demand m_1 is $m_1 = 0.5Y$ and, since the money supply is $125 billion,

$$m_1 + m_2 = 125 = 0.5Y + \frac{i - 0.04}{-0.0004}$$

from which it follows that the equation for the LM function is $i = -0.01 + 0.0002Y$.

Figure 9-3   General equilibrium   (all values in real terms).

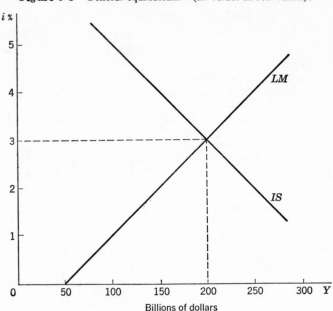

Although the *LM* schedule suggests that several rates of interest are consistent with monetary equilibrium, and the *IS* curve suggests that several rates are consistent with product market equilibrium, there is only one rate of interest and one level of income that is consistent with both. In Figure 9-3 the *IS* and *LM* functions of Figures 9-1 and 9-2 are superimposed. The intersection of the two curves is at an income level of $200 billion with an interest rate of 3 percent.[1] Once these equilibrium values have been found, it is easy

[1] We should be able to find the equilibrium values by solving the *IS* and *LM* equations simultaneously. The *IS* function is $i = 0.07 - 0.0002Y$ and the *LM* function is

$$i = -0.01 + 0.0002Y$$

from which it follows by simple algebra that $i = 0.03$ and $Y = 200$. Given the level of income, savings are
$$S = -50 + 0.5Y = -50 + 0.5 \times 200 = 50$$
which equals intended investment; this can be found from the investment demand schedule to be
$$I = \frac{i - 0.05}{-0.0004} = \frac{0.03 - 0.05}{0.03 - 0.05} = 50$$
Similarly, the level of income of 200 requires transactions balances of
$$m_1 = 0.5Y = 0.5 \times 200 = 100$$
Because the money supply is 125, this releases 25 for speculative purposes. This result is consistent with a 3 percent interest rate because
$$m_2 = \frac{i - 0.04}{-0.0004} = \frac{0.03 - 0.04}{-0.0004} = 25$$

enough to trace back once again through the product market diagrams and verify that the level of investment is $50 billion and the level of savings is $50 billion. Similarly, if we retrace our steps through the money market, we find that at equilibrium the speculative demand is $25 billion and the transactions demand is $100 billion. General equilibrium prevails: there is no tendency for any magnitude to change.

9-3 Government and General Equilibrium

As was noted previously, the condition that must hold at the equilibrium level of income is that total income leakages must equal total compensating expenditures. Thus intended investment plus government expenditures must equal savings plus taxes. This means that the IS schedule, which represents product market equilibrium, becomes[1]

$$I(i) + G = Y - C(Y - T)$$

Chapter 6 considered the effect of adding to the economy of Chapter 5 first $20 billion of government expenditures and then $20 billion of taxes. In similar fashion, let us now take the assumed economy of Section 9-2 and first add $25 billion of government expenditures and then $25 billion in taxes. In Figure 9-4 the IS schedule prior to the imposition of government expenditures and taxes is IS_0.

Government expenditures have the same effect on the level of income as do investment expenditures. We may therefore add the $25 billion government expenditures to the investment demand schedule in quadrant 1. The combined investment demand schedule and government expenditures schedule (what we have been calling "compensating expenditures") is now denoted as $I(i) + G$. Note that if G is added to the investment demand schedule, the horizontal axis of both quadrants 1 and 2 must be changed to $I + G$. The new equilibrium condition is that the compensating expenditures $(I + G)$ must be balanced by an equal amount of leakages $(S + T)$ so that $S + T$ becomes the vertical axis in quadrants 2 and 3.

At a 3 percent interest rate investment expenditures of $50 billion will be

---

[1] Since we are ignoring all but personal savings, we may write

$$S = Y_d - C$$

Disposable income is defined as

$$Y_d = Y - T$$

and since consumption is a function of disposable income we have

$$C = C(Y - T)$$

Combining these expressions gives us the savings schedule

$$S = Y - T - C(Y - T)$$

so that upon adding T to both sides of the equation, we obtain the total leakages schedule

$$S + T = Y - C(Y - T)$$

undertaken, to which must be added the $25 billion government expenditures. This means (quadrant 2) that $75 billion of leakages are now required to match the compensating expenditures. Observe in quadrant 3 that these leakages are generated at an income level of $250 billion. Dropping a perpendicular into quadrant 4, we note that product market equilibrium at a 3 percent rate of interest, instead of being at an income level of $200 billion, is now at $250 billion. If product market equilibrium is found for a number of other interest rates, it will always be the case that for any rate of interest, product market equilibrium is at an income level $50 billion higher than before the addition of the $25 billion of government expenditure. Apparently the IS schedule shifts to the right by $50 billion at all rates of interest. This new schedule is denoted as IS_1 in Figure 9-4.

If the $I(i) + G$ schedule of quadrant 1 shifts by $1, the IS schedule of quadrant 4 will shift by $1 times the multiplier, which in this example is 2. This is so because the increase in investment or government expenditures will require an additional dollar of savings to offset it. Income must therefore rise by enough to generate an additional dollar of leakages. Consequently the shift in the IS schedule will always equal the shift in the $I(i) + G$ schedule times the multiplier—a result that would be expected from the analysis of Chapter 6.

Although the IS schedule will shift by the change in investment or government expenditures times the multiplier, is it also true that the change in income will be of this magnitude? In Figure 9-4 the IS_1 schedule cuts the LM schedule at an income level of $225 billion. Although the multiplier is 2, the level of income rises by only $25 billion. What accounts for this?

Observe first of all that the rate of interest in the new equilibrium position is 3.5 percent. The increase of 0.5 percent over the original level has been caused by the fact that the government cannot borrow $25 billion from the public without a higher yield inducement. Given the assumption that the money supply is fixed, the funds borrowed by the government must come from a reduction in speculative balances and/or from a reduction in transactions balances. In any event, if wealth holders are to be persuaded that government securities are more attractive than the other forms in which they have been holding wealth, interest rates must rise. But this in turn implies that the level of investment will fall, and this means that the level of income will fall. The stimulus provided by the government expenditure is therefore partially offset by a decline in investment spending.

At the new equilibrium rate of interest of 3.5 percent, investment expenditures are only $37.5 billion. Add to this the government expenditures of $25 billion and note that compensating expenditures in the new equilibrium position are, not $75 billion as originally expected, but only $62.5 billion. Thus the net change in compensating expenditures is only $12.5 billion (62.5 − 50.0), which means that the change in income will be 2 (the multiplier) times $12.5 billion or $25 billion.

Figure 9-4 Government expenditures and taxation (all values in real terms).

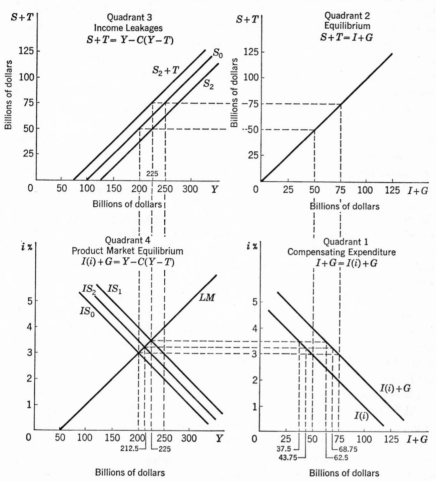

We can now see that one of the virtues of the *IS-LM* model is that it shows that the crude multipliers of past chapters implicitly assume monetary neutrality, i.e., that any change in government expenditures, taxes, or investment would not affect the rate of interest and therefore the level of investment. We now observe, however, that it is conceivable for an increase in government expenditures not to affect the level of income at all. If, through monetary repercussions, an increase in government expenditures of $1 leads to a fall in investment expenditures of exactly $1, there will be no change in income. If, on the other hand, the deficit spending can be financed with no change in interest rates, a full multiplier effect on the level of income will materialize. It is evident, then, that the simple multipliers of Chapters 5 and 6 will hold only if the added transactions resulting from an increase in expenditure can be financed without changes in interest rates. Observe that if the *LM* function is a horizontal line, changes in income will equal the shifts in the *IS* schedule.

Next let us impose a tax of $25 billion to match the government expenditure and assume, as in the simplest fiscal policy model of Chapter 6, that the tax is independent of the level of income. Previous considerations lead us to suppose that $25 billion of taxes will lower the level of income by $25 billion because, the marginal propensity to save being 0.5, $12.5 billion of the tax will be drawn from savings. Leakages therefore rise by a total of only $12.5 billion so that, given a marginal propensity to save of 0.5, the level of income will have to fall by $25 billion in order to eliminate the leakages in excess of compensating expenditures. We would therefore expect the *IS* schedule to shift to the left by $25 billion.

In Figure 9-4 we observe that the $25 billion tax shifts the savings schedule down by $12.5 billion from S_0 to S_2. If we add the tax function to the savings schedule, we obtain the total leakages schedule $S_2 + T$, which is $12.5 billion greater at all levels of income than the S_0 schedule. The combined investment and government expenditures of $75 billion, which are generated at a 3 percent rate of interest, will now be offset by $75 billion of leakages at an income level of $225 billion instead of an income level of $250 billion, as in the previous example. At all other interest rates the same thing will happen: The level of income that yields product market equilibrium at different rates of interest is always $25 billion less than the level prior to the imposition of the tax. The *IS* schedule therefore shifts to the left by the amount of the change in leakages, $b\Delta T$, times the multiplier, or by $b\Delta T/(1 - b)$. After the imposition of the tax, the *IS* schedule is IS_2 of Figure 9-4.

Although the equilibrium level of income prior to the imposition of the tax was $225 billion and the tax causes a leftward shift in the *IS* schedule of $25 billion, the equilibrium level of income falls to only $212.5 billion. Again, monetary effects have kept the full multiplier from working its way out. If the tax proceeds are used to retire the bonds that were issued to borrow the $25 billion previously spent by the government, there will be no net shrinkage in the money supply, although the reduction in consumption caused by the tax will release some money balances from transactions. If monetary equilibrium is to be established, interest rates must fall, investment will be stimulated, and the level of income will rise. The depressing effect of the tax is therefore partly offset by an increase in investment.

Notice that in the final equilibrium situation, the rate of interest is 3.25 percent. At this rate of interest the level of investment is $43.75 billion, whereas at the previous equilibrium rate of 3.5 percent the level of investment was $37.5 billion. Although the tax would tend to lower the equilibrium level of income by $25 billion, the monetary effects of the tax are such as to raise the level of investment by $6.25 billion (from $37.5 billion to $43.75 billion) and the level of income by $12.5 billion. The net effect, as shown in Figure 9-4, is to lower the equilibrium level of income by $12.5 billion.

9-4   Shifts in the *IS* and *LM* Functions

In the last section it was seen that the addition of $25 billion of government expenditures shifted the *IS* schedule to the right by $50 billion because, the marginal propensity to save being 0.5, income would have to rise by $50 billion to generate the additional leakages needed to offset the added $25 billion of government expenditures. Similarly, the addition of a $25 billion tax shifted the *IS* schedule to the left by $25 billion because the level of income would have to fall by $25 billion to offset the additional leakages of $12.5 billion caused by the imposition of the tax. These are but two of the ways in which the *IS* schedule may shift. Some other factors that may cause such a shift in the *IS* schedule, as well as some changes that will shift the *LM* schedule, are considered briefly in this section.

A reduction in intended savings (increase in intended consumption) will shift the savings schedule of quadrant 3 down and thereby reduce the leakages generated at all income levels. This means that the *IS* schedule will shift to the right. Such a change in the savings schedule may result from the introduction of a new product which consumers feel they must have even if it is at the expense of savings. The downward shift in the savings schedule may also result from an increase in the community's wealth. A persistent governmental deficit, for example, may result in the accumulation of such a large stock of liquid assets in the hands of the public that wealth holders no longer feel the necessity of saving at their previous rate. Similarly, the expectation of price increases and shortages of consumer goods may bring about a fall in the savings schedule and lead to a burst of consumer buying of the kind that occurred at the start of the Korean War.

The *IS* schedule will shift to the right if the investment demand schedule shifts to the right. Such a shift may occur as a result of an innovation, as the result of additional housing requirements brought about by population increases, and as the result of better profit expectations in the future. In all these cases, the *IS* schedule will shift by the amount of the shift in the investment demand schedule times the multiplier, or, what amounts to the same thing, the reciprocal of the marginal propensity to save.

Shifts in the *LM* schedule may result from monetary policy, from changes in expectations, and from changes in payments practices. If the Federal Reserve Open Market Committee decides to pursue an expansionary monetary policy, it will purchase government bonds on the open market. Wealth holders trade part of their stock of government bonds to the Federal Reserve System in return for bank deposits. This means that the money supply schedule of quadrant 2 of Figure 9-2 shifts to the right, a greater volume of money is available for both transactions and speculative purposes at all rates of interest, and the LM curve of quadrant 4 shifts to the right.

Changes in expectations are likely to make their presence felt in the money market by shifts in the speculative demand for money. If, for example, investors become accustomed to a low rate of interest, the fear of capital loss that usually accompanies a low rate may gradually become less powerful. Thus the m_2 schedule will shift to the left, and a greater volume of transactions, and therefore income, can be supported at all rates of interest. This means that the LM schedule shifts to the right.

Changes in payments practices will change the volume of transactions that a given money supply will support. If individuals are paid twice as often as before, the average idle deposits that must be held for transactions purposes will decline by one-half. This means that the m_1 schedule of quadrant 3 of Figure 9-2 will rotate in a clockwise fashion, and so also will the LM schedule. In the United States there has been a steady advance in the rapidity with which checks are cleared and in the rapidity with which payments and collections are made. All such changes tend to reduce average transactions balances relative to the volume of transactions. In addition, we may well imagine the size of the reduction in the "k ratio" that has resulted from the increasing use of the pay-as-you-go tax as opposed to the once-a-year payment. Imagine the increase in transactions balances that would be required if, instead of paying taxes each week or each month, we were once again to go back to the system of paying all our income taxes once a year.

9-5 "Real" Versus "Monetary" Sources of Income Change

The present model of income and interest-rate determination is a useful tool for the analysis of many macro-economic problems. One very interesting application, which we present here in order to increase the reader's familiarity with the model, is to the problem of identifying the sources of the disturbances that cause the level of income to change.[1]

Changes in income that occur as the result of shifts in the consumption or investment functions or in government tax and expenditure policies may be denoted as "real" disturbances. Changes in income that stem from changes in the money supply or from changes in liquidity preference may be denoted "monetary" disturbances. In Figure 9-5(a) we assume that the IS schedule shifts from IS_0 to IS_1. This real disturbance causes the level of income to rise from Y_0 to Y_1 and the rate of interest to rise from i_0 to i_1. In Figure 9-5(b) income increases from Y_0 to Y_1 because of a shift in the LM curve caused by, for example, an increase in the money supply. In this case, however, the rate

---

[1] The discussion is adapted from J. L. Stein, "A Method of Identifying Disturbances Which Produce Changes in Money National Income," *Journal of Political Economy*, 68:1–16, 1960.

Figure 9-5   Identifying real and monetary disturbances   (all values in real terms).

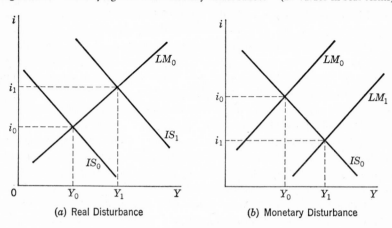

(a) Real Disturbance   (b) Monetary Disturbance

of interest declines. Consequently, it is apparent that a real disturbance may be distinguished from a monetary disturbance by observing that in the case of the former income and the interest rate move in the same direction whereas in the case of the latter they move in opposite directions.

The analysis can be pushed a bit further by dividing monetary disturbances into two components: disturbances that arise as a result of a change in the money supply, and disturbances that arise as a result of a shift in liquidity preference, i.e., a change in the quantity of money demanded for speculative purposes. Let us call the former "money supply" disturbances and the latter "liquidity" disturbances. Notice that both liquidity and money supply disturbances of a sort that raise the level of income tend also to lower the rate of interest. How then are we to tell which of the two has caused income to change?

The answer can be found by observing the behavior of velocity. Recall the quantity equation introduced in Chapter 8,

$$MV = pY$$

and rewrite the equation as

$$V = \frac{pY}{M} \qquad (9\text{-}5)$$

Velocity, V, is the ratio of money income to the money supply. Since the demand for money is

$$\frac{M}{p} = kY + L(i) \qquad (9\text{-}6)$$

we may combine Equations (9-5) and (9-6) to obtain

$$V = \frac{1}{k + L(i)/Y} \qquad (9\text{-}7)$$

From this expression we notice that changes in the velocity of money can be observed by observing changes in the ratio of the quantity of money demanded for speculative purposes, $L(i)$, to the level of income.

From Equation (9-7) we can readily see that a rise in income due to a real disturbance must be accompanied by a rise in velocity. Since income and the interest rate both rise, idle balances are released from speculative holdings and move into transactions balances. Consequently, the ratio $L(i)/Y$ declines, and velocity increases. The average dollar apparently turns over more rapidly under the impact of a real disturbance that raises the level of income.

A money supply disturbance that causes income to rise is associated with a fall in the interest rate. Since the fall in the interest rate increases the quantity of money demanded for speculative purposes, the rise in income cannot be proportionately as large as the increase in the money supply, so that the ratio of speculative balances to income increases and velocity falls. In this case, therefore, the numerator of the expression $L(i)/Y$ increases proportionately more than the denominator.

Finally, in the case of a liquidity disturbance, income rises because wealth holders no longer wish to hold as large a quantity of idle balances as before. They dispose of the surplus idle balances by buying bonds, and this lowers the interest rate, raises the level of investment and income, and thereby effects a transfer of speculative to transactions balances. Velocity, in this case, must rise. Even though the fall in the interest rate tends to increase the quantity of idle balances that wealth holders wish to hold, this increase cannot be enough to offset the initial decline in speculative holdings. Complete offset would occur only if the level of income, and therefore the transactions demand, failed to change at all. Thus, in general, a liquidity disturbance that raises the level of income is associated with a fall in the interest rate and an increase in velocity.

The results are summarized in Table 9-1. A real disturbance can be identified as one in which income, the interest rate, and velocity all move in the same direction. A money supply disturbance can be identified as one in which income moves in the opposite direction to the interest rate and velocity. A liquidity disturbance can be identified as one in which income and velocity move in the same direction while the interest rate moves in the opposite direction.

Table 9-1 Identification of disturbances that cause income to rise

Type of disturbance	Change in Y	Change in i	Change in V
Real	+	+	+
Money supply	+	−	−
Liquidity	+	−	+

In his study of income changes over the period 1919–1958, Stein, by observing income, interest rate, and velocity changes, found that "real factors were mainly responsible for 21 out of 39 year-to-year changes in money income."[1] Money supply factors were mainly responsible for 11 year-to-year changes, and liquidity factors were mainly responsible for 6 year-to-year changes.

As we have seen, a shift to the right of the *IS* schedule will, in general, raise the level of income and the rate of interest. A shift to the right of the *LM* function, on the other hand, will raise the level of income and lower the rate of interest. These general results are not, however, always obtained. Strangely enough, it is the extreme cases in which these results do not hold that have caused much controversy among economists. In the next chapter we shall look at these extremes and their implications for policy.

[1] Stein, *op. cit.*, p. 11.

chapter 10

The demand for money
and stabilization policy

10-1   Introduction

Under what conditions is monetary policy effective in changing the level of real income? Under what conditions is it ineffective? Under what conditions is fiscal policy effective? Under what conditions is it ineffective? When should an "integrated" monetary-fiscal policy be used? Do alternative assumptions about the demand for money and the shape of the investment demand schedule make any difference?

10-2   A Keynesian-classical-intermediate Model

Consider the hypothetical speculative demand function of Figure 10-1. It is assumed that between interest rates of 2 and 6 percent the speculative demand for money is inversely related to the rate of interest. However, when the rate of interest rises to 6 percent the interest loss from holding idle balances becomes so great and the expected risk of capital loss resulting from a further rise in interest rates becomes so small that the speculative demand disappears. On the other hand, once the rate of interest falls to 2 percent, the interest loss is so low and the risk of capital loss so great that investors would just as soon hold idle money balances as earning assets. When increases in the money supply reduce the interest rate to 2 percent, further increases will not affect the rate of interest. The region above 6 percent will be recognized as the region within which the classical assumption (Chapter 8) of no speculative demand holds, while the region of speculative demands of $100 billion or more will be recognized as the Keynesian "liquidity trap" region.

Given this speculative demand function, let us trace out the LM curve on the assumption that the money supply is $125 billion and the ratio of transactions balances to the level of income is 0.5. For interest rates between 2 and 6 percent the derivation is straightforward, following the lines of the last

Figure 10-1   Monetary policy   (all values in real terms).

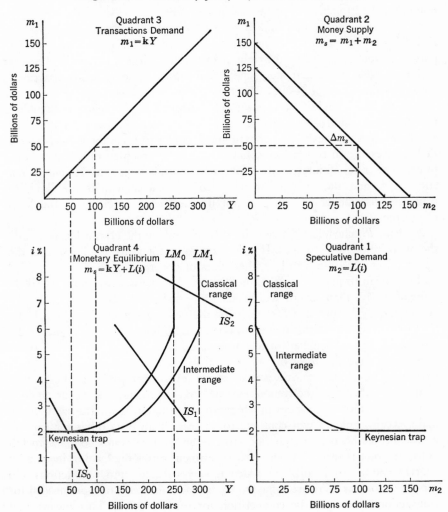

chapter. But what about the classical range? For an interest rate of 7 or 8 percent the same transactions balances are released as for a 6 percent rate. The same level of income is therefore associated with any rate of interest of 6 percent or more. This means that for all interest rates of 6 percent and above the *LM* curve becomes a vertical line.

Next consider a speculative demand of $125 billion. Evidently this is just as consistent with a 2 percent rate of interest as a speculative demand of $100 billion. But since the available transactions balances would be reduced to zero, the level of income that can be supported would be zero, and thus we observe that monetary equilibrium is consistent with all levels of income between zero and $50 billion at an interest rate of 2 percent. For levels of income below $50 billion the *LM* function must be a horizontal line.

Next consider an increase in the money supply of $25 billion resulting from a Federal Reserve purchase of government bonds on the open market. This purchase produces a shift to the right of $50 billion in the *LM* function because each dollar added to the money supply will support $2 of added transactions. How will this monetary policy affect the level of income?

1. If the *IS* schedule (*IS₀*) cuts the *LM* schedules in the Keynesian liquidity trap region, the increase in the money supply does not affect the level of income at all. In this case wealth holders are quite willing to trade their bonds to the Federal Reserve in return for money without the premium of a higher bond price. The rate of interest therefore remains the same, investment is not stimulated, and the level of income remains unchanged. If the liquidity trap prevails, monetary policy is totally ineffective in changing the level of income.

2. If the *IS* schedule (*IS₂*) cuts the *LM* schedule in the classical range, quite the opposite picture emerges. If sellers are to be found for the bonds that the Federal Reserve wishes to buy, the prices of government bonds must be bid up by enough to persuade wealth holders that other assets are now relatively more attractive than government bonds. Only under these conditions will they accept money balances in exchange for the government bonds. There being no speculative demand for money to hold, wealth holders will take these new money balances and use them to purchase other earning assets. These other assets may take the form of new capital investment (new securities) or of purchase of existing securities. New capital investment will raise the level of income and therefore the transactions demand for money. However, as long as some idle money balances in excess of those required for transactions remain, wealth holders will continue to compete with each other for earning assets. Hence bond prices continue to rise and interest rates continue to fall until the point is reached where new investment raises the level of income by exactly enough to absorb the added money balances into transactions. To repeat, as long as there are some money balances in excess of those needed for transactions, there will be competition for earning assets. This means that

interest rates will continue to fall and investment will continue to rise until
the idle balances are absorbed. The level of income must therefore rise by
$\Delta m_s/\mathbf{k}$, where Δm_s is the change in the money supply.

3. If the *IS* schedule (IS_1) cuts the *LM* functions in the intermediate range,
the increase in the money supply succeeds in increasing the level of income,
but not by as much as in the classical case. Whereas in the classical case the
rate of interest falls by enough to absorb the whole addition to the supply
of money into transactions, in the present case part of the increase will be
absorbed into speculative holdings. Thus investment will not increase by as
much as in the classical case, and the level of income will rise by only a fraction
of $\Delta m_s/\mathbf{k}$.

The next step is to do an about-face and inquire into the effectiveness of
fiscal policy. Consider Figure 10-2 in which the three-range *LM* function is
reproduced together with six *IS* schedules. IS_0, IS_1, IS_2 are the same *IS* schedules
as in Figure 10-1. $IS_{(0+g)}$, $IS_{(1+g)}$, and $IS_{(2+g)}$, are the schedules that result from
an increase in government expenditures. How effective is the increase in
government expenditures?

1. In the Keynesian region the government expenditures cause income to
rise by $Y_0' - Y_0$, an amount equal to the full multiplier times the change in

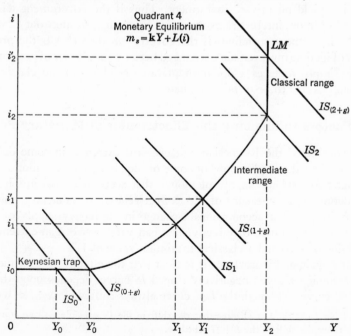

Figure 10-2 Fiscal policy   (all values in real terms).

government expenditures.[1] Since we have assumed that the government expenditure is not tax-financed and since we assume a fixed money supply, the funds are obtained by borrowing from the public. In other words, the fiscal policy is what we have called a "pure" fiscal policy. As long as the liquidity trap prevails, the funds can be borrowed from speculative balances without an increase in the rate of interest. Since therefore the level of investment will not be affected by government borrowing, income will rise by the full multiplied amount of the government expenditures increase.

2. In the intermediate range, government expenditures succeed in increasing the level of income from Y_1 to Y_1'. This increase is not, however, as great as the increase in the Keynesian region. In this intermediate range governmental borrowing apparently necessitates an increase in the rate of interest because without such an increase it is impossible to pry the needed balances away from private holdings. But when the rate of interest rises, the level of investment falls, with the consequence that the expansionary effect of government expenditures is somewhat dampened by a fall in investment.

3. In the classical range, the shift in the IS schedule from IS_2 to $IS_{(2+g)}$ has no effect whatsoever on the level of income and produces an even greater rise in the rate of interest than in the intermediate range. Because not a single speculative dollar exists, the borrowing of funds from the public necessitates interest-rate increases sufficient to drive marginal investors into lending to the government by making the return on government bonds greater than the prospective yield on private investment. Thus if the government wishes to borrow $25 billion, interest rates must rise by enough to snuff out $25 billion of private investment spending. If the government then spends the proceeds, the level of income must remain unchanged because each dollar of governmental spending simply replaces a dollar of private spending. In the classical case fiscal policy seems to be of no use whatever.

10-3   Factors Influencing the Effectiveness of Monetary Policy

Having considered the Keynesian and classical extremes in some detail, let us now consider the implications of some of the alternative assumptions about the demand for and the supply of money that were discussed in Chapter 8. Let us define as our measure of the "effectiveness" of monetary policy the change in income that accompanies a change in the money supply of $1. As we have seen, the range of effectiveness can vary between an extreme Keynesian value of zero and a classical maximum value of $1/\mathbf{k}$.

Looking again at Figure 10-1, it is clear that the effectiveness of monetary policy, assuming a given negatively sloped IS curve, depends upon the slope of the LM curve. Although the LM curve always shifted by $\Delta m_s/\mathbf{k}$, we found

[1] Remember from the last chapter that the shift in the IS schedule will be equal to the multiplier times the shift in the $I + G$ schedule.

monetary policy to be completely ineffective when the slope of *LM* was zero; partially effective when it was positive; and completely effective when it was infinite.

The different values of the slope of the *LM* schedule in the different ranges were the consequence of the speculative demand for money. In the absence of a speculative demand, *LM* had an infinite slope; with speculative demand inversely related to the rate of interest, *LM* had a positive slope; and with infinitely elastic speculative demand, *LM* had a zero slope. Let us now see what happens to the slope of the *LM* curve when we assume, first, that the transactions demand for money and, second, that the supply of money are both sensitive to interest rate changes.

Considering first the transactions demand, we found in Chapter 8 that it would pay wealth holders to enter the bond market more and more frequently during an income-expenditure period as interest rates rise. This means that as interest rates rise, average transactions balances fall so that the transactions demand for money is inversely related to the rate of interest.

In Figure 10-3, LM_0 is drawn on the assumption that the transactions demand for money is not affected by the rate of interest and that the relevant transactions demand curve in quadrant 3 is m_{t_4}. LM_1, on the other hand, is drawn on the assumption that at an interest rate of 6 percent m_{t_6} relates the transactions demand to the level of income; m_{t_4} relates the transactions demand to the level of income when the rate of interest is 4 percent; m_{t_2} is appropriate for a 2 percent rate; and m_{t_8} represents an 8 percent rate. Since we now have a whole family of transactions demand schedules, each one appropriate to a particular rate of interest, we must, in deriving the *LM* schedule, trace through the quadrants by starting with different interest rates in quadrant 1 and pick the transactions demand curve in quadrant 3 that is appropriate to the particular interest rate with which we began in quadrant 1.

LM_1 is less steeply sloped than LM_0. There is now no pure classical range because there is no longer a fixed relationship between money balances and the volume of transactions despite the fact that there is no speculative demand. This flattening out of the *LM* schedule implies that the more interest-elastic transactions and precautionary demands become, the less (more) effective does monetary (fiscal) policy become.

Let us consider next the possibility that rising interest rates cause banks to activate excess reserves and thereby increase the money supply. A useful way to approach this problem is to assume that there is no speculative demand for money and that the transactions demand is insensitive to interest-rate changes. In this way the effect of interest elasticity of the money supply can be compared with the classical *LM* function.

In Figure 10-4 quadrant 1 is left blank to denote the absence of speculative demand, and the absence of interest sensitivity of transactions demand means that there is only one transactions demand function in quadrant 3. Beginning

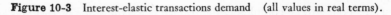

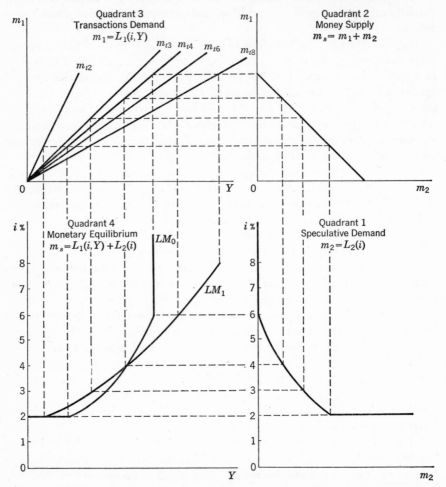

Figure 10-3   Interest-elastic transactions demand   (all values in real terms).

with interest rate i_0 we assume that the money supply is m_{i_0}. Since there is no
speculative demand for money, all balances are available for transactions.
Consequently, the level of income that can be supported is Y_0. If the interest
rate rises to i_1, banks activate excess reserves so that the money supply now
becomes m_{i_1}, and the income level that can be supported becomes Y_1. Similarly,
a rise in the interest rate to i_2 causes a further increase in the money supply
so that income level Y_2 yields monetary equilibrium. Without any increase in
reserves a time must come when interest-rate increases induce no further
increases in the supply of money. Consequently, the slope of the LM curve
becomes steeper as the interest rate rises and eventually becomes vertical as
in the classical case.

Figure 10-4   Interest-elastic money supply   (all values in real terms).

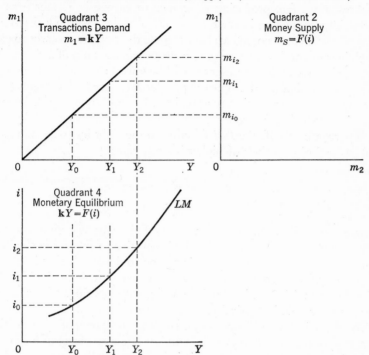

Notice that our present assumption produces an *LM* curve that takes on a shape similar to that attained when we assumed the existence of a speculative demand on the part of the public. Indeed, it may very well have been the case that during the great depression of the 1930s, what appeared to have been a liquidity trap caused by a highly elastic demand for money may have been partially caused by a highly interest-elastic supply of money resulting from bank behavior. Certainly banks held large quantities of excess reserves and appeared to make little effort to convert these reserves into earning assets.

But what does this kind of situation imply about the effectiveness of monetary policy? The money supply function implied by our present discussion might be written

$$m_s = F(i,R)$$

where R is the volume of bank reserves measured in real terms. An increase in bank reserves brought about by Federal Reserve purchase of bonds automatically increases the money supply by an equivalent amount (refer to the discussion of money supply in Chapter 8 if the reasons for this are not clear), and will tend to produce a further increase in the money supply as banks use their excess reserves to purchase earning assets. But the consequence of this is that interest rates fall, producing reluctance to engage in further expansion. During a deep depression interest rates may already be so low that Federal Reserve purchases may not induce banks to use their excess reserves to expand their holdings of earning assets. As a consequence, the ratio of a change in the money supply to a change in reserves will be only 1:1, whereas the potential ratio may be as high as 5:1. Thus the Federal Reserve's leverage effect on the money supply may, during such periods, be severely reduced. What this suggests is that at low interest rates it may take a far more sizable Federal Reserve purchase to shift the *LM* function to the right by some amount than it would take during periods of higher interest rates.

10-4 Monetary Policy and Interest-inelastic Investment Demand

Another reason why monetary policy may fail to be effective stems from the circumstance that investment may be insensitive to changes in the interest rate. As we saw in Chapter 7, there is reason to doubt whether interest-rate changes, even if they could be brought about, could make a significant contribution toward raising the level of investment during periods of slack demand. In the extreme case of a vertical investment demand schedule, the *IS* schedule will also be vertical (see Figure 10-5), so that monetary policy, even though interest rates can be made to change, will not affect the level of income.

In classical monetary assumptions it is implicit that the investment demand

Figure 10-5   Interest-inelastic investment demand   (all values in real terms).

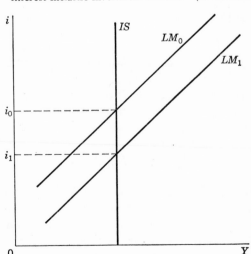

schedule is interest-elastic.[1] If the ratio of real cash balances to the level of real income is fixed, an increase in the money supply must find its way into new transactions in the form of either consumption or investment expenditures. If consumption expenditures are insensitive to changes in the interest rate, which nearly everyone assumes to be the case, investment must be interest-elastic; if it is not, existing security prices will be bid up to a value of infinity, and interest rates will fall to zero. If this possibility is ruled out, it must follow that either the investment demand schedule or the demand for money is elastic with respect to the rate of interest.

In conclusion, it appears to be the elasticity of demand for money that is crucial from the policy point of view. If the rate of interest cannot be made to fall as a result of Federal Reserve action to increase the supply of money, the shape of the investment demand schedule is irrelevant. If, on the other hand, an increase in the money supply succeeds in reducing the rate of interest, the level of investment must necessarily rise. If it does not, the increase in the supply of money will cause interest rates to continue falling until the liquidity trap is reached.

[1] J. Tobin, "Liquidity Preference and Monetary Policy," *Review of Economics and Statistics*, 29:124–131, 1947.

chapter 11

The level of employment (1)

11-1 Introduction

The discussion thus far has been based on the notion that the economy can be divided into two markets—a market for final goods and services and a market for money. But this is not sufficient. We must add a third—the market for factors of production—in order to determine the level of employment. On the surface the task does not look difficult. Each firm in the economy will have a production function, i.e., a relationship between the level of output and various combinations of factor inputs; and thus we may visualize an aggregative production function for the economy as a whole. Such a function may be written

$$Y = X(N,K^*)$$

where N is the level of employment and K is the size of the capital stock of the economy. In a short-run analysis of the kind we have been performing in this part of the book, it is assumed that K is fixed (this is denoted by the asterisk) so that with a given level of output (or real income) the level of employment will be determined.

However, the matter is not as simple as it appears. The *IS-LM* intersection is a position at which the market for goods and services and the money market are simultaneously cleared. But the level of production that is implied by this

Figure 11-1   An excess supply of labor   (all values in real terms).

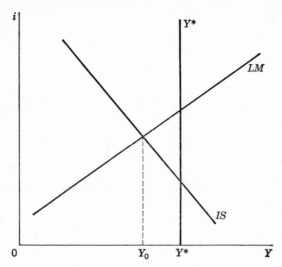

intersection may require the use of less labor than is willing to work at the existing rate of remuneration. In other words, equilibrium in the product and money markets may be accompanied by disequilibrium—specifically, excess supply—in the market for labor services. In Figure 11-1 the vertical line labeled Y^* denotes the level of real income that would be produced if all the resources of the economy were fully employed.[1] Since the IS-LM intersection is to the left of Y^*, the present situation implies the existence of labor market disequilibrium. In this chapter our problem is to find out whether a situation of the kind depicted in Figure 11-1 can be sustained. Will not excess supply in any market cause prices to fall, and will this not, in turn, set off forces that disrupt the IS-LM equilibrium? Finally, will these price adjustments continue until all markets are cleared?

11-2   The Factor Market and the Interest-investment Mechanism

To make headway with our present problem, we need to consider a few elements of the theory of the business firm. The theory teaches that a firm in a competitive industry will hire workers up to the point where the value of the marginal product (marginal product multiplied by the price of output) just

[1] For simplicity we are assuming here that there is only one full-employment level of output. Actually, it would be more sensible to speak of a full-employment zone. Output can be expanded by inducing labor to work overtime and by luring additional people into the labor force.

equals the cost of the factor. Assuming that pure competition prevails, this profit maximization condition, for the economy as a whole, may be written

$$w = pX_n$$

or

$$\frac{w}{p} = X_n$$

where w is the money wage rate, p is the level of prices, w/p is the "real" wage rate, and X_n is the marginal physical product of labor. The demand for labor may therefore be written as

$$N_d = D\left(\frac{w}{p}\right)$$

which states that the demand for labor is a function of the real wage rate. Since, according to the law of diminishing returns, the marginal product of labor declines as more workers are hired, increased employment necessitates a fall in real wages.

On the supply side the matter is more complicated. For the moment we shall adopt the classical assumption that the supply of labor, as well as the demand, depends upon the real wage. It is argued that in a world of rational human beings no one will be so foolish as to imagine that he will be better off if both wages and prices double. If an individual does feel better off under these conditions, he is said to be subject to "money illusion." In the absence of money illusion a change in the quantity of labor supplied will take place only if the real wage changes. Consequently, the classical labor supply function may be written as

$$N_s = S\left(\frac{w}{p}\right)$$

The labor demand and supply functions are shown in Figure 11-2. The real wage rate is measured on the vertical axis, and the quantity of labor is measured on the horizontal axis. The demand curve for labor is negatively sloped in line with the assumption of diminishing returns. The supply curve is positively sloped on the assumption that higher real wage rates will be needed to induce additional workers to become employed. At real wage rate $(w/p)_0$ the quantity of labor demanded by business is N_0. Workers, however, are willing to offer N_1 units of labor, which means that there is an excess supply of labor. When more workers are willing to work at the going real wage rate than business is willing to hire, we have "involuntary unemployment." Should the real wage fall to $(w/p)^*$, involuntary unemployment would be eliminated, and the economy could then be said to be operating at full employment.

Looking at Figure 11-2, it appears that all that is needed to restore full employment is a fall in real wages. Is there a mechanism via which this may happen? If the labor market is competitive, an excess supply of labor would

Figure 11-2   The labor market: classical case.

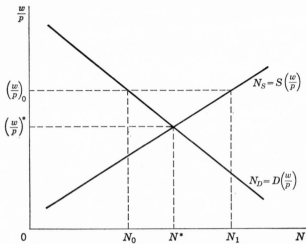

cause workers to compete with each other for the available jobs by offering to work for lower money wage rates. If the level of prices remains constant, the fall in money wages means that real wages will fall and the level of employment will increase. However, if the wage fall should be accompanied by a corresponding fall in the level of prices, real wages will remain the same and employment will not increase. The classical economists believed that real wages could be reduced by a fall in money wage rates, while Keynesians believe that this is not necessarily the case. Let us see where they differ.

A fall in money wages will lower marginal production costs and, as suggested by the theory of the firm, will lead to an increase in output and employment. But will the increase in output be bought? Because the marginal propensity to consume is less than unity, only a fraction of the added output will be taken off the market by consumers, so that the remainder must be in the form of intended investment if the increased level of output and employment is to be sustained.

If intended investment fails to increase, however, unintended inventory accumulation takes place, prices fall, and output and employment fall back to their original levels. In the absence of an increase in intended investment, the level of output at which intended investment and savings are again equal must be the original level of output; since this is associated with a particular real wage, we may infer that prices will fall in proportion to the wage cut.

The present argument can best be illustrated by a diagram similar to those introduced in Chapter 5. In Figure 11-3 the aggregate demand $(C + I)$ schedule cuts the 45-degree line at income Y_0. The full-employment level of income is at Y^*. Since the level of income is less than the full-employment

Figure 11-3   Effect of a fall in wages and prices   (all values in real terms).

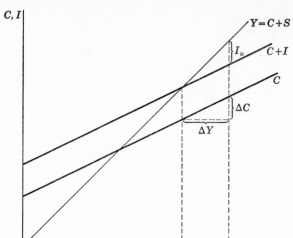

level, there must be an excess supply of labor. As a consequence, money wages will be falling. Suppose that the fall in money wages causes business firms to produce $\Delta Y = Y^* - Y_0$ additional units of output. If there are no taxes, the increased output creates additional disposable income in the same amount. But since the marginal propensity to consume is less than unity, the increase in consumption, ΔC, is less than ΔY and the difference represents unintended accumulation of inventories, I_u. As we saw in Chapter 5, equilibrium will not be restored until unintended investment is eliminated, and this means that prices will fall and output will return to the original level Y_0. Because the absence of unintended investment implies that firms are operating at their profit-maximizing output levels, and because the same level of output implies that the same amount of labor will be hired as before the fall in wages, the fall in prices must have been in exact proportion to the fall in money wages. Real wages remain the same; the labor market clearing mechanism fails to operate.[1]

To a classical economist such a result is inconceivable. He would argue that as long as there is an uncleared market, in this case the labor market, and as long as competition puts pressure on wages and prices, the real value of the

[1] J. M. Keynes, *The General Theory of Employment, Interest and Money*, Chap. 19, Macmillan & Co., Ltd., London, 1936; papers by A. P. Lerner and J. Tobin in S. E. Harris, ed., *The New Economics*, Chaps. 10 and 40, Alfred A. Knopf, Inc., New York, 1950; W J. Fellner, *Competition Among the Few*, Alfred A. Knopf, Inc., New York, 1949, pp. 266–272; F. Modigliani, "Liquidity Preference and the Theory of Interest and Money," *Econometrica*, 12:45–88, 1944; T. Wilson, *Fluctuations in Income and Employment*, Chap. 10, Sir Isaac Pitman & Sons, Ltd., London, 1942.

Figure 11-4 Effect of a fall in the price level: classical case   (all values in real terms).

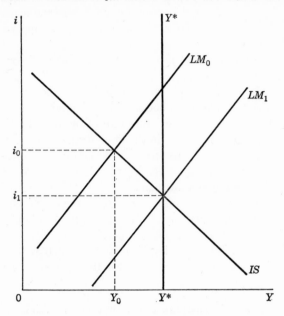

money supply will increase, and this will force down interest rates, raise the level of investment, and increase the level of income and employment.[1] Since prices and wages must continue to fall as long as there is some involuntary unemployment, investment and income must continue to rise until unemployment is eliminated. In Figure 11-4 the original intersection of *IS* with LM_0 is at income level Y_0 and interest rate i_0. As wages and prices fall, the real value of the money supply increases, and this means that the *LM* curve shifts to the right. The rate of interest therefore falls and intended investment and income rise. Since wages and prices continue to fall as long as income is less than Y^*, the *LM* curve will continue to shift to the right until unemployment is eliminated. Consequently, the final equilibrium position is where LM_1

---

[1] Recall from Chapter 8 that the real value of the money supply is given by the ratio of the actual, measurable, or nominal, supply of money, M, to the price level, p. Thus, since

$$m = \frac{M}{p}$$

a fall in the price level would have the same effect on the real value of the money supply as would an increase in nominal money balances due, for example, to a Federal Reserve purchase of securities on the open market. In terms of the four-quadrant money market diagram, the fall in the price level would be represented by an outward shift of the money supply curve in quadrant 2. This would mean that at any arbitrary rate of interest additional money balances would be available for transactions purposes so that a higher level of income would be associated with monetary equilibrium, i.e., the *LM* curve would shift to the right.

cuts *IS* at *Y** and interest rate i_1. In terms of Figure 11-3, wage-price declines
will raise the investment schedule to the point where the aggregate demand
schedule cuts the 45-degree line at *Y**. Unemployment, apparently, tends to
eliminate itself automatically.

The Keynesian would rebut this argument with the theory of liquidity
preference. The fall in prices caused by the wage cut will, to be sure, increase
the real value of the money supply. But this will not affect the rate of interest
or the level of intended investment because in the liquidity trap the demand for
money is infinitely elastic at the existing rate of interest. In Figure 11-5 the
IS-LM intersection at income Y_0 is in the liquidity trap range. The rise in the
real value of the money supply acts to shift the *LM* curve from LM_0 to LM_1,
but this obviously has no effect on the interest rate. The money balances that
are released from transactions demands by the fall in the price level are
hoarded by wealth holders, who make no attempt to convert them into earning
assets. The rate of interest remains the same, and the level of investment and
income remain constant at Y_0. The Keynesian therefore believes that an
"underemployment equilibrium" level of income, such as Y_0, may persist
and that there is no automatic tendency for the economy to return to full
employment.

Figure 11-5   Effect of a fall in the price level: Keynesian case   (all values in real terms).

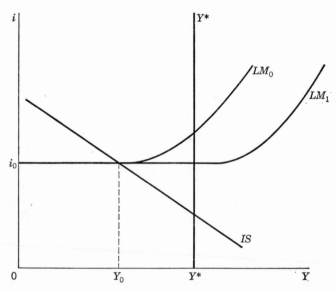

There is a problem in the Keynesian solution. If a fall in wages and prices
fails to reduce the level of unemployment, why will wages and prices not
continue to fall indefinitely? This apparently does not happen; money wages
tend to be sticky in the downward direction. In an environment characterized

by widespread unionism workers can defend themselves against wage cuts. A previously hard-won money wage increase, moreover, tends to be maintained despite shrinking employment.

In recognizing these institutional facts of life, Keynes broke away from the classical theory of labor supply. Instead of assuming that the supply of labor depends on the real wage, he assumed that labor is subject to money illusion and that the supply of labor is a function of the money wage rate. In Figure 11-6, w_0 is the historically given money wage rate and p_0 is the ruling price level. At money wage w_0 workers will offer anywhere between zero and N^* units of labor. Thus the labor supply curve is a horizontal line at w_0/p_0. Although the money wage rate cannot be made to fall, it will rise when all those who are willing to work at w_0 are employed and additional workers are desired. Consequently, the labor supply curve bends up sharply once N^* has been reached. In Figure 11-6 the labor demand schedule cuts the supply schedule at N_0. Consequently, the distance $N^* - N_0$ measures involuntary unemployment—the number of workers willing to work at the existing level of real wages that do not find employment.

Since the money wage rate is assumed to be downwardly rigid (and since a fall in wages, even if it could be brought about, would produce a proportional drop in the price level), the restoration of full employment can come about only through a real wage fall resulting from an increase in aggregate demand and the price level. If such a rise in the price level materializes, the entire labor supply schedule shifts down, and involuntary unemployment is eliminated. Thus at real wage w_0/p_1 the labor demand schedule cuts the supply schedule at N^*, where all who are willing to work at the new real wage are employed.

Figure 11-6   Labor market: Keynesian case.

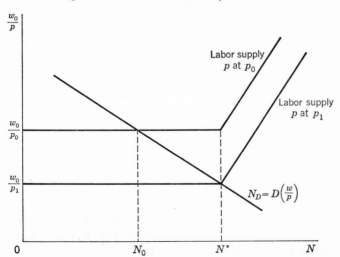

Notice that even though the real wage has fallen, the number of workers willing to work at the new real wage is the same as at the old real wage, a result that follows from the assumption of money illusion.

In summary, money wage cuts resulting from competition in the labor market leave the level of employment and the real wage unchanged in the Keynesian system. Consequently, we may call the level of employment N_0 in Figure 11-6 an underemployment equilibrium. In the classical analysis, on the other hand, competition on the labor market will continue until the fall in money wages brings about the fall in real wages needed to restore full employment.

We have seen that the issue of whether there is a unique equilibrium level of income and employment or whether there are several possible equilibrium levels seems to hinge primarily on the nature of the demand for money. If the demand for money is infinitely elastic with respect to the rate of interest, there will be no labor-market clearing mechanism regardless of the nature of the labor supply function. But the labor supply function is important in another respect: If the demand for money is elastic, if at the same time competition on the labor market leads to money wage reductions, and if no change in the level of employment takes place, the end result would be that money wages and prices would fall indefinitely. It is clear, however, that in our existing institutional framework wages and prices are extremely sticky in the downward direction.

11-3 Formal Models of Income and Employment Determination

Given a constant capital stock, the production function of the economy

$$Y = X(N,K^*)$$

indicates that once the level of income is known, the level of employment will automatically be determined. Similarly, if the level of employment has been determined, the level of income must be known. Although the Keynesian and classical models are general equilibrium systems in which the equilibrium values of the variables are simultaneously determined, it is nevertheless useful to think of the determination of the equilibrium values in terms of a definite sequence. In the classical model the sequence runs from the level of employment to the level of income, consumption, and investment; then to the rate of interest; and finally to the price level. In the Keynesian system it is helpful to think of the sequence as running in the other direction. The consumption and investment functions, together with the monetary equilibrium relation, determine the rate of interest and the level of income, which, in turn, determines the level of employment.

The Keynesian underemployment system can be formalized as follows. If the price level is initially held constant and the nominal money supply is given, product market equilibrium

$$I(i) = Y - C(Y)$$

together with monetary equilibrium

$$\frac{M}{p} = \mathbf{k}Y + L(i)$$

serve to determine the level of income, consumption, investment, savings, the rate of interest, and the way money balances are split between transactions and speculative purposes. The level of income being known and the capital stock being fixed, the production function

$$Y = X(N, K^*)$$

determines the level of employment. Consequently, the demand for labor together with the downwardly rigid money wage

$$N = N_d = D\left(\frac{w_0}{p}\right)$$

adds the equation needed to determine the price level.

Next let us formalize the classical system. The real wage and the level of employment are determined by labor market equilibrium

$$D\left(\frac{w}{p}\right) = S\left(\frac{w}{p}\right)$$

Since the level of employment is now known, the level of income is determined by the production function

$$Y = X(N, K^*)$$

Since we know the level of income, the product market equilibrium equation

$$I(i) = Y - C(Y)$$

determines the rate of interest and the way in which aggregate expenditures are divided between consumption and investment. Finally, since both the level of income and the rate of interest are known, the monetary equilibrium equation

$$m_s = \frac{M}{p} = \mathbf{k}Y$$

serves only to determine the level of prices.

Observe that in the classical model the rate of interest is independent of the size of the money supply and that the sole function of the money supply is to determine the price level. The reasons for this, though highly interesting, are not pertinent to our immediate line of inquiry, and further discussion of the classical model will therefore be postponed to Chapter 13, in which these questions will be examined in detail.

11-4 Additional Notes on Money Wage Rates, Money Illusion, and Employment

The Keynesian argument that the liquidity trap would prevent wage-price flexibility from restoring full employment was indeed a startling one. It was, however, met by a classical rejoinder. The distinguished economist A. C. Pigou argued that even though the liquidity trap might bar the way to an increase in employment via the path of changes in interest rates and investment, falls in wages and prices would sooner or later restore full employment because price declines would lead to an increase in consumption.[1] The mechanism, commonly known as the "Pigou effect," works as follows: A fall in the price level means that the real value of the stock of liquid assets held by the public rises. This being the case, consumers will cut down on their current savings because a smaller nest egg (in money terms) will, after the price decline, be necessary to make purchases planned for the future. This means that as long as markets remain uncleared, wages and prices will fall, so that consumption will continue to increase until full employment is restored.

Although the value of the liquid assets held by a creditor increases as prices fall, the real value of the corresponding debtor's obligations also increases. Presumably the Pigou effect would fail to materialize at all if the "wealth effects" of price changes affected debtor and creditor symmetrically. The effects, however, are held to be asymmetrical because a large portion of the liquid assets held by the public is in the form of government obligations—the stock of currency and government debt. Since government consumption is not supposed to be affected by a change in the real value of government obligations, there will be a net change in consumption resulting from a fall in the price level.

Some additional possible consequences of a money wage cut are the following:

1. A fall in wages and prices will induce foreigners to buy more from us and at the same time will make it easier for domestic producers to sell abroad. This means that the net export of goods and services, and therefore aggregate demand, will rise so that the level of employment will increase.

---

[1] A. C. Pigou, "The Classical Stationary State," *Economic Journal*, 53:343–351, 1943; and "Economic Progress in a Stable Environment," *Economica*, New Series, No. 14:180–188, 1947; D. Patinkin, "Price Flexibility and Full Employment," *American Economic Review*, 38:543–564, 1948.

2. A money wage cut involves a redistribution of income from workers to dividend earners, who tend to be the higher-income groups. If, as is likely, the marginal propensity to consume of high-income groups is lower than that of low-income groups, each dollar taken from a wage earner and given to a dividend earner will result in a net fall in consumption expenditures. A money wage cut may therefore cause a fall in aggregate consumption; if this redistributive effect is significant, a cut in money wages may actually cause an increase in real wages rather than a decline.

3. It is practically inconceivable that money wages could instantaneously be cut across the board. But piecemeal money wage reductions will foster the expectation that further cuts are in the offing. Acting on this expectation, entrepreneurs will cut back production, make current sales out of inventory, and postpone new plant and equipment expenditures. The adverse expectations induced by the wage cut may therefore totally defeat its intended effect.[1]

4. We have seen that Keynes believed labor to be subject to money illusion. In other words, labor was supposed to be far more conscious of changes in money wages than of changes in the price level and would therefore be likely to consider an increase in money wages as an increase in real wages even if prices rose in proportion to the wage increase. With respect to the labor market, this implied that if money wages remained unchanged, an increase in the price level would not be noticed by workers, who thus would offer the same supply of labor even though real wages had fallen.

There is no reason to suppose that money illusion is confined to labor supply. A similar phenomenon may, for example, be expected to exist with respect to consumption behavior. If money wages and prices fall and consumers notice the fall in money income but not the fall in prices, they will be under the illusion that real income has fallen. Recall from the discussion of the consumption function in Chapter 5 that when real income falls, the percentage of income consumed rises. Thus if consumers think their real income has fallen, they will spend a greater percentage of their money income than previously. This means that the consumption function out of real disposable income will shift up as a result of the wage cut and that the level of income will, to some degree, rise.

Probably the greatest source of money illusion is the Federal income tax structure. Income tax rates are based on money income. If money income and prices both fall, leaving real income unchanged, taxpayers nevertheless shift into lower brackets and pay a smaller percentage of their income in the form of taxes. A proportional fall in wages and prices will therefore result in an increase in real disposable income and an increase in consumption.

As long as we are on the subject of money illusion, we should point out that the existence of money illusion does not necessarily imply irrational behavior on the part of those whose economic behavior is not in strict conformity

[1] Wilson, *op. cit.*, p. 69.

with the classical "homogeneity postulate."[1] The primary reason for this is that workers, consumers, and businessmen all make long-term contracts that are fixed, not in real, but in money terms. A wage earner, for example, may still have many years of payments to make on the mortgage on his home. If wages and prices decline in the same proportion, his real wage will be the same. But the real value of his debt burden will increase, and he may therefore be obliged to reduce his current consumption expenditures. Although the worker appears to be subject to money illusion, his decision to consume less may be based on a perfectly rational calculation. Since workers tend, in general, to be debtors, a fall in money wages, even though real wages remain the same, will be regarded as a serious real loss.

Whether money illusion is rational or not, it is important to emphasize that from the point of view of the economy as a whole, money illusions are in general stabilizing. The Federal income tax structure, for example, causes tax collections to fall by a greater proportion than wage decreases even though

---

[1] A fancy way of saying that the supply of labor is a function of the real wage is to say that the function is homogeneous of degree zero. In general we may write

$$N_s = S(w,p)$$

as the labor supply function. In the absence of money illusion a proportional increase in w and p will not affect the amount of labor supplied. To a mathematician this means that the labor supply function has the property of zero degree homogeneity. In general, an nth order homogeneous function has the property that if all the independent variables are multiplied by a constant, the dependent variable will be multiplied by that same constant raised to the power n.

Mathematically, if

$$y = f(x,z)$$

then
$$y\mathbf{u}^n = f(x\mathbf{u},z\mathbf{u})$$

and if $n = 0$, $u^n = 1$, so that

$$y = f(x,z) = f(x\mathbf{u},z\mathbf{u})$$

which means that multiplication of the two independent variables by a constant does not change the value of the dependent variable.

Therefore, in the case of the labor supply function,

$$N_s = S\left(\frac{w}{p}\right) = S(\mathbf{u}w,\mathbf{u}p)$$

and since $\mathbf{u}$ is an arbitrary constant, we can let $\mathbf{u} = 1/p$ so that

$$N_s = S\left(\frac{w}{p}\right) = S\left(\frac{w}{p}, 1\right)$$

which is to say that the supply of labor depends only on the ratio of w to p, the real wage rate.

If workers are subject to money illusion, the labor supply function will not be homogeneous, and hence it is said that the homogeneity postulate is denied. In this connection see W. W. Leontieff, "Postulates: Keynes' General Theory and the Classicists," in S. E. Harris, ed., *The New Economics*, Chap. 10, Alfred A. Knopf, Inc., New York, 1950.

prices may have fallen in the same proportion. Since this raises real disposable income, the effect is clearly stabilizing. Similarly, during inflationary periods tax collections increase in greater proportion than increases in money income even though prices may have risen in proportion. The effect is to reduce real disposable income and real consumption expenditures and is therefore again stabilizing.

11-5   Summary and Conclusion

This chapter may be summarized as follows:

1. In the classical view there is only one equilibrium level of employment, which is determined by labor market competition. Since there is only one equilibrium level of employment, there is only one equilibrium level of income, which must necessarily be the full-employment level. In the absence of wage-price rigidities, there will be an automatic tendency for all markets to be cleared and for full employment to be restored.

2. In the Keynesian view the level of employment is determined by the level of income, which in turn depends upon aggregate demand. Since there is no presumption that competition on the labor market exists, or that if it did exist, real wages would fall, "underemployment equilibrium" is a possibility.

3. The question of whether money wage cuts will raise the level of employment depends primarily on the nature of the demand for money. In the absence of other effects, a money wage cut will leave the level of employment unaffected in the liquidity trap extreme, while in the classical extreme of a fixed ratio of money balances to the volume of transactions, money wage cuts will restore full employment.

4. The effect of money wage cuts on the level of employment will depend to some extent on the importance of the Pigou effect, on the significance of foreign trade, on the effect of money illusion on consumption, on money illusion in the tax structure, on the effect of a redistribution of income on consumption, and finally on the nature of the expectations induced by the wage cut.

Although our discussion of the level of employment is not yet finished, it is useful at this juncture to take stock. To suppose that a money wage cut, as a practical policy device, is feasible in our present-day institutional environment would be to lose touch with reality. Apart from other considerations, the fall in real wages needed to restore full employment could always be achieved by monetary and fiscal, as opposed to wage-price, policy. Since these tools are feasible, while money wage cuts are not, they are the ones that will be employed.

But it would be foolish to infer from this that it is pointless to consider the effectiveness of wage cuts on the level of employment. In the first place, the typical classical economist believes that money wage cuts can restore full employment; if that is so and if he is opposed to remedies that restore full employment by raising the price level, he is apt to promote policies designed to restore wage-price flexibility. While centrally enforced wage cuts are unrealistic, a strong antitrust policy, designed to destroy the monopoly power of unions and enterprises, is not beyond the realm of possibility. Because price flexibility is a necessary feature of an automatically regulating economic system, monopoly, apart from other reasons, is anathema to the traditional economist.[1] The Keynesian, less convinced of the importance of wage-price flexibility, is apt to be a less enthusiastic trust buster than his classical counterpart.

Second, the question of whether money wage cuts will be effective in restoring full employment is really the same as the question of whether or not the economy has an automatic steering wheel. An economist who believes that full employment at stable prices is the norm to which the economy will return after a disturbance from equilibrium will prescribe radically different policies from the economist who believes that full employment is an accidental state that cannot be maintained, or even achieved, without considerable assistance from governmental policy.

Third, the discussion of money wage cuts has focused attention on the most vital of the differences between Keynes and traditional economists, namely, the theory of liquidity preference, which, as we saw in Chapter 10, was the vital part of the issue between monetary and fiscal policy. We now see that this is the vital difference between an automatically adjusting economy and one in which several equilibrium levels of employment are possible.

[1] The view that stabilization policy of any description is doomed without vigorous action to restore competition is expressed most lucidly by Henry Simons, *Economic Policy for a Free Society*, Chap. 5, University of Chicago Press, Chicago, 1948.

chapter 12

The level of employment (2)

12-1 Introduction

The discussion of employment theory between the Keynesians and their critics left a number of loose ends which we shall attempt in this chapter to tie together. By removing the assumption that pure competition prevails in product markets and by adding a few added assumptions, all of which seem to conform to the realities of the world, we can show that:

1. Under depression conditions the level of employment can be changed without changes in real wages.

2. The classical assumption of a labor supply dependent on the real wage does not, contrary to accepted doctrine, determine a unique level of employment, output, and real wage even though a labor market clearing mechanism exists.

3. Money wage cuts and increases in the supply of money through monetary policy will not increase the level of investment even though interest rates can be made to fall. Indeed, the interest rate as an economic calculator is largely irrelevant during depression.

12-2 The Movement of Real and Money Wages

It follows directly from the labor demand function

$$N_d = D\left(\frac{w}{p}\right)$$

and the law of diminishing returns that in the short run an increase in the level of employment cannot be brought about without a fall in the real wage. Most economists, accepting the labor demand function as written above, assume that a fall in real wages is a natural by-product of emergence from depression. Noting that money wages rise as output rises, Keynes expressed the opinion that "the change in real wages associated with a change in money wages, so far from being usually in the same direction, is almost always in the opposite direction."[1] In other words, Keynes and most economists believed that even though money wages rise during recovery, prices rise even faster so that real wages fall. But when the issue was subjected to statistical analysis,[2] it was found that real wages actually increase as output and employment increase. Apparently there is something wrong with the notion that the demand for labor is a decreasing function of the real wage.

In a later article[3] Keynes acknowledged the fact that real wages seem to increase as output increases, although he refused to abandon the assumption of diminishing returns in the short run. He suggested instead that real wage increases would be compatible with employment increases if the assumption of pure competition were abandoned. Whereas a pure competitor will hire workers up to the point where the wage equals the value of the marginal product (marginal product multiplied by price), a monopolist will hire workers up to the point where the wage equals the marginal revenue product (marginal product multiplied by marginal revenue). Since marginal revenue mr can be written

$$mr = p\left(1 - \frac{1}{e}\right)$$

where p is the price of output and e is the price elasticity of demand, we may write

$$w = p\left(1 - \frac{1}{e}\right)X_n$$

or

$$\frac{w}{p} = \left(1 - \frac{1}{e}\right)X_n$$

as the condition for maximum profit. This implies that the demand for labor can now be written

$$N_d = D\left(\frac{w}{p}, e\right)$$

[1] J. M. Keynes, *The General Theory of Employment, Interest and Money*, Macmillan & Co., Ltd., London, 1936, p. 10.

[2] L. Tarshis, "Changes in Real and Money Wages," *Economic Journal*, 49:150–154, 1939; and J. T. Dunlop, "The Movement of Real and Money Wage Rates," *Economic Journal*, 48:413–434, 1938.

[3] J. M. Keynes, "Relative Movements of Real Wages and Output," *Economic Journal*, 49:34–51, 1939.

Under these conditions output increases are compatible with real wage increases as long as demand elasticities increase with increases in aggregate demand.

In the following sections the assumptions of imperfect competition will be retained. It will, however, be shown that even though demand elasticities remain unchanged, employment increases are not incompatible with real wage increases. It will, in fact, be assumed that demand elasticities remain unchanged since this will help to avoid repetition and to simplify the exposition.

12-3   A Model of a Depression Economy

It should be recognized that although a certain stock of capital goods K^* exists, this does not, unless the stock of capital goods is indivisible, necessarily mean that K^* will be employed in the sense that it is utilized in the production process. A cigarette factory with 100 machines will, in times of slack demand, use somewhat less than 100 machines because substitution between labor and machines is not perfect. The firm may therefore utilize 60 machines together with some labor even though labor costs are variable whereas machine costs are fixed in the short run.

If the period of slack demand persists, the idle equipment may gradually be reduced. But since this can normally take place only by a slow process of depreciation and obsolescence, the typical depression can be expected to be characterized by widespread excess capacity, which, if equipment is divisible and the production function is characterized by ranges of zero returns, may for purposes of analysis be considered unemployed.

If the present view of the matter is acceptable, the marginal productivity of labor (labor demand) schedule of Figure 11-2 merely becomes one of many possible labor demand schedules. In that figure, if the real wage is $(w/p)_0$, the optimum factor mix may warrant the level of employment N_0. The labor demand schedule shows the increments to output that can be obtained by adding successive units of labor to the given initial factor mix. If, however, it is decided that the additional output can be produced more profitably by bringing another existing machine into operation, the labor demand schedule shifts to the right. Under these assumptions, an increase in aggregate demand can restore full employment by a shift in the demand curve for labor and/or by a fall in the real wage. As long as the stock of capital goods is divisible, as long as excess equipment is available, and as long as zero marginal returns to capital are possible, increases in employment may be achieved without real wage adjustments.

A formal model similar to the models of the previous chapter can be constructed quite simply. Write the production function as

$$Y = X(N,K) \qquad K \le K^*$$

where K is to be interpreted as capacity in use, which in the short run may vary between zero and K^*, where K^* is capacity in existence at the beginning of the production period. To find the factor mix, consider the following analogies from the theory of the individual firm. Assume that labor and machinery are the only factors of production used by the firm, that equipment is divisible, that factors are of homogeneous efficiency, and that the firm's production possibilities for the output levels y^*, y_1, and y_0 are as represented by the isoproduct curves of Figure 12-1, in which the quantity of machinery is measured on the vertical axis and the quantity of labor is measured on the horizontal axis.

Suppose that full employment for this firm justifies a level of output y^* and that the tangency of the factor price line is at (k^*, n^*). Now suppose that the desired level of output drops to y_0. Since the firm has available k^* units of capital which can be reduced only by gradual depreciation and obsolescence (which we ignore for the sake of simplicity), output of y_0 will be produced with k_0 units of machinery and n_0 units of labor. Since capital costs are sunk costs and not variable in the short run, the factor price line at less than k^* is, in effect, vertical, i.e., the variable cost of utilizing another machine is zero. It therefore pays the firm to adjust to a decline in output by laying off workers up to the point where the marginal product of capital is zero. If the level of

Figure 12-1 Determination of the factor mix for an individual firm at output levels y_0, y_1, and y^*.

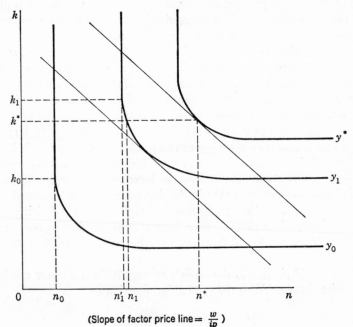

(Slope of factor price line $= \dfrac{w}{\overline{w}}$)

output in this situation is still greater than the desired amount, it will pay to begin shutting down machinery and laying off workers simultaneously. The process continues until the desired level of output y_0 is achieved, at which point the optimum factor mix warrants the use of k_0 machines and the hiring of n_0 workers.

Let us call this Case A and incorporate it into an aggregative model. Assume that a rigid money wage w_0 prevails and that $K < K^*$. Under these conditions

$$I(i) = Y - C(Y) \tag{12-1}$$

defines product market equilibrium. Monetary equilibrium is expressed by

$$m = \frac{M}{p} = kY + L(i) \tag{12-2}$$

The production function

$$Y = X(N,K) \qquad K \leq K^* \tag{12-3}$$

gives the relationship between factor inputs and output. To these equations we must add the profit-maximizing relations,

$$\frac{w}{p} = \left(1 - \frac{1}{e}\right) X_n \tag{12-4}$$

and

$$0 = \left(1 - \frac{1}{e}\right) X_k \tag{12-5}$$

Assuming a given real money supply, Eqs. (12-1) and (12-2) give product and monetary equilibrium and therefore determine i, Y, C, S, and I. Y having been determined, the factor mix is given by the production function in Eq. (12-3) and by the condition in Eq. (12-5) that the marginal product of capital equals zero. Finally the addition of Eq. (12-4) gives the price level.

As a consequence of a mild slump the desired level of output may fall only from y^* to y_1. In this case—call it Case B—the marginal product of capital cannot be made equal to zero by worker layoffs. Since in the short run new equipment cannot be obtained, output of y_1 will be produced with k^* units of capital together with n_1 units of labor. In the aggregate this implies that Eq. (12-3) becomes

$$Y = X(N,K^*) \tag{12-6}$$

which further implies that Eq. (12-5) can be eliminated because the level of employment is now determined by the production function, since Y is known.

Note that Case B corresponds to the usual formulation of the Keynesian system because all existing capital equipment is in use while only the intensity of utilization is subject to change. In a modern industrial economy in which factors of production are highly specialized and imperfect competition keeps product prices from being bid down so that excess capacity is absorbed, it is doubtful whether Case B has very much relevance unless the fall in demand is slight. It is practically inconceivable that the output adjustment that results from a fall in demand will ever be achieved entirely by a fall in employment. Certainly in a deep depression it is reasonable to suppose that both men and machines will be idle.

12-4 The Implications

When demand falls from the full employment level, the existence of divisible capital equipment implies that a portion of the capital stock will be unemployed. From this it follows that output can be expanded by hiring more labor, by bringing additional existing machines into use, or by both. In essence this means that there is more than one attainable marginal productivity of labor schedule and that employment can be increased both by a shift in the schedule and by a movement along it. It follows that there may be many possible real wage rates that are compatible with labor market equilibrium.

The fact that the demand for labor depends not only on the real wage but also on the level of aggregate demand means that regardless of the labor supply schedule, there is no unique equilibrium level of employment. Writing the classical labor supply function as

$$N_s = S\left(\frac{w}{p}\right)$$

and the demand for labor implied by Case A as

$$N_d = D\left(\frac{w}{p}, Y\right)$$

a market clearing mechanism such that $N_d = N_s$ will yield some equilibrium level of employment. There is, however, nothing unique about this level of employment since it also depends upon the particular level of aggregate demand that prevails.

The analysis adds weight to Keynes' belief that interest-rate changes will not stimulate the level of investment. As long as there is excess capacity, there is no reason why investment should take place because the effective return on new investment, unless in types of equipment not currently in existence, is zero. Additions to the money supply via money wage cuts or monetary policy will therefore succeed only in reducing interest rates to the point where all the added balances are absorbed into speculative holdings.

Monetary policy, even if the conditions of Case B prevail, is likely to encounter frustration. Refer once again to Figure 12-1. Assume that the desired level of output is y_1; then consider the point (k^*, n_1'), where k^* is capacity in existence and n_1' is the level of employment that would exist if k could be increased to k_1. In the long run y_1 can be produced (1) by obtaining an additional $k_1 - k^*$ units of capital, i.e., by investing; (2) by hiring an additional $n_1 - n_1'$ units of labor; or (3) by some intermediate combination of investment and additional labor. If relative factor prices do not change as a result of the fall in demand from y^* to y_1, it is clear that y_1 will be produced by adding more labor rather than by investing, for at the point (k^*, n_1)

$$\left| \frac{x_n}{w} \right| > \left| \frac{x_k}{ip} \right|$$

where x_n and x_k are the firm's marginal products of labor and capital, respectively. For investment to be stimulated, the interest rate would have to fall by an amount sufficient to rotate the factor-price line clockwise beyond k^*. As capitalism advances toward heavier industry—which means more specialized factors of production—the necessary change in interest rates becomes greater.

Finally, observe that Case A may, after a period of decumulation or as a result of recovery from a slump, merge into Case B. This suggests that our model has certain implications for the supply of output with respect to the price level. Where it is possible to increase output by shifting the labor demand schedule, the supply of output will be elastic with respect to the price level. When it is no longer possible to shift the labor demand curve without further capital accumulation, additional increases in output can be realized only by a movement along the labor demand schedule. But since this is possible only if real wages fall and since existing institutional arrangements all but preclude money wage cuts, the point at which Case A merges into Case B is the point where the supply of output with respect to the price level becomes less elastic

chapter 13

Full employment, the price level, and the theory of interest

13-1 Introduction

Part II has dealt with an environment in which the productive resources of the economy are nearly always assumed to be partly unemployed. It is now time to round out the discussion by supposing that factor markets are cleared so that the supply of output, call it Y^*, is fixed. Given this assumption, let us observe the effects on our aggregative variables of changes such as an increase in the money supply or an increase in investment demand. This procedure will help to prepare the ground for subsequent consideration of inflation; and it will help to put the real versus monetary interest theory controversy into its proper perspective.

13-2 The Price Level and the Rate of Interest at Full Employment

Consider the familiar *IS-LM* diagram in Figure 13-1. The diagram is identical with previous figures with the exception that a vertical line is drawn at Y^* to denote the fact that once Y^* is reached, the supply of output is fixed and cannot, as has been assumed thus far, adjust automatically to aggregate demand. At the point where the *IS* curve cuts Y^*, the interest rate i_0 equates the demand for goods and services with the full-employment supply. This interest rate we shall call the "natural" rate. As we shall see subsequently, it is determined uniquely by the demand for investment funds and the supply of savings at full employment.

If the *LM* curve also happens to cut Y^* at i_0, the *market* rate of interest will equal the *natural* rate. General equilibrium of factor, product, and money markets is established since at that rate the demand for goods and services equals the full-employment supply, and just the right amount of money balances is made available for a Y^* volume of transactions.

Starting with the equilibrium situation specified above, what is the effect of an increase in the money supply? Assume that the nominal money supply is increased by ΔM dollars. The effect of this increase in the money supply is to shift the *LM* curve to LM_1 and to lower the market rate of interest to i_1. But at i_1 the supply and demand for goods and services are no longer in equilibrium because, investment having been stimulated by the fall of the market rate of interest, the total demand for goods and services is $Y_1 - Y^*$ in excess of what can be supplied. Prices are therefore bid up so that the real value of the money supply, $m_s = M/p$, begins to fall. This means that a particular value of nominal money balances is no longer adequate to make the real transactions previously made. Wealth holders are therefore induced to sell earning assets to supplement their transactions balances; interest rates rise; and excess demand is gradually eliminated as the increase in the interest rate causes investment to decline.

What will be the final solution? As long as the *LM* schedule is to the right of the original schedule (LM_0), there will be excess demand for goods and a

Figure 13-1   Full-employment general equilibrium   (all values in real terms).

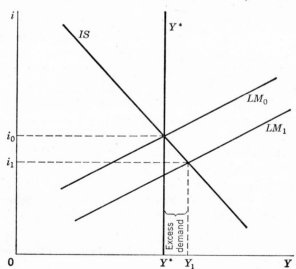

Figure 13-2 The liquidity trap and full employment   (all values in real terms).

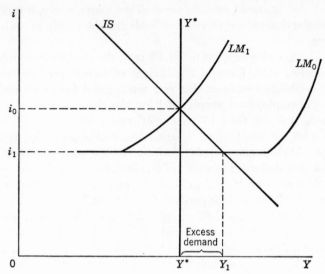

continuation of price increases. Evidently, then, equilibrium will not be restored until price increases have brought the real value of the money supply back to its original level. In other words, the LM curve will shift back to LM_0, where the market rate of interest once again coincides with the natural rate. We may therefore conclude that:

1. The increase in the nominal supply of money produces a proportional change in the price level.

2. The natural rate of interest, i_0, is reestablished as the equilibrium market rate of interest. Under full-employment conditions the equilibrium rate of interest is independent of monetary factors.[1]

Both conclusions are in direct conformity with the classical view of interest and the price level. Observe, moreover, that these results have been obtained without abandoning Keynes' assumption of a speculative demand for money.

Do these classical results always hold true at full employment? What, for example, would happen in the unlikely event that the assumption of full employment was combined with the liquidity trap hypothesis? In Figure 13-2 the establishment of the liquidity trap at market rate i_1 creates a situation in which excess demand of $Y_1 - Y^*$ prevails. Thus again the price level rises, and the LM schedule shifts to the left. As long as the market rate is below the natural rate, prices will continue to rise, so that ultimately there is no alternative but

[1] These results are spelled out by D. Patinkin, "Keynesian Economics and the Quantity Theory," in K. K. Kurihara, ed., *Post-Keynesian Economics*, Rutgers University Press, New Brunswick, N.J., 1954.

to suppose that the *LM* schedule must shift until the trap is escaped. Since final equilibrium is not established until the *LM* curve shifts to LM_1, we may infer that the liquidity trap is purely a depression phenomenon. At full employment the demand for money cannot possibly be infinitely elastic with respect to the rate of interest except in the practically inconceivable case in which the natural rate of interest happens to be the same as the liquidity trap rate.

Next let us turn to the effect of changes in the demand for goods and services as the result of a decreased desire to save, an increase in investment demand, or an increase in government expenditures. If an increase in government expenditures causes the *IS* schedule of Figure 13-3 to shift from IS_0 to IS_1, the natural rate of interest rises to i_1. Thus, if the market rate is at i_0, there must be excess demand for output of $Y_1 - Y^*$ so that competition for the available supply causes prices to rise and the *LM* curve to shift upward until, at LM_1, the market rate of interest coincides with the new natural rate.

Figure 13-3 Changes in the natural rate of interest (all values in real terms).

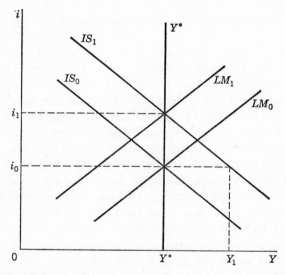

In the new equilibrium the same level of real income prevails as before the change except that it is now higher priced. The rise in the interest rate causes money balances to be released from speculative holdings and makes it possible to finance the same volume of real transactions with the same nominal supply of money at a higher level of prices. The existence of the speculative demand for money therefore leaves open the possibility that an increase in investment demand can lead to a rise in the price level—a possibility that could not materialize in the nonspeculative demand world of the classical model.[1]

[1] See the appendix to this chapter at the end of the book for proof of these results and derivation of the magnitudes of the changes in the interest rate and the price level.

In the full-employment world in which the level of output is fixed we can make the following provisional conclusions:

1. An increase in the money supply will bring about a proportional change in the price level as long as the natural rate of interest is in excess of the rate of interest at which the demand for money is infinitely elastic.

2. The natural rate of interest cannot be altered by monetary changes. The rate depends, rather, on the position of the IS schedule in relation to the full-employment supply of output.

3. The price level is uniquely determined by the nominal money supply only in the absence of a speculative demand for money. A shift in investment demand or in the savings function or in government expenditures or taxation, by affecting the interest rate, either releases or creates a shortage of speculative balances, thereby affecting transactions balances and the price level.

13-3 Real and Monetary Theories of Interest

It seems appropriate to explore further the question of why the assumption of full employment produces such a radical difference in the determination of the rate of interest. The question, moreover, is at the heart of a controversy that has caused much heated debate, namely, is the equilibrium rate of interest determined by real factors such as the productivity of investment and the savings habits of the community, or is interest a purely monetary phenomenon.[1]

Traditionally, it has more or less been taken for granted that the interest rate is determined by real factors and that influences from the monetary sphere were in the nature of short-run disturbances that could not change the natural, and therefore the equilibrium, rate of interest. The natural rate, it will be remembered, is the rate which equates the demand for goods and services with the full-employment supply. Since it is established where the IS schedule cuts Y^*, the natural rate must depend on the shape of the investment demand schedule and on the full-employment level of savings. Since the natural rate, in

[1] The most complete exposition of "real" interest theory is Irving Fisher, *The Theory of Interest*, Kelley and Millman, Inc., New York, 1954. While Fisher thought that both the "impatience to spend income," which necessitates an interest premium if present consumption is to be foregone, and "opportunity to invest it" were the relevant factors, the so-called "Austrian school" as represented, for example, in F. A. von Hayek, "The Mythology of Capital," *Quarterly Journal of Economics*, 50:199–228, 1936, emphasized the importance of savings, while F. H. Knight, "Capital and Interest," *Encyclopedia Brittanica*, Vol. 4, pp. 779–801, 1946, emphasizes the investment side. The general equilibrium approach is implicit in the famous paper by J. R. Hicks, "Mr. Keynes and the Classics: A Suggested Interpretation," *Econometrica*, 5:147–159, 1937, and is expounded in an interesting fashion by H. M. Somers in "Monetary Policy and the Theory of Interest," *Quarterly Journal of Economics*, 55:488–507, 1941. The papers by F. A. von Hayek, F. H. Knight, J. R. Hicks, and H. M. Somers, as well as an exposition by J. M. Keynes of his own purely monetary theory, may be found in Fellner and Haley, ed. for American Economic Association, *Readings in the Theory of Income Distribution*, Richard D. Irwin, Inc., Homewood, Ill., 1946.

classical theory, is the only possible market *equilibrium* rate of interest and since it depends on the investment demand schedule and the volume of full-employment savings, it is regarded as a "real" phenomenon dependent on the "productivity" of investment (reflected in the shape of the investment demand schedule) and the "thriftiness" or savings habits of the community.

In contrast to this view Keynes argued that since full employment is but one possible equilibrium level of employment, there is nothing natural about the natural rate and that the rate of interest is a monetary phenomenon determined by the intersection of the demand for and the supply of money. This rate, moreover, is an equilibrium rate; if there is no reason why the economic system should automatically adjust to full employment, there is, by the same token, no reason why the market rate should approach the natural rate.

The extremes have been tempered by those writers who regard interest determination as a general equilibrium matter and who therefore hold that the equilibrium rate of interest depends on both real and monetary factors.

Let us first consider the classical real interest theory. To make it more general than we have thus far made it, we should first introduce the possibility that savings may be a function of the rate of interest as well as of the level of income. The average person presumably has a strong preference for present consumption over future consumption. In other words, if he has the choice of receiving a dollar now or a dollar a year from now, he will, barring distortions introduced by taxation, most certainly take the dollar now. If, therefore, he is to be persuaded to forego the dollar now, he must be paid a premium equal to or greater than his marginal rate of time preference, i.e., an amount that will make the utility of the dollar received today equal to or smaller than the utility of the sum he will collect in a year if he lends the dollar. Presumably a higher rate of interest will induce an individual to forego some present consumption in favor of future consumption.

On this basis we may draw the savings schedule $S(i)_0$ plotted against the rate of interest in Figure 13-4, and we may suppose that as the rate of interest rises, the community will be persuaded to increase its savings.[1] Superimposed

---

[1] The whole issue of the effect of interest changes on the volume of savings is rather cloudy. There is no evidence that savings are significantly affected by reasonable changes in interest rates, although large changes could, on a priori grounds, surely be expected to affect savings. A complication arises from the possibility that for some individuals, and for the community as a whole if we assume a high enough interest rate, the savings schedule may assume a negative slope. To some extent this may be due to the fact that some individuals save toward a lump sum of wealth in the future. If an individual's goal is to have available a pool of funds totaling $20,000 when he retires at the age of sixty-five, an increase in the rate of interest will enable him to put aside a smaller sum each year and still reach the desired goal. Similarly, while an increase in the rate of interest will induce him to substitute future consumption in place of current consumption, the high rate so improves his future income prospects that he may tend to save less today. There is thus the possibility that at high enough interest rates the *income* effect may overcome the *substitution* effect and thus produce a backward bend (negative slope) in the savings schedule.

on this savings schedule we plot the familiar negatively sloped investment demand schedule $I(i)_0$, which defines the expected future returns on new investment.

Given the investment demand schedule and the savings schedule, it can easily be seen that the equilibrium rate of interest must be the rate i_0 at which the two schedules cross. If the current market rate of interest happens to be i_1, savers are willing to withhold an amount S_1 from current consumption. But since the demand for investment funds is only I_1, there will be an excess supply of savings, and the interest rate falls. As this happens, the amount of savings offered declines, and what were marginal investment projects at i_1 now become profitable. Ultimately the market is cleared at i_0, where evidently the equilibrium rate of interest is that rate that just makes the marginal rate of time preference equal to the return on the last dollar of investment. Notice that the rate i_0 is the natural rate referred to previously; to say that investment equals full-employment savings is the same as to say that aggregate demand equals the full-employment supply of output.

If an innovation shifts the investment demand schedule to $I(i)_1$, the resources required to exploit the innovation must, given the assumption of full employment, come from the willingness of savers to reduce current consumption and increase savings. The inducement to do this is the higher rate of interest that results from the bidding by investors for the available supply of savings. In Figure 13-4 the increase in the interest rate to i_1 induces savers to increase

Figure 13-4   Savings, investment, and the natural rate of interest   (all values in real terms).

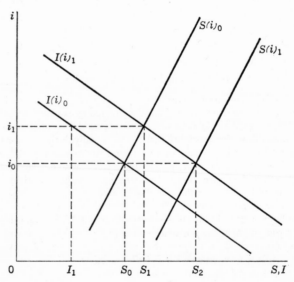

savings by $S_1 - S_0$ (and therefore reduce consumption by an equivalent amount) so that investment may increase by that same amount.

But what would happen if the shift in the investment demand schedule occurred when there were unemployed resources available? In this case the shift in the investment demand schedule need not cause the interest rate to rise at all. The existence of unemployed resources implies that there is no need to induce the public to release resources from consumption. Idle resources may simply be activated by the use of idle money balances held by individuals or by the banking system. When this happens the level of income rises; and since savings also depend on the level of income, the savings schedule, plotted with respect to the rate of interest, shifts to the right. In Figure 13-4, if the savings schedule shifts to $S(i)_1$ as a result of the increase in income brought about by the increase in investment, the equilibrium rate of interest will not rise at all.

It may clarify matters if we realize, following Horwich,[1] that the investment demand schedule is nothing more than the supply of new securities, while the savings schedule is simply the demand for new securities. Prior to the innovation, the demand and supply for new securities are exactly balanced off at i_0. The innovation, by shifting the investment demand schedule to $I(i)_1$, increases the supply of new securities. If the economy is at full employment, the savings schedule (demand for new securities) cannot shift, so the increased supply of new securities lowers security prices and raises the rate of interest. On the other hand, if unemployed resources exist, it is possible for the investment and savings schedules to shift by equal amounts, which means that the supply of and demand for new securities shift by equal amounts so that the rate of interest will not change. If, in this situation, the interest rate does change, the change must be due to the fact that the higher level of income causes wealth holders to sell some securities in order to supplement their transactions balances. Notice, however, that this will affect the rate of interest only if the demand for money is not perfectly elastic.

What general conclusions can be drawn? In Figure 13-5 the intersection of IS_0 with LM_0 is to the left of Y^* at i_0 and Y_0. Since this is a point of less than full employment, the supply of output is able to adjust to the demand, so that the intersection is a point of general equilibrium. If the IS schedule shifts to IS_1, the level of income rises to Y_1 while the interest rate remains unchanged. This is the case of the liquidity trap in which the equilibrium rate of interest is the rate at which the demand for money becomes infinitely elastic. If the IS schedule shifts further to the right to IS_2, the level of income again rises, but this time the rise is accompanied by an increase in the rate of interest to i_2. Here the liquidity trap is escaped and the equilibrium rate of interest is established at the point of intersection of the IS and LM curves. In this range of the

[1] G. Horwich, "Money, Prices, and the Theory of Interest Determination," *Economic Journal*, 67:625–643, 1957.

LM function, where the demand for money is neither zero nor infinitely elastic with respect to the rate of interest, the interest rate is determined by the combined equilibria of the product and money markets and can be changed either by monetary factors (a shift in the *LM* schedule) or by real factors (a shift in the *IS* schedule).

Finally, suppose that the *IS* schedule shifts to IS_3 so that the intersection of IS_3 with LM_0 is to the right of the full-employment level of income at interest rate i_3'. Since it is now impossible for the supply of output to adjust to the demand, the price level must rise and the *LM* curve must shift to the left. In the final equilibrium the *LM* schedule will have shifted to the point where monetary equilibrium is exactly consistent with equilibrium between the demand for and the supply of goods. This must be the rate i_3 that just balances full-employment savings with investment.

It may reasonably be argued that the Keynesian solution (i_0) and the "general equilibrium" solution $(i_2$ at $Y_2)$ are not true equilibrium solutions because they depend on rigidities in the wage-price structure. In the absence of such rigidities, the existence of uncleared markets would cause prices and wages to fall and would therefore increase the real value of the money supply. In the Keynesian case this would have no effect on the rate of interest and therefore on the level of investment and income. But this would keep markets from becoming cleared, and pressure on wages and prices would continue so that ultimately they would all approach zero. As was seen earlier, compatibility of the liquidity trap with the existence of positive levels of wages and prices necessarily assumes the existence of downward wage-price rigidities.

Figure 13-5　Determination of the equilibrium rate of interest　(all values in real terms).

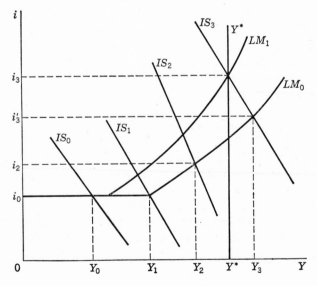

The case in which the equilibrium rate of interest is determined by both real and monetary factors also depends on the assumption of wage-price rigidities in the downward direction. Since Y_2 is at less than full employment, there are uncleared markets; so that if wages and prices fall, the real value of the money supply will increase. Since the (Y_2,i_2) solution is in a range where the LM curve has a positive slope, the increase in the real value of the money supply will cause the rate of interest to fall either to the point where investment increases by enough to restore full employment or to the point where the demand for money becomes totally elastic (the LM curve becomes horizontal). In the first case the final equilibrium will be the classical natural rate at full employment, and in the latter case it will be the Keynesian liquidity trap rate. The rate i_2 can therefore be maintained only if costs and prices are *absolutely* rigid in the downward direction.

In the final analysis it appears that the theoretical issue seems to depend on whether one insists that equilibrium in a market means a cleared market or whether one is willing to regard an uncleared market, with wage-price rigidities thwarting the possibility of clearance, as a suitable definition of equilibrium.

13-4   Assets and the Rate of Interest

Having taken considerable pains in the preceding sections of this chapter to show that the rate of interest is determined by real factors when the economy is at full employment, we are now going to do an about-face and show that the results of the preceding sections are valid only if savings are independent of the level of wealth. In a fundamental paper, L. A. Metzler[1] showed that under the assumption of full employment and flexible prices, increases in the money supply would lower the rate of interest if brought about by an open-market purchase of securities. However, if the money supply were increased without a corresponding reduction in the holdings of the earning assets of the public, the interest rate would remain the same. According to Metzler, therefore, the interest rate, even in the classical world of full employment, is partially determined by monetary factors.

In this section let us take a brief look at the considerations that lead to Metzler's result. The subject, while relevant for its own sake, is important for two additional reasons. First, although we have attempted to be explicit about the monetary effects of fiscal policy, we have not been very careful to specify whether the method of increasing the money supply makes any difference. The present analysis will allow us to remedy this deficiency. Second, if it is true that the monetary authority can affect the equilibrium rate of interest when the economy is at full employment, it follows that the monetary authority can affect the rate at which the economic system grows. Since a once-for-all

[1] L. A. Metzler, "Wealth, Savings, and the Rate of Interest," *Journal of Political Economy*, 59:93–116, 1951.

monetary policy can permanently lower the interest rate and raise the level of investment, the monetary authority can accelerate the rate of capital accumulation.

The way the money supply is increased clearly makes a difference. For example, an increase in the money supply resulting from an open-market operation might have different effects from an increase in the money supply stemming from gold production. In the former case the public gives up bonds in return for money, thereby reducing its holdings of earning assets. But in the latter case, there is no such exchange. It is likely, then, that if "wealth" is an important determinant of consumption expenditures, as most modern writers believe to be the case, the two methods of increasing the money supply may produce different effects on the rate of interest and the price level. Note that if the level of wealth is a variable that affects consumption, and if the level of wealth can be affected by monetary policy, the IS and LM curves will no longer be independent of each other.

The real wealth of the public may be defined as the sum of the net government obligations in the hands of the public plus the capitalized value of the earnings that result from the ownership of capital. If the full-employment level of income is Y^* and if a proportion, a, of this income consists of corporate profits, and if all profits are paid out as dividends, the real value of common stock, K', will be[1]

$$K' = \frac{aY^*}{i}$$

If all common stock is in the hands of the public, if there is no government debt, and if all money is in the form of currency, the real value of private wealth, W, may be written

$$W = \frac{aY^*}{i} + \frac{M}{p}$$

Now suppose, as suggested by Pigou (Chapter 11) and Friedman (Chapter 5), that consumption depends upon the level of wealth. This would imply that

$$C = C(Y,W)$$

In combination with the investment demand schedule this consumption function implies the IS curve

$$I(i) = Y - C(Y,W)$$

Since we are assuming full employment (holding Y fixed at Y^*), the new

[1] The prime is added to distinguish K in the sense of the value of capital ownership from K in the production function sense of units of productive power. In a long-run equilibrium sense the two quantities would be equal. In the short run a fall in the rate of interest raises the real value of K'. But this does not mean that the economy is capable of increasing the level of production.

IS schedule implies that the rate of interest is a function of the level of wealth. If wealth increases, consumers will want to spend more for consumption. But if the economy is at full employment, a rise in consumption cannot take place unless investment declines, and this means that the rate of interest must rise. Thus we see that the rate of interest is an increasing function of the level of wealth.

We are now ready to inquire into the effect of an increase in the money supply brought about by Federal Reserve purchases of privately held common stock.[1] In Figure 13-6 we assume that the economy is in equilibrium at full employment with interest rate i_0 and income level Y^*. Now suppose that the Federal Reserve increases the money supply by purchasing securities. The *LM* schedule shifts to the right, and the market rate of interest drops to i_1. Here, however, there is excess demand of $Y_1 - Y^*$ so that the price level begins to rise, as does the rate of interest. The *LM* schedule begins to shift back toward LM_0.

In the analysis of Section 13-2 the *LM* curve would have had to shift all the way back to LM_0 before equilibrium was again restored. But now that consumption depends on wealth, this will not happen. To see why this is so, let us in fact suppose that it does happen. If *LM* shifts back to LM_0, the rate of interest will be back at its original level, which means that each unit of common stock held by the public will have the same value as it did before the open-market operation. Moreover, the shift back to LM_0 implies that the price level has risen in exact proportion to the increase in the money supply. Consequently, the real value of the money supply is the same as it was before the open-market operation. But this must mean that the public is poorer. The real value of its stock of money is the same, as is the real value of *each unit* of common stock; but the *number* of units of common stock the public now owns is less than before.

These considerations imply that the *IS* curve must shift because the reduction in the level of wealth causes consumption to fall. If full employment is to be sustained, investment must rise to compensate for the fall in consumption, and this means that the rate of interest at which *IS* cuts the Y^* vertical line must fall. In Figure 13-6 the final equilibrium might be somewhere in the neighborhood of i_2. The *LM* curve shifts back, not to LM_0, but to LM_2; and the *IS* curve shifts to IS_2 as a result of the change in the level of wealth. The monetary authority can, apparently, change the natural rate of interest.

If the money supply had been increased by gold production, the increase would not have been accompanied by a reduction in private holdings of securities, so that a rise in the price level in proportion to the increase in the money supply would leave the real value of wealth unaffected and would cause the *IS* schedule, and therefore the natural rate of interest, to stay put.

[1] Recall that we are assuming that there is no government debt so that an open-market operation would have to be conducted by trading in private securities.

Figure 13-6 Wealth and the natural rate of interest   (all values in real terms).

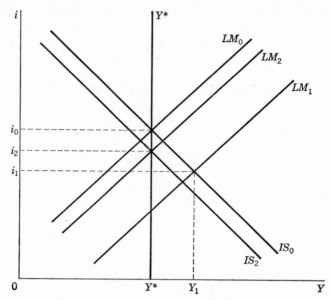

In summary, the present analysis implies that if consumption depends on wealth as well as on current income, a change in the money supply occurring in consequence of an open-market operation will affect the natural rate of interest. Thus the conclusions of the preceding sections of the chapter that pointed toward a view of money as neutral must be modified in the light of the effect of wealth on the level of consumption.

chapter **14**

International trade and the level of income

14-1 Introduction

Up to this point we have concentrated on the theory of income determination without complicating the analysis by considering the effects of domestic policy changes on trading relations with the rest-of-the-world or the effect of foreign economic policy on the domestic economy. In this chapter let us open the economy to trade and consider explicitly the effects of international trade upon the level of income.[1]

The United States was for a very long period in the position where she could virtually ignore her trade relations with other countries. As a large-scale net creditor, as a net exporter of goods and services, and as a haven for foreign capital, the United States continued for a long time to add to her gold balances. The gold drain that has occurred since the late 1950s has been a new and bewildering experience for most Americans. Our understanding of the cause

[1] Among the many excellent general discussions of this topic are L. A. Metzler, "The Theory of International Trade," in H. S. Ellis, ed. for American Economic Association, *A Survey of Contemporary Economics*, Vol. 1, Chap. 6, Richard D. Irwin, Inc., Homewood, Ill., 1949; T. C. Schelling, *International Economics*, Parts III and IV, Allyn and Bacon, Inc., Englewood Cliffs, N.J., 1958; and C. P. Kindleberger, *International Economics*, Chap. 4 and Part IV, Richard D. Irwin, Inc., Homewood, Ill., 1953.

of the gold drain and its effects upon domestic policy will be aided if we digress for a moment to look at the balance-of-payments accounts.

The balance-of-payments account is an accounting of the money values of the flows of capital, goods, and services across a country's borders during a given period of time. As its name implies, it must always balance. When the account is struck at the end of the year, it will always show that the debits equalled the credits. What, then, do people mean when they speak of an "unfavorable balance?" To understand this phrase, we should look at the composition of the accounts. Table 14-1 presents figures for selected years from the United States balance-of-payments account.

In its general form a balance-of-payments account includes three classifications of transactions. First, there are what are called current transactions. These include such things as payments for imports and exports, payments for shipping and insurance services, tourist expenditures, and interest and dividend payments. They are, in short, payments representing current flows of goods and services. Second, there are what are called capital transactions including both long-term and short-term flows. These include such things as the purchase and sale of securities, investment in foreign branch plants, and changes in accounts held in foreign banks. In addition, there is a type of capital flow that does not originate in the normal course of world trade. This includes unilateral transfers such as loans, gifts, and grants between individuals and governments in different countries. Third, there are monetary gold flows, the balancing item in the accounts.

The role of these monetary gold flows in international trade can perhaps be illustrated in the following manner. Suppose, for example, that the United States exports more than she imports and therefore accumulates credits against foreign countries. In the normal course of events, the United States would lend, in the form of commercial credit, the dollars that enabled foreigners to buy more from America than they sold to her, or Americans would buy foreign securities or invest abroad and provide foreigners with dollars in that way. If such were the pattern, there would be only very small net transfers of monetary gold between countries to balance foreign trade accounts. Suppose now that the American government considers it necessary to make large volumes of foreign aid available to foreign countries. If this aid is used to buy American goods, the money flows back in payment for American exports. However, if the money is loaned to country A, which uses it to buy goods from country B, and country B does not want to buy any goods from the United States but wishes instead to increase its gold reserves, the dollars will flow back to the United States but gold will flow to country B. In the world in which we live, foreign aid is a necessary expenditure. How then can the gold outflow be stopped?

One way to stop the outflow might be to raise tariffs against foreign goods, thereby reducing sales of foreign goods to the United States and obliging

Table 14-1 The United States balance of international payments, selected years 1935–1961 (millions of dollars)*

	1935	1937	1939	1949	1951	1953	1955	1957	1959	1960	1961
Current account											
Exports............	3,265	4,553	4,432	16,061	20,333	21,335	22,328	29,168	25,683	28,778	29,531
Imports............	3,137	4,256	3,366	9,702	15,142	16,644	17,937	20,923	23,537	23,188	22,923
Balance............	128	297	1,066	6,359	5,191	4,691	4,391	8,245	2,146	5,590	6,608
Capital account											
Net capital flows†..	1,876	1,302	2,286	− 358	− 176	856	379	−2,694	1,521	−3,021	−3,156
Net unilateral transfers.......	− 182	− 235	− 178	−5,387	−4,962	−6,708	−4,811	−4,753	−4,398	−4,271	−4,194
Balance...........	1,694	1,067	2,108	−6,195	−5,138	−5,852	−4,432	−7,447	−2,877	−7,292	−7,350
Changes in gold stock‡....	−1,822	−1,364	−3,174	− 164	− 53	1,161	41	− 798	731	1,702	742

* In this table a negative sign indicates an outflow of funds.

† Includes errors and omissions.

‡ − means gold purchase by the United States.

Source: 1935–1957, U.S. Bureau of the Census, *Historical Statistics of the United States, Colonial Times to 1957,* Series U182–U192, U.S. Government Printing Office, Washington, 1960. 1959, U.S. Bureau of the Census, *Statistical Abstract of the United States, 1961,* Table 1188, U.S. Government Printing Office, Washington, 1961, p. 865. 1960–1961, U.S. Department of Commerce, *Survey of Current Business, June, 1962,* Table 4, U.S. Government Printing Office, Washington, 1962, pp. 16–17.

foreigners to use up their dollar balances to buy American exports. Such a policy would no doubt be ineffective because foreigners would raise their tariffs against American goods. Americans might then allow domestic interest rates to rise, thereby encouraging foreigners to invest their excess dollars in the United States. However, this policy might conflict with domestic policy if it were felt that interest rates should be held at low levels in order to stimulate the domestic level of income. Finally, the United States might increase the dollar price of gold, i.e., might pay less gold per dollar received or, in other words, devalue the dollar. If one views the stability of the dollar as an important factor in stimulating world trade and economic strength, then this too does not appear to be an acceptable solution. The United States can suggest that other countries ought to shoulder a larger part of the foreign aid burden, but most of the adjustment will certainly have to come from an expansion of exports—a goal that will be difficult to achieve if the economy is faced with inflationary pressure.

The foregoing paragraph suggests that the attempt to maintain balance-of-payments equilibrium may be in serious conflict with the desire to maintain domestic income and price stability and with the needs of military security. A country may, for example, be at the full-employment level of income with a stable level of prices while exporting more than it imports. But this means that another country is importing more than it exports. This cannot go on indefinitely because an indefinite excess of imports over exports would ultimately exhaust the credit of the net importing country. The net importing country would therefore have to take steps to export more or to import less, and this would have adverse income effects on the country that was originally a net exporter. As we shall see subsequently, the balance of payments of the various countries would normally tend to adjust automatically to yield a long-run balance. But these equilibrating forces may produce such severe income and price effects that governments will try to counteract the adjustment process by resorting to offsetting monetary and fiscal policies or by resorting to direct controls over the volume of trade. The present reluctance on the part of the United States government to take serious steps in the direction of reducing the level of unemployment is partly attributable to the fear that expansionary monetary-fiscal policies will cause the price level to rise and that this will make it more difficult for our exporters to compete in foreign markets. Similarly, the state of the domestic economy would appear to call for a policy of low interest rates and easy money. It is feared, however, that such a policy will cause capital to be withdrawn and reinvested in foreign countries where interest rates are higher.

In this chapter we shall first examine the nature of the automatic mechanisms by which the balance of payments would normally be brought into equilibrium. We shall then assume that domestic income and price levels are taken as fixed by policy and examine the nature of the direct controls that governments may utilize as a substitute for automatic equilibrating mechanisms. Before we do this, however, we need to integrate international trade into our national accounting framework.

Net national product including foreign trade may be defined as

$$Y = C + I_r + G + (X - M)$$

where $(X - M)$ represents exports minus imports. Thus a positive net export balance is an addition to income in the same way that a positive level of investment is an addition to income. As before, income receipts are divided into

$$Y = C + S + T$$

When we replace realized investment (I_r) by intended investment (I) and equate the two foregoing expressions, we obtain the equilibrium condition

$$I + G + X = S + T + M$$

which, as usual, implies that income leakages must equal compensating expenditures. Exports, like investment and government expenditures, are contributions to the domestic income stream, while imports, like savings and taxes, are leakages.

14-2 Automatic Mechanisms of Adjustment

The international gold standard still occupies a cherished place in the hearts of those given to nostalgia. In its full flowering, a period covering roughly the years 1880–1914, it served as an international system of payments and adjustment which, when all countries played the game, promoted world-wide trade freedom. The intellectual foundation of the theory of the gold standard is embodied in the famous classical "specie-flow" mechanism. The basic simplicity of the theory makes it a convenient place to start the discussion. As in classical income theory, it assumes that the equilibrium level of output is the full-employment level.[1] Under a gold standard, the major trading countries of the world fix their domestic currencies in terms of gold and stand ready to buy and sell gold at the fixed rate to any and all. Thus an American would be perfectly willing to accept British pounds in payment of a debt because he could at any time transfer his pounds into gold and then exchange the gold for dollars.

Given this basic rule of convertibility, let us suppose that the trading world consists of two countries, A whose currency is alphas and B whose currency is betas. Now suppose that because of differences in the price levels between the two countries, A exports more to B than she imports from B. Exporters in country A will accumulate beta balances in B which they will eventually turn

[1] G. von Haberler, *The Theory of International Trade*, Part I, The Macmillan Company, New York, 1950, provides a thorough and detailed discussion of the classical theory.

into gold to ship back to A to exchange for alphas. The gold movement will reduce bank reserves in B and will cause a contraction of the money supply, an increase in interest rates, and a fall in the price level. At the same time, A will experience rising bank reserves, a loosening of credit, falling interest rates, and a rising price level. Because of these price changes, A becomes a more expensive market in which to buy and a better market in which to sell, while the opposite takes place in B. Exports from A begin to decline while exports from B rise. The net effect, apparently, will be a reversal of the balance of trade as well as a reversal of gold flows.

Notice that as long as both countries remain on the gold standard, neither one can do anything to prevent an ultimate adjustment. Country B may, for example, attempt to stave off the adjustment by allowing its gold reserves to flow out. However, as long as B remains on the gold standard, eventual tightening of credit is inevitable. Given the full-employment assumption, the balance-of-payments equilibrating mechanism is a purely monetary one. Trade imbalances are ironed out through changes in the money supply, interest rates, and prices. When an outflow of gold from B develops, the market rate of interest rises above the natural rate, aggregate demand is less than the full-employment supply, and prices fall. In country A the market rate of interest is forced below the natural rate by the increase in the money supply, aggregate demand exceeds the full-employment supply, and prices rise. Country A becomes a good seller's market and country B a good buyer's market.

As part of its general revision of macro-economic theory, the Keynesian analysis brought with it significant alterations in the classical theory of international trade adjustment.[1] The new theory, by allowing the level of real income to be a variable subject to change, explained what empirical studies had long made known as a fact—that the balance of payments between countries tended to adjust much more rapidly than could reasonably be accounted for by the relatively slow changes in price levels.[2]

Consider once again the case in which B increases its imports from A, and suppose that the increase is caused by a change in consumer tastes in B. The resulting trade imbalance must, of course, be financed by a capital movement which will, except in a liquidity trap situation, produce adjustment tendencies. But there is another mechanism at work. As A's exports rise, the increase in its net foreign balance increases the level of income, first in the export industries and then throughout the economy as a result of secondary induced expendi-

---

[1] Joan Robinson, *Essays in the Theory of Employment*, The Macmillan Company, New York, 1937, made the first attempt to apply Keynesian theory to the theory of international adjustment.

[2] J. H. Williams, *Argentine International Trade under Inconvertible Paper Money, 1880–1900*, Harvard University Press, Cambridge, Mass., 1920; J. Viner, *Canada's Balance of International Indebtedness, 1900–1913*, Harvard University Press, Cambridge, Mass., 1924; F. W. Taussig, *International Trade*, The Macmillan Company, New York, 1928.

tures. The increase in income will cause consumption to rise and, since part of the added goods will be bought from abroad, will raise the level of imports. In country B, since consumer tastes have shifted from domestic to foreign goods, there will be a decline in domestic income and therefore in consumption and imports from A. Thus income changes causing A to increase its imports and B to decrease its imports offset a part, or in some cases all, of the initial imbalance.

In summary, the balance of payments between countries A and B will tend to adjust automatically as a consequence of two developments. First there will be a direct income effect stemming from the fact that an export surplus in country A and an import surplus in B will raise the level of income in A and lower it in B. This in turn causes A's imports to rise and B's imports to fall, thereby offsetting part of the initial disequilibrium. In addition, there will be indirect effects caused by the money flow between the two countries. A's money supply increases, while B's decreases. Interest rates fall in A, investment is stimulated, and money income rises, while exactly the opposite takes place in B. These indirect effects on the level of money income will not take place in the event that the demand for money in both countries is infinitely elastic with respect to the rate of interest. In this extreme Keynesian case the whole burden of adjustment is placed on the direct income effects.

Direct income effects will not, in general, produce complete offsets to balance-of-payments disturbances. If investment, government expenditure, and taxes are constant, an autonomous increase in exports from country A of ΔX_a due to a change in tastes in country B will cause three induced effects to occur in country A. First, the increase in income in country A will cause imports to rise by some amount ΔM_i; second, the increase in income will cause savings to increase by some amount ΔS; and finally, the fall in income in B due to the original diversion of expenditures from domestic production to goods produced in A will induce a fall in B's imports, and therefore in A's exports by some quantity ΔX_i. If income is to be restored to the equilibrium level in A, the change in compensating expenditures must be equal to the change in leakages. Consequently, it must be the case that

$$\Delta X_a - \Delta X_i - \Delta M_i = \Delta S \qquad (14\text{-}1)$$

The left-hand side of the equation is the net change in the balance-of-payments surplus, and this, apparently, must equal the change in savings. Since A's export surplus must equal B's import surplus, it follows that savings in B must change by an equal amount (though in the opposite direction) as savings in A.

From Eq. (14-1) we may next observe that if the initial autonomous change in exports is to be just offset by the induced increase in imports and subsequent reduction in exports, the net change in savings in both countries would have to be zero. This means that complete offset will materialize only if the marginal propensity to save in one of the two countries is zero. Furthermore, since there would be no change in savings in either country, the country with the zero marginal propensity to save will undergo the whole burden of income adjustment while the income in the other country will be unaffected. If the marginal propensity to save in country B is equal to zero, the autonomous increase in their imports (A's exports) will lower their income level by an amount that induces a fall in imports of exactly the same amount as the initial increase. Income in country A will therefore remain constant, and this means that there will be no induced change in A's imports. Consequently, Eq. (14-1) reduces to

$$\Delta X_a - \Delta X_i = 0$$

On the other hand, if the marginal propensity to save in country A is zero, the autonomous increase in A's exports will increase income to the point where imports rise by exactly the amount of the original autonomous change in exports, so that income in B will remain constant. In this case Eq. (14-1) becomes

$$\Delta X_a - \Delta M_i = 0$$

In general, we may expect the marginal propensities to save in the two countries to be greater than zero. This means that the direct income effects will not yield complete adjustment of the balance of payments and that both countries will be subject to income changes as the result of autonomous changes in the balance of payments.

14-3 Exchange Rate Variations

The automatic mechanisms of adjustment discussed in the preceding section are predicated on the assumption that public policy will permit the requisite income and price changes to take place. Price and income stability is, however, not always considered secondary to balance-of-payments equilibrium. In many countries it is national policy to utilize monetary-fiscal measures to offset disturbances originating at home or abroad that affect the balance of payments. If a policy of full employment is pursued, especially if that policy is accompanied by inflationary pressure, trade deficits would tend to be perpetuated, and perhaps even aggravated, unless alternative means for achieving balance can be found.

One possible approach to the problem is to permit exchange rates between currencies to fluctuate.[1] To illustrate how this works, consider again the case in which B increases its imports from A. The imbalance will be noticed in B by a flow of capital to A to finance the imbalance. If the exchange rate between

[1] R. Nurske, *International Currency Experience*, League of Nations, Geneva, 1944, pp. 117–122, presents an illuminating discussion of the French experience with freely fluctuating exchange rates during the early 1920s.

alphas and betas is not fixed, the increased flow of betas will cause a fall in the alpha price of betas; this has the effect of making goods produced in B cheaper for the residents in A and goods produced in A more expensive for residents in B.

Thus it is possible to obtain assistance from another automatic mechanism of adjustment. If exchange rates are pegged, the balance of payments can be adjusted automatically only by internal price and income changes. But if the exchange rate is allowed to fluctuate, price levels may remain fixed, while foreign markets may become more or less attractive markets in which to buy or sell by virtue of fluctuations in the rate of exchange between currencies.

For reasons which we shall discuss subsequently, fluctuating exchange rates are universally unpopular. Governments prefer to maintain sets of fixed exchange rates between currencies and to adjust these from time to time by government action. If the exchange rate between alphas and betas is 4:1, an automobile produced in A costing 2,000 alphas will cost 500 betas in country B. A bicycle produced in B costing 25 betas will cost 100 alphas in A. If betas are devalued to the point where 1 beta is the equivalent of 2 alphas, the immediate consequence will be for the price of A's cars to double in B, while the price of B's bicycles will fall to 50 alphas in A. Presumably, the devaluation would stimulate the purchase of bicycles by A's citizens and reduce the purchase of cars by B's citizens, thereby helping to achieve equilibrium on the balance of payments. But whether improvement will, in fact, result from devaluation depends on rather more involved considerations.[1]

If B devalues, its people are almost certain to spend fewer alphas on A's cars. The devaluation is first noticed by importers of cars in B, who find that they have to put up more betas to purchase a car from A than they did before. This means that they must raise the price of cars to buyers in B, and this in turn will reduce the quantity of cars purchased. But the reduction in the number of cars purchased by B's citizens means that car producers in A will observe a fall in the demand for cars; if the elasticity of supply of cars in A is not infinite, this will cause car prices in A to fall. This means that B's citizens now buy fewer cars and at the same time pay a smaller price, in terms of alphas, for each car. The net effect is therefore the desired one of reducing the quantity of alphas spent by country B on imports.

There would be only one case in which B would not spend fewer alphas than before. If the demand for A's cars in B is infinitely inelastic, the rise in the beta price of cars will not reduce car purchases in B; there will therefore be no fall in the demand for cars noticed by A's car producers and no fall in the alpha price of cars. B therefore buys the same number of A's cars and spends the same number of alphas on them; this implies that the devaluation has

[1] Voluminous literature exists on the effect of devaluation on the balance of payments. Joan Robinson, "The Foreign Exchanges," *Essays in the Theory of Employment*, The Macmillan Company, New York, 1937, remains the classic discussion of the problem.

simply had the effect of increasing the beta price of A's cars in proportion to the devaluation.

While this is an extreme case, it had, in the years immediately following World War II, a certain amount of practical relevance. Many of the commodities imported by European countries from the United States were absolutely essential and had extremely low demand elasticities. This implied that devaluation would not be effective and would, in any case, not be a solution to the problem on any long-run basis. What was obviously needed was assistance in rebuilding capital equipment so that ultimately the need for imports would be reduced and the capacity to expand exports would be increased. Happily, the United States, through the Marshall Plan, undertook to cancel the balance-of-payments deficits of European countries.

On the export side, devaluation by B not only may be ineffective but may operate in such a perverse way that A ends up importing more bicycles while spending a smaller total alpha sum on them. If A's demand for bicycles has an elasticity of less than unity, the percentage fall in the alpha price due to devaluation will be greater than the percentage increase in quantity bought so that total alpha expenditures on bicycles will decline. In such a case devaluation, viewed purely from the export point of view, will have a perverse effect on the balance of payments unless it happens that the supply of bicycles of country B cannot be expanded. If B's supply of bicycles is perfectly inelastic, the beta price of bicycles will rise in exact proportion to the devaluation, and there will be no net change in alpha earnings on exports.

If A's demand for bicycles is highly elastic, B's alpha earnings will increase as long as the supply of bicycles is elastic; the effect will be negated if the supply of bicycles is inelastic. Thus, even if A's demand for bicycles is elastic, the desired effects of devaluation may be thwarted by an inability to expand export capacity. Since this is most likely to be the case at or near full employment, balance-of-payments equilibrium may necessitate a shrinkage of income and may be impossible to achieve by devaluation alone. At full employment it is likely that a large proportion of the effect of devaluation will be frittered away in the form of higher prices so that balance-of-payments equilibrium, despite governmental attempts to maintain full employment, may ultimately require the pursuit of deflationary policies.

The easiest way to see that devaluation may not be a substitute for deflationary monetary-fiscal policies is by returning again to the definition of income, substituting intended investment, I, in place of realized investment, I_r, and writing the expression as

$$Y - (C + I + G) = X - M \qquad (14\text{-}2)$$

The level of domestic production is given by Y; $C + I + G$ represents aggregate domestic demand, or "absorption." If domestic production is in excess of absorption, and if there is no unintended investment, the country must be enjoying an export surplus — i.e., $X - M$ will be positive. On the other hand, if consumers, investors, and the government absorb more output than the country produces, this must mean that the country is borrowing foreign resources and therefore encountering an export deficit (import surplus).

Observe from Eq. (14-2) that essentially there are only two ways to eliminate an import surplus. One way is to increase output without a corresponding increase in absorption. Alternatively, if output remains constant, exports can be increased and imports reduced by a reduction in domestic absorption. When the economy is at full employment, the latter alternative is the only one available to it, and this means that it will be impossible to eliminate a balance-of-payments deficit without a reduction in some component of domestic demand. An increase in taxes, for example, would reduce consumption. Since some consumption goods are imported while others are produced with materials that are all, or partly, imported, the increase in taxes causes imports to decline automatically. Since the tax increase also releases domestic resources, the resources will be available for the expansion of exports. It is here that devaluation becomes important. By making production for export relatively more profitable than for domestic consumption, the devaluation provides a relative price incentive toward transfer of resources into export industries.

Devaluation is an unpopular policy. It has, quite foolishly, become a matter of national pride to maintain the value of the currency in relation to foreign currencies. Of a more substantive nature is the objection that the prospect of devaluation may give rise to damaging speculative activity. If a devaluation by country B is anticipated, A's buyers will defer purchases of B's goods until after the devaluation, while B's buyers will hasten to purchase A's goods prior to devaluation. The effect may be to worsen the imbalance and to make it appear that a more drastic devaluation will be necessary than would be required under normal circumstances. Although governments would like to keep prospective devaluation a secret, traders can watch changes in a country's gold and foreign exchange reserves and can, from the knowledge that a severe drain is in process, infer that devaluation is not far off.

Another circumstance that makes devaluation unpopular is the fact that it causes the "terms of trade" of the devaluing country to deteriorate. Insofar as prices in A and B do not change in proportion to the devaluation, B will, after the devaluation, be obliged to give up more real resources (bicycles) in exchange for a unit (a car) of foreign resources. Such deterioration in the terms of trade implies that real income will be transferred from B to A.

In view of the difficulties that the United States is encountering in balancing its international accounts and in raising economic activity to tolerable levels, the policy of freely fluctuating exchange rates is beginning to look attractive to those who see no point in allowing the economy to go through a wringer of the kind imposed by a de facto gold standard. How lovely it would be if we could concentrate on reducing the level of unemployment and raising the rate of economic growth and not have to worry about whether gold was flowing in or out.

Suggestions to unpeg the exchange rate are usually greeted with horror. It is argued that freely fluctuating exchange rates inevitably create adverse expectations. For example, a fall in the price of betas relative to alphas will give rise to the expectation that further falls are likely. Acting on this expectation, A's importers will defer purchases of B's goods in anticipation of a further fall in the exchange rate, while B's importers will rush to purchase additional quantities of A's goods. Since such behavior means that alphas become even scarcer relative to betas, the fall in the exchange rate, rather than restoring equilibrium, promotes a further fall in the price of betas relative to alphas.

The foregoing argument is based on the notion that expectations are "extrapolative," i.e., a movement of price in one direction creates the belief that further movements in the same direction are in the offing. Generalized to all prices, such expectations would soon mean the complete collapse of the price system. While there have been periods when a fall in prices undoubtedly gave rise to the expectation of further falls, there is no particular reason to single out the price of foreign exchange as any more susceptible to destabilizing expectations than any other price. Moreover, release from exchange-rate pegging could allow governments to create the kinds of stable domestic economies that are conducive to price stability and price-stabilizing expectations.

Another argument that has frequently been heard is that freely fluctuating exchange rates would introduce an added element of uncertainty into international trade and that this would reduce the volume of trade. We see no particular reason why international trade should be singled out as an area requiring special price stabilization. We have attempted such stabilization in domestic agriculture, and it is not an exaggeration to assert that the policy has not been a howling success.

Among the other arguments, most are of such little value as to warrant only passing reference. We hear of the dangers of "speculative raids" and "attacks" on the dollar, and we are told that the United States, as the world's banker, has an obligation to guarantee the value of the dollar to those who hold dollars. Since we do not guarantee the owner of a share of common stock that the price of his share will never drop, it is difficult to see why we should go out of our way to guarantee the value of the dollar vis-à-vis foreign currencies.

We hasten to emphasize that we do not pretend to be experts in the area of international payments arrangements. However, we believe that the subject of more appropriate payments arrangements ought to be discussed and considered more fully than it has been to date. The de facto gold standard under which we are struggling is clearly a technically deficient arrangement. It is obvious that when central banks stand ready always to purchase their own currencies in exchange for gold at a fixed price, country A will sooner or later be subjected to a gold crisis; and when country A is not in the throes of such a crisis, it is very likely that country B will be suffering from one.

14-4 Tariffs, Quotas, and the Balance of Payments

Modern governments wish to maintain domestic price and income stability. Yet devaluation is not always a suitable alternative and may not be effective unless accompanied by deflationary monetary-fiscal policies. This dilemma is one of the reasons why governments frequently resort to direct devices of trade obstruction such as tariffs and quotas, which, as nearly all economists agree, thwart efficient resource allocation and reduce the combined real incomes of the affected countries.[1]

Suppose that the imbalance in B's trade account results from a situation that is likely to take a long time to cure. For example, there may be an inflation in B resulting from a high level of investment expenditures combined with a large defense budget. In such a case B's accumulated foreign exchange reserves may not be sufficient to stand the expected drain without resort to devaluation or some other policy. If B refuses to devalue or to pursue deflationary monetary-fiscal policy, it may impose direct controls upon the volume of trade by means of import quotas upon A's goods. Importers in B must then apply to their government to buy A's currency because there is an excess demand for it at the unchanged price. This excess demand will be rationed out of the market, not by price changes, but by allowing B importers to buy only that amount of A's currency that A importers make available at the fixed exchange rate. B's importers are, in effect, given ration tickets in an amount depending primarily upon the volume of exports. Since the quota reduces the physical quantity of imports, the alpha price of cars will fall so that B buys fewer cars and pays a smaller alpha sum per car. Quota systems therefore cannot fail to reduce the quantity of the foreign currency spent on imports.

Since the exchange rate remains fixed and the alpha price of cars falls while the beta price rises, a tremendous surplus profit is realized by the importers lucky enough to obtain a quota. If for no other reason, quota systems are undesirable because they put a great premium on obtaining a quota and discriminate most severely against those importers who do not have enough friends in high official places, even though they may be far more efficient than those who obtain quotas. If the government were to grant import licenses on the basis of competitive bidding and were to turn the receipts over to the Treasury, the system would be less discriminatory because the lowest-cost firms would be able to submit the highest bids. In addition, auctioning quotas

---

[1] If a country imposes a tariff, it can, if there is no retaliation, increase its welfare at the expense of other countries. Tariff retaliation will, however, reduce the welfare of all countries. See T. de Scitovszky, "A Reconsideration of the Theory of Tariffs," *Review of Economic Studies*, 9:89–110, 1942.

has the added advantage of removing purchasing power from the hands of the public.

Although the use of import quotas will prevent the need for a domestic adjustment, quota systems cause a real loss because they perpetuate inefficient resource allocation. Country B's citizens are obliged to shift their purchases to domestic cars which are produced less efficiently and yield less satisfaction, while country A's car producers must retrench and shift resources into less desirable uses.

Although the need for import quotas may decrease over time, there is little effective guarantee that quotas will in fact be removed. The fact that B has to impose controls is in effect a sign that devaluation and/or deflationary policies should be undertaken. But since the quotas take the place of such unpopular policies, the required domestic adjustments may never be undertaken. Since quota systems, like tariffs, create politically powerful vested interests, they may be very difficult to remove.

A tariff is a less damaging form of direct control than a quota. Its effects are practically identical to devaluation except that they are restricted to the import side, where devaluation is likely to do the most good. Tariffs raise the price of imported cars to B's consumers and reduce the over-all demand for A's cars, thereby causing the alpha price to fall, so that B buys fewer cars and pays fewer alphas per car.

Tariffs are generally regarded as less offensive than quota systems in that they give the price system a chance to adjust to some extent. A new importer of materials who is able to convert imported materials into final product more cheaply and efficiently than existing firms will displace an older, less efficient firm. But if all the quotas have been assigned, the new producer, despite his superior efficiency, will be unable to expand his business. Tariffs shelter the home market from foreign competition, whereas quotas go beyond this in sheltering inefficient domestic producers from competition by both foreigners and their own nationals.

14-5   Some Final Notes

It would not be surprising if someone inferred from the previous discussion that since foreign trade is such a nuisance, it should be abolished. This approach is comparable to treating a nose cold by cutting one's head off; but to an appalling extent this is the attitude that prevails in many business and government circles. While economists can agree on precious few things, there seems to be virtual unanimity with respect to the beneficial effects of international trade. Just as it would be ridiculous to prohibit trade between Alabama and Indiana, it would be absurd to prohibit trade between the United States and Japan. If trade between the states were prohibited, Alabama would have to divert some of its resources from cotton production, in which she is efficient, to corn production; Indiana farmers would have to divert resources from corn production to cotton production. The loss in real income for the states would indeed be monumental.

Gains result from trade even if Indiana can produce both cotton and corn more efficiently than Alabama. Indiana is then said to have an absolute advantage in the production of both cotton and corn. Alabama, on the other hand, would then have only a comparative advantage in the production of cotton. But since cotton production in Indiana would necessitate a diversion from corn production, in which she is even more efficient, it pays Indiana to specialize in the production of corn, where her absolute advantage is the greatest, and to trade with Alabama for cotton, where Alabama's comparative disadvantage is the least.

The notion that it pays to specialize and trade even though one economy is more efficient in the production of all commodities than another was first advanced by David Ricardo.[1] The validity of this "law of comparative advantage," as it is known, is so obvious and incontrovertible that one wonders how it could be so frequently forgotten.

The cause of free trade encounters countless obstacles, some of which, it must be admitted, have a compelling short-run validity. The principal obstacle is the circumstance that it is virtually impossible simultaneously to maintain full employment and price stability, balance-of-payments equilibrium, and pegged exchange rates. By pegging the exchange rate, the adjustment process is deprived of one of its degrees of freedom. The burden of adjustment is then placed upon income and price changes. Since these, too, are intolerable, recourse is sought in "beggar-my-neighbor" tariff, quota, and exchange-control policies. Since the neighbor is unlikely to react kindly to such measures, he retaliates in kind. Before the dust has cleared, the world economy finds itself in the position of the 1930s, when world trade had largely degenerated into a series of bilateral barter agreements between nations. In a world consisting of individual nations, each jealous of its sovereignty, in which international cooperation is undertaken only as long as such cooperation is in the narrow interests of the individual participants, the cause of free trade, as well as of peace and other "incidental" goals, is apt to be subjugated to selfish ends.

Trade restrictions arise from causes other than those emphasized thus far. The reason for such restrictions may be largely noneconomic, and therefore the economist has little to say about them in his professional capacity. A developing country may well place restrictions on trade with others in order to develop an industrial system of its own, in the hope that it will eventually be able to compete freely with them. It may wish to conserve domestic capital and attract foreign capital. National defense may also be used as an argument for restriction of trade. The American watch industry is protected by high

[1] David Ricardo, *Principles of Political Economy and Taxation*, Chap. 7, J. M. Dent & Sons, Ltd., London, 1948.

tariff walls on the ground that the skills of precision machinists must not be allowed to die out.

Some degree of trade restriction is always likely to be with us. Advancing technology, differing resource bases, and changing tastes mean that domestic adjustments must continually be made by all countries, and such adjustments will create a demand for protection. But the compelling arguments in favor of freer trade have induced nations to band together in cooperative agencies[1] ready to assist in the adjustment process so that no country is forced, in an effort to protect its domestic economy, to engage in policies that are likely to result in mutual retaliation. This assistance may take the form of loans to finance declining foreign exchange balances or assistance in setting the terms of a controlled devaluation. In return, the country that has run into difficulty must give evidence that it is trying by use of domestic policy to adjust the imbalance, if more than a very short-run cause is involved.

There is hope that the experience of the 1930s will encourage nations to cooperate in seeking the benefits of an increasing volume of trade. Success in such an endeavor requires that deep and prolonged depressions be averted in the future. Under conditions of relative stability, it may be possible to look forward to a period of normal trading relationships in which balance will be maintained by slight changes in exchange rates. Indeed, if free trade becomes established, the increase in real income that will result will make the processes of adjustment that much easier.

[1] T. C. Schelling, *International Economics*, Part V, Allyn and Bacon, Inc., Boston, 1958, contains an extended discussion of the operation of such international agencies.

part III

Growth and Fluctuations in Economic Activity

chapter 15

Introduction to macro-economic dynamics

15-1 Introduction

We are now about to embark on a discussion of problems that economists call "dynamic" in contrast to the "static" analysis of Part II. Our first task is to inquire into the meaning of these terms. One general rule among many economists is that a "dynamic" model is a "good" model, whereas a "static" model, the kind other people invent, is a "bad" one. Unhappily, this definition will not suffice for our purposes.

A broad and rather loose notion of a dynamic model is one in which time becomes introduced as an explicit variable. Now that we are about to consider the determinants of the rate of growth of the economy, it is obvious that we have to know over what period of time the economy grows by a certain percent. Similarly, during inflation the price level, by definition, is not in equilibrium; it is, rather, changing at some rate per unit time. If we were told that the price level had risen by 10 percent we might be bored, mildly concerned, or downright panic-stricken, depending upon whether the 10 percent increase had taken place over a period of a century, a decade, or a year. It goes without saying that the study of business cycles—the ups and downs in economic activity—is also a dynamic problem.

Except for the multiplier process of Chapter 5, the models of Part II are "comparative static" models. The solutions to the equation systems define equilibrium values for the variables. A shift in one of the functions due, for example, to a change in the money supply or government expenditures, causes the equations to give a new equilibrium point as a solution. The models did not make explicit the process by which the variables of the system move to the new equilibrium. We did, to be sure, discuss the process of adjustment from one equilibrium to the next. But the various adjustment processes were in no way implied by the equations themselves. The models would have been truly dynamic only if we had specified how the variables behave when the system is out of equilibrium.

If we were reasonably sure that an increase in the money supply would lower the rate of interest and raise the level of income to a new equilibrium level, as implied by the models of Part II, and if we were not particularly concerned about how long it took to get to the new equilibrium point, there would be no pressing reason to complicate our comparative static models by specifying exactly how adjustments to disequilibrium take place. Unfortunately, however, we cannot always be sure that the equilibrium solutions predicted by comparative static models will actually be attained. The equilibria may be "unstable," i.e., if the variables of the system happen to be at the equilibrium point, they will tend to stay there; but should the equilibrium be disrupted by some disturbance, a progressive divergence from, rather than a movement toward, the equilibrium point will occur. Thus the comparative static solutions may be irrelevant. For example, although an increase in the money supply leads our models of Part II to predict a rise in income and a fall in the rate of interest, we may never get to this position. The changes may, in fact, be in a direction opposite to that predicted by the static model.

These as yet unsupported assertions lead to a fundamental proposition: It is frequently impossible to determine the effect of a shift of a function in a comparative static model without examining the underlying dynamic process of adjustment. This proposition, developed by P. A. Samuelson[1] and called by him the "correspondence principle," is a good place to begin our discussion of macro-dynamic problems.

15-2   Dynamic Adjustment and the *IS-LM* Model

Throughout Part II we assumed that the investment demand equation was $I = I(i)$. However, in Chapter 7 we took note of the fact that it might be reasonable to write

$$I = I(i,Y)$$

The inclusion of the level of income as an independent variable in the invest-

[1] P. A. Samuelson, *Foundations of Economic Analysis*, Chap. 9, Harvard University Press, Cambridge, Mass., 1947, especially pp. 276–283.

ment demand equation does not at first seem like much of a change. But, as we shall see, it introduces some formidable and intriguing new problems.

With the new investment demand function the equation for the *IS* schedule becomes

$$I(i,Y) = Y - C(Y) \qquad (15\text{-}1)$$

The first thing we must notice is that the *IS* schedule is no longer necessarily negatively sloped. Recall from Chapter 7 that with the new investment demand equation there will be a whole family of investment demand curves in quadrant 1. Thus in Figure 15-1 income Y_0 is associated with investment demand schedule $I(i,Y_0)$. Consequently, interest rate i_0 equates intended investment and savings at income level Y_0. Similarly, when the level of income is Y_1, the relevant investment demand schedule is $I(i,Y_1)$, so that by tracing around the four quadrants we observe that interest rate i_1 gives product market equilibrium.

Figure 15-1 Product market equilibrium   (all values in real terms).

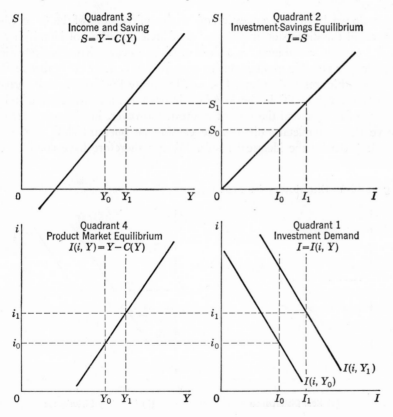

In the present example the *IS* schedule has a positive slope, although the slope may also be negative. If we define **h** as the "marginal propensity to invest," i.e., the increase in investment that is induced by a $1 increase in income, the *IS* curve will have a positive slope if **h** is greater than the marginal propensity to save and a negative slope if the reverse is the case. Let us see why this is so.

When investment increases to a new level, the level of income rises until savings have risen by an amount equal to the increase in investment. But given our present assumption about investment demand, the increase in income induces further increases in investment. If the marginal propensity to invest is greater than the marginal propensity to save, savings cannot rise fast enough to balance intended investment with savings. The level of income would therefore tend to keep rising indefinitely, and product market equilibrium would never be attained. However, equilibrium can be restored if the rate of interest rises and reduces intended investment. Consequently, when the marginal propensity to invest exceeds the marginal propensity to save, product market equilibrium implies that as the level of income rises, the rate of interest must also rise.

Why do we dwell on the question of the sign of the slope of the *IS* schedule? First, recall the discussion in Chapter 9 of Stein's method of identifying the disturbances that cause income to change. If the *IS* curve has a positive slope, it is no longer possible to distinguish a real from a monetary disturbance. This is shown in Figures 15-2(*a*) and 15-2(*b*). In Figure 15-2(*a*) a real disturbance causing an upward shift in the *IS* schedule has the expected effect of raising the level of income and the rate of interest. However, in Figure 15-2(*b*) we observe that a monetary disturbance causing an outward shift in the *LM* schedule produces the identical result. We can therefore have confidence in

Figure 15-2 Disturbances that cause income to change (all values in real terms).

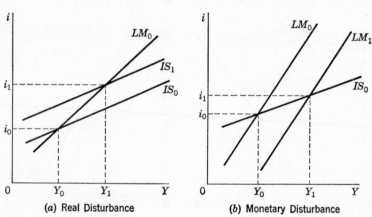

(*a*) Real Disturbance   (*b*) Monetary Disturbance

Stein's method only if we are convinced that the marginal propensity to invest is less than the marginal propensity to save.[1]

The second problem, which is more pertinent to our present line of inquiry, is that the static equilibrium points defined by the intersection of the *IS* and *LM* curves may now become unstable. That is to say, even though a shift in the *IS* or *LM* functions from one position to another shifts the equilibrium position of income and the interest rate, it is now no longer clear whether the new equilibrium will in fact be reached.[2]

In Figure 15-3 the *IS-LM* curves are represented with their conventional shapes. We assume that the initial equilibrium is at i_0 and Y_0 and that the equilibrium is disturbed by a shift to the right of the *LM* curve.

Figure 15-3 Dynamic adjustment: Case 1 (all values in real terms).

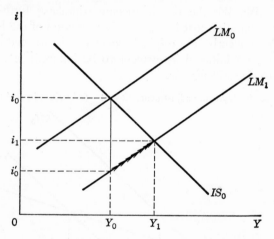

We wish now to trace the process of adjustment to the new equilibrium point Y_1, i_1. To do this, we need to introduce some dynamic assumptions about how the system behaves when it is out of equilibrium. Accordingly, let us assume that the rate of interest adjusts instantaneously to monetary disturbances and that the speed of adjustment in the product market is equal to the difference between investment and savings (that is to say, the difference between aggregate demand and what is currently being produced). The assumption of instantaneous money market adjustment allows us to trace the

---

[1] Some economists have found additional reasons for being skeptical of Stein's analysis. See the complaints of Clark Warburton, "Forces Producing Disturbances in the Value of Output," *Journal of Political Economy*, 69:587–604, 1961; and Martin J. Bailey, "A Method Sometimes Identifying Disturbances Which Produce Changes in Money National Income, *Journal of Political Economy*, 69:288–292, 1961; and Stein's reply, "What Changed Money Income? A Reply," *Journal of Political Economy*, 69:292–294, 1961.

[2] See the appendix to this chapter at the end of the book for a restatement of the subsequent analysis in mathematical terms.

path of income and the interest rate along the *LM* curve from which, by our assumption, we can never depart.

Referring again to Figure 15-3, the shift in the *LM* curve together with our assumption about interest rate adjustments implies that the interest rate falls immediately to i_0'. But at i_0' with income level Y_0 intended investment exceeds savings. Consequently, income begins to rise. As the level of income rises, the quantity of money demanded for transactions purposes increases so that the interest rate also begins to rise. The adjustment now continues upward (following the arrows) along the *LM* curve until Y_1 and i_1 are reached. At this point intended investment again equals savings, and equilibrium is restored.

Suppose next that the *IS* curve has a positive slope, as shown in Figure 15-4. The shift in the *LM* curve causes the interest rate to fall immediately to i_0'. This again means that intended investment exceeds savings and that income must therefore rise. But the rise in income stimulates further investment because of our assumption that investment is a function of the level of profits and income. Consequently, the original monetary disturbance causes income to rise; this causes additional investment to be induced; and this, in turn, causes income to rise still further.

Figure 15-4   Dynamic adjustment: Case 2   (all values in real terms).

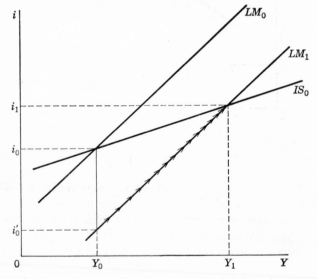

Will income continue to rise indefinitely, or will a new equilibrium point be found? In the present case the rise in income causes the interest rate to rise and to dampen investment more rapidly than the rise in income stimulates further investment. In other words, the rate of interest that keeps the money market in equilibrium rises more rapidly than the rate of interest that keeps the product market in equilibrium. Consequently, a new stable equilibrium point will be reached at Y_1 and i_1. The path of adjustment again follows the arrows upward along the LM curve.

Finally, consider the third case shown in Figure 15-5. This differs from the second case in that the IS curve is now assumed to have a steeper slope than the LM curve. If we knew nothing about the adjustment process, we would assume that the shift in the LM curve to LM_1 would cause the equilibrium level of income to fall to Y_1 and the rate of interest to fall to i_1. Such a fall in income does not seem to be a very sensible result. And, indeed, our dynamic analysis will show that the point i_1 and Y_1 cannot be attained. The point Y_0, i_0 is also an unstable equilibrium point from which the system would tend to diverge the moment the equilibrium is disturbed.

As before, the shift in the LM curve causes the interest rate to fall immediately to i'_0. Consequently, investment exceeds savings, and, contrary to what the static model predicts, income, instead of moving down to Y_1, rises. The rise in income causes additional investment to be induced. In the previous case the rise in income eventually caused the transactions demand and therefore the interest rate to rise fast enough to keep income from expanding indefinitely. But in this case the actual interest rate (along the LM curve) rises less rapidly than it would have to rise (along the IS curve) in order to bring intended investment into equilibrium with savings. Thus at Y_2, for example, the interest rate that equates savings and investment (i_2) is in excess of the rate of interest

Figure 15-5 Dynamic adjustment: Case 3 (all values in real terms).

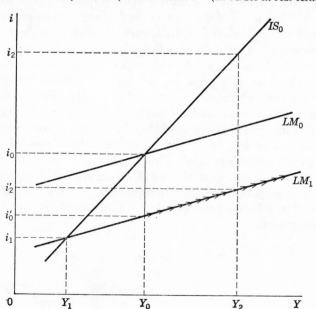

that gives monetary equilibrium (i_2') by more than at lower income levels. Income therefore continues to rise and at an increasingly rapid rate.

In the case just considered the system is said to be "unstable," and the intersection points of the IS and LM curves are said to be "unstable equilibrium" points. As long as we assumed that the IS curve was negatively sloped, we did not have to worry about this problem. Indeed, even a positively sloped IS curve produced an unstable system only when the slope of the IS curve was assumed to be greater than the slope of the LM curve.

15-3 Some Implications of the Analysis

We have seen that the introduction of dynamic assumptions about how the system behaves when it is out of equilibrium is sometimes necessary to verify whether the results of comparative static analysis are meaningful. The equilibrium point Y_1, i_1 of the third case in the preceding section was unobtainable and irrelevant. But we did not know this until we examined the dynamic properties that underlie the model. Accordingly, we can now appreciate Samuelson's remarks: "It is the task of comparative statics to show the determination of the equilibrium values of given variables (unknowns) under postulated conditions (functional relationships) with various data (parameters) being specified." However, "in order for the analysis to be useful it must provide information concerning the way in which our equilibrium quantities will change as a result of changes in the parameters taken as independent data."[1]

As Samuelson has shown, the correspondence principle goes still farther. Recall that stability required the slope of the LM curve to be greater than the slope of the IS curve. The slope of the IS curve depends upon the values of the marginal propensity to save, the marginal propensity to invest, and the slope of the investment demand schedule with respect to the rate of interest. Similarly, the slope of the LM curve depends on the values of the slope of the demand for money with respect to the level of income (the **k** ratio) and the slope of the speculative demand for money function. As we have seen, the parameter that has caused all the trouble is the marginal propensity to invest. Although we have no a priori, and very little empirical, knowledge about its value, the correspondence principle allows us to infer something about it. If we assume that the system is stable, and if we are reasonably confident about our dynamic assumptions, we can, from knowledge about the values of the other parameters, infer the range of values within which the marginal propensity to invest must lie.

[1] Samuelson, *op. cit.*, p. 257.

chapter 16

Fundamentals of growth economics

16-1   Introduction

The models of aggregate economic behavior that we considered in Part II demonstrate that the maintenance of full employment requires that the leakages generated at the full-employment level of income be offset by an equivalent volume of compensating expenditure. To say that a given level of investment is necessary to maintain full employment is to assume that the labor force and the productive capacity of the economy do not change. Such an assumption may well be justified when dealing with very short periods of time. For example, it is not unreasonable to assume that the increase in the productive capacity of the American economy resulting from net investment in one year is so small that it can safely be ignored within the context of the analysis of Part II. But the cumulative effects of continued net investment over a longer period of time cannot be ignored, and therefore a certain amount of reorientation is required for the longer view.

The static models of Part II failed to bring out the fact that investment has a dual character. While investment expenditures are a component of aggregate demand, they are made for the purpose of increasing productive capacity. This means that they expand the potential supply of output at the same time as they increase current income. Thus a positive level of net investment means that the supply of output is capable of continued increase over time, and full utilization of this capacity will necessitate continued increases in aggregate expenditure in the future. In addition, if, as seems to be the case, the absolute volume of full-employment savings increases over time, increasing absolute amounts of investment must be forthcoming in every year if full-employment savings are to be balanced by equivalent investment expenditures. But as the absolute flow of investment increases every year, the capital stock of the economy increases by larger and larger amounts; and this means that income must increase by larger and larger amounts to maintain full employment. The economy must, in other words, run faster and faster if full employment is to be maintained.

Productive capacity not only grows as a result of net investment expenditure, but also becomes more efficient as the result of technical progress. By technical progress we mean improvements in the efficiency of the stock of capital that result from technological and organizational changes and improvements in the quality of the labor force that result from improved education, training, and health.[1] As a consequence of technical progress the productivity of capital and labor has been increasing, and this, to a large extent, is what has permitted Americans to enjoy an ever-rising standard of living.

Finally, in addition to capital growth and technical progress, population and the labor force grow with time, and this growth both creates the potential for a greater supply of output and provides some or all of the additional demand needed to ensure that the output is absorbed.

The purpose of this chapter is to explore the consequences of the dual character of investment and the effects of technical progress and population growth. We begin our study of this topic with an extension of the simple Keynesian model in which the dual character of investment is highlighted, but in which there is assumed to be no technical progress and in which the labor force is assumed to grow at the same rate as the capital stock. Given these assumptions, the rate of growth of income that utilizes existing capacity will also provide full employment for the growing labor force.

16-2   A Model of an Expanding Economy[2]

To derive the rate of growth of income that would be necessary to maintain full employment, we shall construct a highly simplified model in which there

---

[1] The most important element of technical progress in the economy of the United States appears to be the steady improvement in the quality of the working force. See T. W. Schultz, "Investment in Human Capital," *American Economic Review*, 51:1–17, 1961.

[2] The simple model presented here follows the approach of E. Domar, "Capital Expansion, Rate of Growth and Employment," *Econometrica*, 14:137–147, 1946. A similar earlier approach is that of R. F. Harrod, "An Essay In Dynamic Theory," *Economic Journal*, 49: 14–33, 1939. See also W. J. Baumol, *Economic Dynamics*, The Macmillan Company, New York, 1951.

is assumed to be no government or foreign trade. We shall also assume that over time consumption is a fairly constant proportion of income. With these assumptions we may write the familiar expression

$$Y = C + I$$

as the definition of equilibrium income and

$$C = \mathbf{b}Y$$

as the consumption function. The savings function then must be

$$S = (1 - \mathbf{b})Y$$

Suppose we begin from a full-employment level of income Y^* in year zero. This will be associated with savings of $S^* = (1 - \mathbf{b})Y^*$. If full employment is to be maintained, these savings must be matched by an equal amount of intended investment, I^*.

To determine the effect of the investment of I^* in year zero upon the productive capacity of the economy, we shall introduce the simple linear production function

$$Y^* = \mathbf{s}K$$

where $\mathbf{s}$, the capital coefficient, is the average value, for the economy as a whole, of the relationship between the capital stock and the level of output. If the capital stock of the United States is $1,800 billion and the value of $\mathbf{s}$ is 0.35, then the American economy, fully employed, can produce output worth $630 billion in one year.[1]

In the present model we begin by assuming investment of I^* in year zero. Since I^* constitutes an addition to the capital stock of $\Delta K = I^*$, the full-employment level of output increases by

$$\Delta Y^* = \mathbf{s}\Delta K$$

or since $$\Delta K = I^* = S^* = (1 - \mathbf{b})Y^*$$
we have $$\Delta Y^* = \mathbf{s}(1 - \mathbf{b})Y^*$$

Finally, by dividing the above expression through by Y^* we obtain

$$\frac{\Delta Y^*}{Y^*} = \mathbf{s}(1 - \mathbf{b})$$

which says that the percentage change in full-employment output resulting from the investment of I^* in year zero is $\mathbf{s}(1 - \mathbf{b})$. In other words, output in year 1 will be $\mathbf{s}(1 - \mathbf{b})Y^*$ in excess of what it was in year zero. Clearly, if full

[1] Since $\mathbf{s}$ obviously has something to do with the production function $Y = X(K,N)$, which has been referred to several times previously, let us earmark $\mathbf{s}$ for more thorough consideration later.

employment is to be maintained in year 1, the required amount of investment must also grow at the same rate as the rate of growth of output.

To clarify the nature of this growth process and the important role played in it by **b** and **s**, let us consider a few numerical examples. In Table 16-1 we post the levels of income, consumption, investment, and aggregate demand $(C + I)$, that give full employment through time if $(1 - b) = 0.20$ and $s = 0.25$. We begin in period zero with a full-employment equilibrium level of income of 100. Of this income 80 is spent for consumption goods, so that full employment necessitates investment spending of 20. Investment of 20 means that the full-employment output of the economy in period 1 will be $20 \times 0.25 = 5.0$ in excess of the full-employment level of period zero. Out of this new higher level of income of 105.0, the amount consumed will be 84.0 (105×0.8). It follows that investment in period 1 must be 21.0 if full employment is to be maintained. But this investment in period 1 again raises the full-employment level of output for period 2 to 110.25, which means that a new higher level of investment must be undertaken in that period if full employment is to be maintained.

Table 16-1   Required growth of income   (b = 0.80, s = 0.25)

Time	Y	C	I	C + I
0	100.00	80.00	20.00	100.00
1	105.00	84.00	21.00	105.00
2	110.25	88.20	22.05	110.25
3	115.76	92.61	23.15	115.76
4	121.55	97.24	24.31	121.55
5	127.63	102.10	25.53	127.63
6	134.01	107.21	26.80	134.01

Notice from Table 16-1 that income in any period is just 5 percent greater than in the preceding period, but that the absolute difference between the level of income in any two periods becomes larger and larger. Notice, further, that the rate of growth of 5 percent could have been calculated directly had we substituted the values for **b** and **s** in the formula for the required rate of growth of income derived above, i.e., $s(1 - b) = 0.20 \times 0.25 = 0.05$, or 5 percent.

What is the consequence of a fall in the marginal propensity to consume? The formula $\Delta Y^*/Y^* = s(1 - b)$ suggests that the required rate of growth must rise. To illustrate why this is so, suppose that **b** falls to 0.50 while **s** remains at 0.25. With income of 100, savings were 20 in period zero; assuming a **b** value of 0.50, they would rise to 50. It follows that investment in period zero must also be 50 instead of 20. Thus the full-employment level of output in period 1 will be $50 \times 0.25 = 12.5$ in excess of the previous period, instead of the 5.0 obtained with a **b** value of 0.80. Clearly, a fall in the marginal propensity to consume implies that the required rate of growth must rise, since such a fall means that a higher level of intended investment is required to balance full-employment savings. As illustrated in Table 16-2, the required rate of growth with a **b** value of 0.50 rises to 0.50 × 0.25 = 12.5 percent.

Table 16-2   Required growth of income   (b = 0.50, s = 0.25)

Time	Y	C	I	C + I
0	100.00	50.00	50.00	100.00
1	112.50	56.25	56.25	112.50
2	126.56	63.28	63.28	126.56
3	142.38	71.19	71.19	142.38
4	160.18	80.09	80.09	160.18
5	180.20	90.10	90.10	180.20
6	202.72	101.36	101.36	202.72

Instead of a fall in **b**, suppose that advances in technology increase the value of **s** to 0.40 so that $10 of net investment produces an annual product of $4 instead of $2.50. In this case the output of the economy must increase at a faster rate than before because each dollar that is invested increases the full-employment level of output by more than previously, which means that the rate of growth of aggregate expenditure that is necessary to maintain full employment must rise. Table 16-3 shows that with a **b** value of 0.80 and an **s** value of 0.40 the required rate of growth rises to 8 percent.

Table 16-3   Required growth of income   (b = 0.80, s = 0.40)

Time	Y	C	I	C + I
0	100.00	80.00	20.00	100.00
1	108.00	86.40	21.60	108.00
2	116.64	93.31	23.33	116.64
3	125.97	100.78	25.19	125.97
4	136.05	108.84	27.21	136.05
5	146.93	117.54	29.39	146.93
6	158.68	126.94	31.74	158.68

Before we complicate the model presented here, let us emphasize the importance of the lesson it teaches. Consider, for example, the paradox that President Eisenhower could accurately claim in 1953 that production and employment were higher than ever before, while Walter Reuther could complain, with equal justification, that unemployment was severe. What appears to be a paradox becomes, in the light of the present analysis, a perfectly plausible state of affairs. Output must grow over time at a certain rate if full employment is to be maintained. If the level of output does not grow fast enough, even though some growth justifies the President's statement, unemployment will be the net result. Apparently, then, output was higher in 1953 than in 1952, but not enough higher to absorb the additional resources that the process of capital and population growth made available. There is nothing paradoxical about the fact that continuing unemployment may be accompanied by an unprecedentedly high level of income.

16-3 The Razor's Edge

The type of model that we have been considering in this chapter has frequently been called a "razor-edge" model because of its precarious balance and behavior when there is a slight deviation from the required rate of growth. The economy appears to teeter, prepared to shoot off into hyperinflation or into deep depression at any moment. While this circumstance suggests less about the real world than about the oversimplified nature of the model, it is nevertheless interesting to note, as the model points up, that overinvestment will lead to capital scarcity, while underinvestment will lead to excess capacity. Apparently, if entrepreneurs invest too much, it will look as if they have invested too little, while if they invest too little, it will appear as if they have invested too much.

Consider Figure 16-1, in which the growth process is given for an s value of 1.0 and a b value of 0.50. At the start there is a full-employment income of 100 and investment of 50. This in turn raises the full-employment level of income in day 1 to 150 so that investment of 75 is required. The full-employment level of income in day 2 therefore becomes 225 so that investment of 112.5 is required. Evidently the required rate of growth of investment and income in this case is 50 percent.

Now suppose that businessmen underinvest in period zero, i.e., instead of investing 50, they invest only 40. As a result of this insufficient investment, the equilibrium level of income will be 80 instead of 100. Thus there will be excess capacity of 20 because income is below the potential of period zero. In addition, the positive net investment of 40, in period zero, adds another 40 to the potential level of output. Consequently, at the start of period 1 entrepreneurs will discover that there is substantial excess capacity, so that investment will be further reduced, if indeed it does not collapse entirely. Underinvestment therefore leads to excess capacity. Had businessmen invested 50 instead of only 40, they would have found that the demand for goods and services was just sufficient to employ all productive resources.

Suppose, on the other hand, that the rate of growth of money income exceeds the required rate. In this case the volume of investment goods demanded by business will exceed the supply of such goods released by savings. In the face

Figure 16-1   The growth process   (all values in real terms).

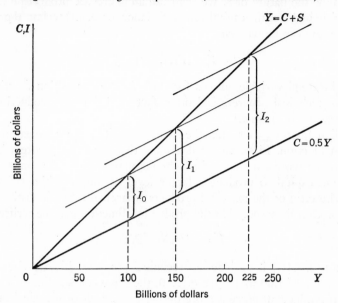

of underproduction in the last period, businessmen will attempt to produce more in the current period. But the increased output of the current period will induce larger investment plans in the next period, causing further underproduction. Thus the attempt to increase output too rapidly leads to renewed attempts to expand more rapidly and continued underproduction. In Figure 16-1, if the level of intended investment in period zero is 60, aggregate demand is in excess of what can be supplied. Prices are thus bid up, and businessmen are moved to increase their investment spending even further in day 1, i.e., far in excess of the required amount of 75, in order to attempt to make up the gap between the demand for goods and their productive capacity. It is, however, these very attempts to catch up that widen the gap.

16-4   The Capital Coefficient and Per Capita Income

The required or full-employment rate of growth has been expressed in terms of the marginal propensity to consume b and the capital coefficient s. By writing $Y = sK$, we were in fact using an extremely simple production function. In this formulation the capital coefficient is some sort of omnibus parameter that incorporates the influences of differential rates of capital and population growth, technical progress, and a host of other factors. It is useful to go behind the scenes and probe into the nature of s to gain a better appreciation of the factors that determine the required rate of growth.

To examine the nature of **s**, we shall use an aggregate production function that explicitly includes the capital stock, the labor force, and technical progress. Such a function can be written

$$Y = F(K,N,t)$$

where t, the trend variable, allows for shifts in the production function that result from technical progress and other factors that cause production techniques to change over time.[1]

To faciliate matters, we shall make two assumptions about the nature of this production function. First, we shall assume that technical progress is "neutral." In other words, a change in technology will allow the same quantity of labor and capital to produce a larger level of output without, however, affecting the ratio of the marginal products (marginal rate of substitution) of the factors. On this assumption the production function may be written

$$Y = A(t)X(K,N)$$

where the term $A(t)$ is an index of technical progress. If $A(t)$ rises from a base-year value of 1.00 to a value of 1.50, the same combination of labor and capital can produce 50 percent more output as a result of technical progress.

The second assumption we shall make about the production function is that it has the property of first-degree homogeneity; that is, if the quantity of both labor and capital double, the level of output will double. In other words, we assume that if K and N are both multiplied by some constant term **u**, Y will also be multiplied by **u**. We may therefore write

$$\mathbf{u}Y = A(t)X(\mathbf{u}K,\mathbf{u}N)$$

and since **u** is an arbitrary constant, we may let $\mathbf{u} = 1/K$ and obtain

$$Y = \left[A(t)X\left(1, \frac{N}{K}\right) \right] K$$

Recalling that $Y = \mathbf{s}K$, we now see that

$$\mathbf{s} = A(t)X\left(1, \frac{N}{K}\right)$$

What is implied by a constant value of **s** that, together with a constant marginal propensity to consume, gives us a constant required rate of growth? Let us assume at the outset that technical progress is absent so that $A(t)$ remains constant. Under these conditions a constant value of **s** and therefore of the required rate of growth requires that both the labor force and the capital

[1] This discussion owes a huge debt to Robert Solow's impressive paper, "Technical Progress and the Aggregate Production Function," *Review of Economics and Statistics,* 39:312–320, 1957.

stock grow at the same rate. A rate of population growth that is lower than the rate at which capital must be accumulated to maintain aggregate demand at the full-employment level will cause **s** to fall steadily. This must happen because if the capital stock grows more rapidly than the labor force, the marginal productivity of capital will fall, and this means that each successive unit added to the capital stock produces less additional output than the preceding unit. The full-employment level of income therefore rises less rapidly, and the required rate of growth is reduced.

From what has been said it appears obvious that innovation and technical progress are absolutely vital if per capita income is to grow. In the absence of an increase in $A(t)$, per capita income (as measured by Y/N, the ratio of output to the labor force) could grow only if the capital stock grows more rapidly than the labor force. But in the long run this is impossible. If the capital stock grows more rapidly than the labor force, **s** will fall, and per capita income will grow at a progressively diminishing rate. Moreover, **s** will continue to fall until the rate of capital growth falls to equality with the rate of growth of the labor force, at which time the rate of growth of per capita income becomes zero. In the long run, therefore, the growth of aggregate output is uniquely determined by, and is equal to, the rate of growth of the labor force, and this in turn implies that per capita income will remain constant.

Technical progress makes it possible for per capita income to grow by allowing the required rate of growth to exceed the rate of growth of the labor force. Thus, while the rate of growth of the labor force needed to raise per capita income in the absence of technical progress would lower the value of **s**, technical progress can offset this by making capital and labor more productive. If $A(t)$ increases, it is possible for per capita income to increase even though the labor force grows more rapidly than the capital stock.

To date, American capitalism has succeeded quite well in achieving a general increase in per capita income. According to Solow's calculations, the value of employed capital per man-hour (K/N) has risen from \$2.06 to \$2.70 over the period 1909–1949. While this increase in K/N would cause the rate of growth of income to slow down, this dampening effect has been more than offset by technical progress. Taking the value of $A(t)$ as 1.00 in 1909, Solow calculates a 1949 value of 1.809.

Whether we shall enjoy steady growth of per capita output at full employment in the future or whether we shall "stagnate" is a question that warrants serious consideration. The next section is devoted to a survey of some of the most prominent theories of stagnation.

16-5 Secular Stagnation

Economic growth, by any reasonable definition, implies increasing per capita real income over time. Stagnation implies that per capita real income remains constant, declines, or grows less rapidly than it might. Stagnation may set in for two reasons. First, even though resources are fully employed, the rate of growth of output may be lower than the rate of population growth. Second, though the supply conditions for an adequate required rate of growth may be at hand, the economy nevertheless may fail to achieve its potential because of deficient aggregate demand. In the first case, society suffers from the fact that differential rates of population and capital growth reduce per capita income; in the latter case, it suffers from the fact that demand is frequently insufficient to fully utilize the resources of the economy. In either case the per capita income situation is unsatisfactory.

The problem of predicting the path of development for a capitalist economy is one that has intrigued economists since the time of Adam Smith.[1] Smith, the father of modern economics, regarded a growing population as intimately connected with economic progress. A growing population makes possible, through widening markets, an increasing "division of labor." As the labor force expands, each individual laborer is able to become more and more of a specialist as distinct from a jack-of-all-trades. Because each worker is able to concentrate on the attainment of one or a few skills, his productiveness increases. Moreover, increasing specialization fosters inventiveness—the finding of more efficient ways of doing jobs—and this further increases productivity. As the per capita income level is raised by this process, conditions favorable to population growth develop, and further division of labor is rendered possible.

Smith's theory contains little reference to the role of capital in the growth process; it assumes ever-increasing returns to labor; and like the theories of most economists before the time of Marx, it concentrates its attention exclusively on the supply side of the growth process. Because he was unaware of the notion of diminishing returns, Smith was optimistic about the possibility that growth, once begun, could be a cumulative process of rising per capita income.

Smith's optimism gave way to the pessimism of his illustrious successors Robert Malthus and David Ricardo.[2] Whereas population growth was the mainspring of progress to Adam Smith, Malthus and Ricardo regarded population growth as the evil that caused a steady decline in per capita income, leading ultimately to a "stationary state" in which no economic progress takes place. Indeed, the Malthus-Ricardo analysis predicted such a bleak outlook for capitalism that Thomas Carlyle was moved to dub economics the "dismal science."

[1] Adam Smith, *The Wealth of Nations*, Books I, II, and III, Modern Library, Inc., New York, 1937.
[2] The writings of Malthus and Ricardo are summarized in any number of standard texts on the history of economic thought, for example, F. A. Neff, *Economic Doctrines*, 2d ed., The McGraw-Hill Book Company, Inc., New York, 1950; and R. Heilbroner, *The Worldly Philosophers*, Simon and Schuster, New York, 1953.

According to Malthus, population tends to grow at a geometric rate, doubling every generation, as long as there is an available supply of food. Because of limitations on the supply of land, the food supply cannot, however, be increased at the same rate. Although capital accumulation could affect the race between the expanding population and the "means of subsistence" by increasing the rate at which output increases, the rate of capital accumulation depends on profits; these profits, in turn, were, for reasons explained by Ricardo, adversely affected by the growth of population. Because of the purely biological character of population growth,[1] population inevitably outruns the means of subsistence, profits decline to zero, net investment declines to zero, and the stationary state arrives.

Why do profits decline as population grows? If a growing population is to be fed, argued Ricardo, progressively less fertile land must be taken under cultivation. If landowners are to be persuaded to bring this less efficient land into use, food prices must rise. As food prices rise, those landowners who are fortunate enough to own fertile land earn a surplus, called "rent," over and above the amount needed to induce production. At the same time, the capitalist is obliged to pay higher wages because of the rise in food prices. Thus, if we visualize a pie that represents the total national product, the pie becomes divided, more and more over time, between rents and wages. Eventually profits disappear, and when this happens, net investment falls to zero; the laboring class lives at a subsistence level; and the landowners become the only class accumulating wealth.

The stationary state could presumably be avoided if landowners were to invest their rents in real capital formation. But landowners, suggested Ricardo, are a profligate class that wastes its substance on ostentatious expenditure instead of engaging in productive investment.

In the Western world, the gloomy prognosis of Malthus and Ricardo has happily not been realized. Population has failed to grow as rapidly as predicted by Malthus, and advances in technology, despite occasional setbacks, have held the specter of diminishing returns at bay. This is not to say, however, that the classical theory of economic development is of only incidental interest to the contemporary scene.

In many underdeveloped areas, for example, population continually presses against the food supply, leaving in normal crop years such a slim margin that a moderately bad year produces widespread misery and starvation. Painfully gained increases in output are met almost instantaneously by population increases. At the same time, there exists in such countries a wealthy class that derives its income from ownership of land. By tradition and custom this class is more inclined to spend its wealth for ostentatious accumulation of material

---

[1] Malthus did introduce the concept of "preventive checks," but these were a later addition to the theory; and while modifying the gloomy notion of the stationary state, he did not modify his main conclusions.

property; if it invests its wealth, these investments are likely to be made in foreign countries. Social and political turmoil in such lands frequently stems from growing awareness of the disparity of incomes and the hope that some form of public ownership of land and other resources will lead to general abundance.

The study of economics provides ample opportunity for gratifying a penchant for paradox. On the one hand rapidly expanding population is the bogey that leads to Malthus' stationary state, and advances in the productivity of capital hold out the chief hope that per capita income may rise in the long run; on the other hand it also appears to be possible that stagnation may result from too little population growth and from the fact that advances in technology are "too productive." This weird circumstance arises from the fact that although greater advances in technology relative to population growth make possible a rapidly expanding required rate of growth, these relative rates of growth of population and productivity at the same time make it difficult for the economy to generate sufficient aggregate demand to take advantage of the full-employment potential.

A. H. Hansen has most clearly and systematically expounded the view that the ingredients that make for a high required rate of growth also set up road-blocks because they tend to cause aggregate demand to be deficient.[1] Writing during the 1930s, Hansen was particularly concerned with the question of whether or not the great depression was merely an unusual adjunct of a cyclical trough or whether it foreshadowed a period of long-run stagnation for the American economy.

In the nineteenth and the early part of the twentieth centuries, America developed at an impressive rate. Population grew rapidly while physical output increased at an even faster rate, so that per capita product grew constantly. But as the twentieth century proceeded, the pace of development began to tail off. Looking for the cause of this slowdown, Hansen delineated four principal factors: a declining rate of population growth; the disappearance of the geographic frontier; the growth of the absolute volume of savings; and the tendency for new techniques of production to be capital-saving, i.e., to raise the value of **s**, instead of capital-using.

Hansen saw the expanding population of nineteenth-century America as one of the mainsprings of its growth, and the geographic frontier as one of the inducements for the large increase in population. Expanding population and the settlement of new territory required tremendous investment expenditures for just about everything from houses and schools to railroads and utilities. Here indeed was the ideal outlet that channeled the tremendous volume of savings of the American economy into productive investment.

As the rate of population growth declined because of a declining birth rate

[1] A. H. Hansen, "Economic Progress and Declining Population Growth," *American Economic Review*, 29:1–15, 1939.

and because of rigid immigration restrictions, and as the geographic frontiers became filled, the investment outlets for America's ever-growing volume of savings declined. A slowly growing population does not need many new homes, and once the railroads are built, the need for investment spending declines significantly.

Stagnation due to deficient demand might be prevented by technological developments of the capital-using type, i.e., changes in the mode of production that would increase the average amount of capital needed to produce a particular level of output. But Hansen was not optimistic about the likelihood of such development. Indeed, he believed that advances in technology would increase rather than reduce the value of **s**; this would mean that less new investment would be required to produce additional units of output. Advances in technology, for example, have replaced the railroad with the airplane, a mode of transportation that requires considerably smaller investment outlays.

Hansen's analysis came on the heels of the revolutionary work of Keynes. Accepting the Keynesian conclusion that full employment is but one of several possible equilibrium levels of employment, Hansen argued that given the level of savings that the American economy tends to generate at the full-employment level of income, it would become increasingly difficult to balance off these leakages with investment expenditures because of the gradual drying up of investment opportunities. Full employment might be attained occasionally at the peak of a cycle, but the long-run trend would be one of substantial underemployment.

Perhaps as a result of World War II and the conditions attending its aftermath, the American economy's problem over the years 1940–1955 was quite the opposite of the problem that concerned Hansen. Instead of deficient aggregate demand, demand was in excess of what the economy could supply, with the result that we suffered inflationary pressures during the period. However, since the middle of the 1950s the economy appears to have reverted to secular unemployment and excess capacity. Hansen's analysis now appears to be not nearly as obsolete as it was thought to be during the early postwar years, especially since it now seems reasonably clear that the problem is one of fairly persistent demand deficiency. In any case, stagnation of the deficient demand variety is a very real danger that we would do well to bear firmly in mind, especially since, as some economists argue, capital expansion cannot indefinitely exceed the rate of population growth.[1] Let us close this section by inquiring into the reasons for this.

In the absence of technical progress, a falling ratio of N to K implies a progressive fall in the marginal productivity of capital. The investment demand schedule would shift steadily to the left, so that the generation of sufficient investment would require a steady fall in the rate of interest. Since there is a

[1] A. Murad, "Net Investment and Industrial Progress," In K. K. Kurihara, ed., *Post-Keynesian Economics*, Rutgers University Press, New Brunswick, N.J., 1954.

limit to the extent to which the interest rate can be depressed, the time will surely come when investment will be insufficient to maintain full employment. It is of course true, as was pointed out in Section 16-4, that the required rate of growth will also fall when N/K falls, and thus full employment will require a progressively lower rate of investment growth. But whether stagnation sets in because of insufficient demand or because of a falling required rate of growth, it is clear that the absence of technical progress will produce dire consequences for the economy.

Technical progress tends to produce a rise in the marginal product of capital and thus stimulates investment. If, however, the capital stock grows more rapidly than the labor force, might it not be impossible to find sufficient labor to run the new machines? If it takes exactly one worker to run one machine, the capital stock cannot increase more rapidly than the working force. The only thing that can happen is that old machines are replaced by newer, more efficient machines. But this amounts to saying that net investment is zero, which further implies long-run stagnation if positive net investment is required to balance savings at full employment.

Is there a way out? If innovation of a labor-saving kind can be found, it would appear that sufficient investment might be generated. Suppose, for example, that there are ten workers and four machines in existence. Suppose further that each machine requires two workers to operate it. If all resources are to be kept busy, eight workers will produce the consumption goods of society, while the two remaining workers can be set to work producing another consumer-good machine. After the machines are produced, there being five machines and ten workers, no further expansion of output and no further investment are possible. However, if the two workers had been set to work to produce a machine that would substitute for workers in producing consumer goods—i.e., another machine (machine B) that takes the place of the workers in running the consumer-good machines (machines A)—workers could be shifted from consumer-goods production into investment-goods production (B machines) and expansion could continue. Thus if each B machine replaces two workers, a time will come when all A machines are run by B machines and the working force can concentrate entirely on the production of both A and B machines.

Are there not likely to be limitations to this process? Although it may be possible to substitute some machines for workers, it is not likely that substitution can be carried out completely. As long as some workers are needed to produce consumer goods, the ten workers will ultimately set a limit to the amount of consumer-goods production that is possible and thus will also set a limit to the number of B machines it will pay to produce. Also, even if it is possible to displace workers entirely in the production of consumer goods, there are still only ten workers available for the production of B machines, so there will be a ceiling to the production of B machines unless someone invents a C machine that replaces labor in the production of B machines. While this latter eventuality is possible, it is unlikely that production at all stages can be carried on without some labor. This being the case, the labor force will ultimately grow so scarce in relation to the capital stock that investment will be more and more difficult to generate.

While the above argument may be technically valid, it has, in a contemporary context, a bit of a hollow ring. Population is exploding all over the place. Given the large annual additions to the labor force, we may, with justification, suggest that the main problem with which the United States economy is now faced is to expand aggregate demand rapidly enough to absorb the available labor supply.

16-6 Concluding Remarks on Growth Economics

Economic growth is, of course, a great blessing. It is what enables the individuals in society to look forward to ever-rising living standards. It is, moreover, a great social solvent. When all can look forward to rising levels of well-being, the pressure for redistribution of the existing pie is reduced. Not to be in favor of economic growth is as heinous a crime in our society as is hostility to dogs and little children. But is it desirable to force-feed economic growth, as many are now urging?

The growth rate has become a symbol of national prestige and is said to be regarded by uncommitted nations as the index by which the performances of the Soviet and United States economies are judged. We leave open the question of whether this consideration ought to be a legitimate guide in the formulation of economic policy. Certain items need, however, to be pointed out in connection with the comparison of American and Soviet growth rates.

What frightens people is the circumstance, known to all amateur mathematicians, that if two quantities A and B grow, and if A grows at a higher percentage rate than B, then A must ultimately become larger than B regardless of how tiny it was at the start. Applied to the American–Soviet comparison, this elementary exercise in differential equations implies that if the Soviet growth rate continues to be higher than the American rate, the Soviet economy will ultimately catch up to and pass the American economy.

However, comparisons of growth rates between nations may not be particularly meaningful. The fruits of economic growth are partly quantitative but also partly qualitative and to that extent not measurable. When a "cost-saving" invention is made, it is possible to measure the effects of the invention on productivity. But when invention and innovation are directed toward product improvement, it is virtually impossible to measure the benefits that accrue. To take an extreme example, suppose that product B is introduced and that consumers switch to this product at the expense of A, which then disappears from the market. Assume next that B sells at the identical price as did A and that consumers buy the same quantity of B as they formerly bought of A. Now the national income will appear to be unaffected by the introduction of product B. But society clearly seems to be better off, as indicated by the fact that consumers prefer product B. During advanced stages of economic development, inventive and innovative activity is apt to become substantially reoriented in the direction of product improvement and away from cost reduction. When the Soviets succeed in raising agricultural output per man-hour, the effects are clearly discernible and readily measurable in the national income. When American enterprise introduces a new product or improves an existing one, the national income statistics may reflect no change whatever. Consequently, we ought to expect the Soviet economy at its present stage of development to show a more rapid growth of national income than the American economy, and we ought not to be too surprised that the rate of growth in the United States, as measured by national income data, has slowed down.

A rapid rate of economic growth enables the economy to expand its national defense, welfare, and foreign aid activities without imposing on other claims on resources. To illustrate, suppose that government expenditures are going to rise at a rate of 5 percent. If income grows at a rate of only 3 percent, either the government will have to scale down its requirements or a progressively smaller proportion of the national product will be available for consumption and investment.

Although it is true that the national income must grow at the same rate as the growth in government expenditures if the ratio of government expenditures to national income is to remain constant, it is not at all certain that it is better to support a growing government sector by force-feeding the growth rate, rather than by retrenching in other sectors. Accelerated economic growth is not bought at zero cost. The rate at which our natural resources are being ravaged in our present frenetic attempts to acquire consumer durable goods is frightening.

It is of course desirable to raise the actual growth rate to the rate required to achieve full employment. But if we do this, the rate at which our nonhuman resources are exploited will rise. However, not to raise the growth rate to the required rate will mean persistent unemployment and the wasting of our human resources. It is because of the belief that we are not utilizing all our human and nonhuman resources effectively that some social critics are trying to prod us into giving up some of our appliances in exchange for better schools and other forms of social capital. The only thing that is clear at this time is that the "growthmanship" debate will be with us for a long time to come.

chapter 17

Inflation

17-1 Introduction

An economy that tries to grow more rapidly than the required rate of growth will suffer from inflation. Inflation may come about because the government attempts to absorb more resources than are released by the private economy at the existing price level. It may come about because various groups in the economy attempt to improve their relative income shares more rapidly than the growth of productivity. It may come about because buoyant expectations cause the demand for goods and services to rise more rapidly than the economy can expand output. And it may come about from interactions between some or all of the above factors.

For purposes of analysis it is useful to classify inflation with respect to its degree of intensity and with respect to its several causal factors. A slowly rising price level we shall denote as "creeping" inflation, while a rapidly rising one we shall denote as "hyperinflation." With respect to causality, we may define "excess-demand" inflation as inflation resulting from the fact that aggregate demand grows more rapidly than the full-employment output potential; "bottleneck" inflation as resulting from changes in the structure of demand; and "cost-push" inflation as resulting from the circumstance that many economic groups in society have the power to force up wages and prices. In this chapter we shall confine ourselves to "classical" or "excess-demand" inflation. "Cost-push" and "demand-shift" inflation, which have been said to characterize the past decade, are such timely problems that we shall consider them in Part IV, where current economic problems are discussed.

17-2   The Consequences of Inflation

When discussing the problem of inflation, we must bear in mind that many economists do not believe the social costs of mild inflation to be very serious, just as some economists believe that mild recession may occasionally be beneficial. If the expectation of a mildly increasing price level serves to stimulate consumer buying and investment spending, mild inflation may increase aggregate real income.

While there is some debate about the seriousness of creeping inflation, there can be little doubt that hyperinflation would produce disastrous consequences. Although hyperinflation has been unknown in the United States since the Civil War,[1] a brief consideration of some elements of hyperinflation will help us to examine some of the problems that may be created by creeping inflation of the type to which we are becoming accustomed in the United States.

Hyperinflation is a phenomenon that usually accompanies war and its aftermath. It is a consequence of attempts to finance government expenditures by currency issue. At first the government deficit may be slight and the addition to the price level insignificant. However, as the price level begins to rise, the government must spend greater and greater nominal amounts of currency to obtain the same quantity of real resources. Meanwhile consumers and investors come to anticipate further price increases and intensify their bidding for real goods and services. Considered in terms of the *IS-LM* model, government expenditures financed by currency creation mean that both the *IS* and the *LM* curves shift to the right. The resulting price increases cause a rush to exchange money balances for goods. This means that the *IS* schedule shifts again and the *LM* schedule rotates downward and to the right because the transactions velocity of circulation increases. The climax of hyperinflation appears when the flight from money is such that the velocity of circulation approaches infinity.[2]

The government cannot indefinitely acquire resources by means of currency issue. When the price level rises at such a rapid rate that the public loses faith in the stability of the monetary unit, trade will no longer be carried on with

---

[1] For an interesting discussion of hyperinflation in the United States see E. M. Lerner, "Inflation in the Confederacy," in Milton Friedman, ed., *Studies in the Quantity Theory of Money*, University of Chicago Press, Chicago, 1956.

[2] See the paper by Phillip Cagan, "The Monetary Dynamics of Hyperinflation," in Friedman, *ibid.*, for a discussion of the effect of price expectations on transactions velocity.

money. Such a flight from currency implies that exchanges will be made on a purely barter basis. Since the government has nothing to barter, it must resort to outright requisition.

We may well imagine how demoralizing hyperinflation would be. A merchant will not sell a good for money in the morning if he expects prices to double by the afternoon. Unless he is given a physical unit of some commodity, he will prefer to hoard his stock of goods rather than make the exchange. Exchange during hyperinflation inevitably degenerates into primitive bartering.

Production is also impaired by hyperinflation. The workers in an automobile plant cannot be paid in anything other than money. It would not do to divide a car into parts and pay workers with fenders, heaters, and radiators. Because they must be paid in money, the workers have no incentive to work, so that production breaks down except in a few areas where it is possible to make compensation in kind. If, as seems unlikely, the car actually gets produced, it is difficult to see how it can be sold because the car producer is not likely to want a car's worth of groceries or a car's worth of paperclips in return.

The social consequences of hyperinflation are no less terrifying than the economic effects. Debtors pursue creditors in order to pay back past obligations with worthless currency. The earnings of fixed-income groups are wiped out. The value of accumulated liquid savings disappears. Some groups in society are able to defend themselves against inflation while others are not. The end result can only be one in which society is set against itself and in which democratic political institutions are placed under intolerable strain.

Hyperinflation replaces industry and thrift with hoarding and speculation. To some extent there is danger that even creeping inflation may have similar, though less drastic, consequences. If the long-run outlook is for a rising price level, the inducement to save may be seriously impaired. Interest rates will rise drastically because of the decline in the supply of real savings and because of expected price increases. Investment and growth may therefore be retarded. Creeping inflation may also produce unfortunate consequences for small savers. Government bonds, insurance policies, savings deposits, and the other forms of fixed-interest-bearing asset holdings that appeal to small savers merely become traps through which the value of savings is eroded by a rising price level. Inflation forces everyone to become a speculator or to upgrade his propensity to consume. In either case, economic growth will be seriously inhibited.

Inflation finally is incompatible with the promotion of free international trade. A rising price level produces an excess of imports over exports and a drainage of gold. Governments that do not have the fortitude to stand firm against the rise in the price level may turn to tariffs and quota systems to avert further drains of foreign exchange. But the resultant restriction in trade reduces real income and further inhibits the growth potential of the economy.

Those economists who argue that creeping inflation is not necessarily an undesirable thing seem to feel that the alternative to creeping inflation is unemployment and a retarded rate of growth. They feel that since prices are flexible only in the upward direction in our present institutional framework, resource allocation through the price system must operate through price increases in areas of the economy that are growing rather than through price decreases in areas that are stagnating. They feel, moreover, that the monopoly power of unions and enterprises is such that price increases are inevitable and that it is better for the government not to pursue contractionary policies since this would cause unemployment rather than a fall in the price level. Finally, they feel that the goal of maximum economic growth is best served by a policy that lifts the dead hand of debt from the economy. They therefore find a policy that discriminates against creditors to the advantage of debtors a congenial one.

We are not among those who feel it necessary to cry havoc each time the price level rises by a small amount. Neither are we comfortable about the "relax and enjoy it" attitude of some economists. There is always the danger that mild inflation may gradually snowball into hyperinflation. Because a steady, though minute, rise in the price level may create such expectations that people will behave in a way that makes further increases inevitable, it would be folly to take a flippant attitude toward mild inflation.

We move on now to an analysis of excess-demand inflation. We shall assume that it is creeping inflation rather than hyperinflation that is under consideration. This will permit us to make the assumption that confidence in the currency has not been badly damaged by price increases and that the transactions velocity of circulation (or the k ratio) remains constant. It must be borne in mind that the conclusions of subsequent sections will be valid only under these assumptions.

17-3   Excess-demand Inflation and the Monetary Sector

The static analysis of Chapter 13 is a convenient starting point for considering excess-demand inflation. To simplify matters, let us suppose that the full-employment level of output in Figure 17-1 remains fixed at Y^*. General equilibrium is established at Y^* and i_0 with price level p_0. An increase in the price level may now come about as a result of an increase in aggregate demand, which shifts the IS schedule to IS_1; the resulting excess demand of $Y_1 - Y^*$ leads to a bidding up of prices so that the real value of the money supply shrinks and the LM schedule shifts to LM_{p_1}, where general equilibrium is again established at the higher interest rate i_1 and higher price level p_1.[1]

---

[1] Throughout this section we shall be utilizing the "money veil" model that takes no account of the effects on the IS and LM functions of an initial reduction of bond holdings by the public in consequence of open-market operations. The conclusions of a more sophisticated analysis would be along the lines of Chapter 13. However, since the more sophisticated model gives the same results as the simpler model with respect to the direction of change in the price level, there is no particular need in our present line of inquiry to be formally precise.

Inflation is a dynamic disequilibrium process. It implies a steady increase in the price level over time. Thus excess-demand inflation implies that the *IS* and/or the *LM* schedules continue to shift upward over time so that excess demand for goods and services is perpetuated and general equilibrium is never established. Although an increase in the price level would normally tend to clear markets, this does not take place if demand continues to increase as fast as prices rise.

Ultimately, an excess-demand inflation that is not nurtured by an expanding money supply must come to an end. When interest rates rise to a high enough level, the demand for money will become totally inelastic with respect to the rate of interest. At this point there are no more speculative balances to be had; attempts to borrow funds either will be frustrated or, because of the resultant increase in interest rates, will come from the abandonment of other ventures. When the demand for money becomes inelastic, all funds are used for transactions purposes, and further increases in aggregate demand can then be financed only by a reduction in expenditures elsewhere in the economy or by an increase in the transactions velocity of money.

Wartime financing in the United States provides a good example of the ingredients of excess-demand inflation. Because tax receipts were insufficient to finance war expenditures, each of the war years produced a Federal budgetary deficit. It therefore became necessary for the Treasury to finance part of its expenditures via the sale of government bonds. Such a steady increase in the supply of bonds would soon have driven bond prices down and interest rates up had it not been for a highly inflationary offsetting policy. All during the war

Figure 17-1   Excess-demand inflation   (all values in real terms).

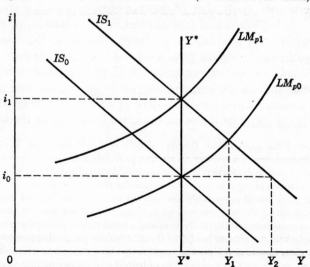

the Federal Reserve System stood ready to purchase government bonds in an amount that would stabilize bond prices and fix interest rates at a constant level. The effect of this policy was to add large amounts to the supply of money. The proceeds of the bond sales to the Federal Reserve were used by the Treasury to pay its bills, which in turn increased deposits and the reserves of the banking system.

The policy pursued by the Federal Reserve during the war, though undoubtedly the only feasible one at the time,[1] provided the means whereby a serious inflationary situation could have developed. The fact that the inflation was, in retrospect, mild is attributable to the fact that investment, prices, and consumer expenditures were all subject to direct control. Excess demand was therefore to some extent suppressed.

The postwar years of the late 1940s were marked by high levels of demand and persistent price increases. The magnitude of these increases was undoubtedly partly due to the fact that the Federal Reserve continued, until 1951, its wartime policy of supporting the government bond market. Thus each time an increase in aggregate demand impinged on the money supply and threatened to raise interest rates, the Federal Reserve, at the behest of the Treasury, would step in and purchase government bonds, thus offsetting the equilibrating effects that rising interest rates would have caused. This situation was ultimately regarded as so intolerable by Congress and by the Federal Reserve itself that the Treasury was, to the great relief of most economists, obliged to sign an accord with the Federal Reserve in 1951, in which the Federal Reserve's powers to function as a monetary stabilizing agency were partly restored.

The inflationary process of the 1940s can be illustrated by referring again to Figure 17-1. Beginning at interest rate i_0 and income level Y^*, and again assuming, quite erroneously, that Y^* does not grow over time, we may suppose that an increase in government expenditures or the relaxation of controls on consumer and investor spending raises the IS schedule to IS_1. Normally this would lead to an increase in the price level and a reduction in the real value of the money supply so that interest rates would rise. In other words, the LM schedule would shift to the left, and the rise in the interest rate to i_1 would choke off the excess demand and thus once again stabilize the price level. But if public policy is such that the prime objective is to stabilize the interest rate

---

[1] In the face of the huge annual Treasury deficit, it is difficult to see how the Federal Reserve could have pursued any other course than to stabilize the government bond market. In the absence of such stabilization, bond prices would undoubtedly have fallen drastically, and the interest burden of the debt would have risen sharply. Under normal circumstances the rise in interest rates would presumably have served to reduce the level of investment. But since investment during the war was subject to direct control, the interest rate was largely irrelevant as an economic calculator. By pursuing a bond-stabilization program, the Federal Reserve not only kept the interest burden of the debt within manageable proportions but also insured investors against capital loss. Thus government bonds became a reasonably attractive form of holding wealth; this may perhaps have helped to increase the rate of savings.

at i_0, the Federal Reserve must purchase the bonds that wealth holders are releasing and thereby increase the money supply and offset the shift in the LM schedule. Under these conditions aggregate demand (the IS schedule) need not even increase over time. Given a fixed full-employment level of output and a fixed level of aggregate demand, there will be a steady increase in the price level as long as the rate of interest that balances the demand for and the supply of goods and services (i_1) is in excess of the rate (i_0) that is pegged by policy. For example, in Figure 17-1 if the pegged rate is i_0 and the natural rate is i_1, there will be persistent excess demand of $Y_2 - Y^*$.

What is the key to the control of excess-demand inflation? If, as seems likely, the demand for money will be highly inelastic with respect to the rate of interest in a full-employment–inflationary situation, monetary control must be the primary anti-inflationary weapon. Consider Figure 17-2 in which the LM function is vertical at the full-employment level of income. General equilibrium is established at Y^* and i_0. In this situation an increase in aggregate demand serves only to raise the rate of interest and has no effect on the price level. This result, as we have suggested, stems from the fact that all money balances are already used for transaction purposes so that any increase in expenditures can be made only at the expense of a decrease elsewhere. In general, therefore, an increase in aggregate demand is inflationary only insofar as the increase makes it possible to sustain the same level of demand at a higher interest rate.

An increase in the money supply, on the other hand, has immediate inflationary consequences. The LM curve in Figure 17-2 shifts to the right, creating excess demand of $Y_1 - Y^*$ and therefore competition for the available supply of output, so that prices rise. The inflationary push does not stop until the

Figure 17-2 Control of excess demand (all values in real terms).

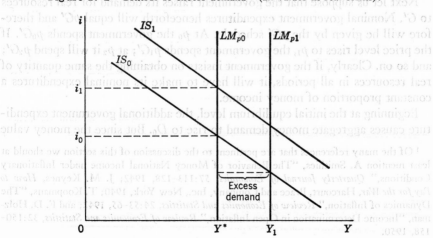

price level has risen by enough to reduce the real value of the money supply to its original level.

17-4   Excess-demand Inflation and Gap Analysis[1]

We have seen that it would be difficult, if not impossible, to sustain excess-demand inflation in the absence of increases in the money supply. A question that should be considered, however, is whether there are forces that would cause inflationary pressure to abate if the monetary authority allowed the money supply to increase in proportion to the rise in prices, or whether the absence of monetary control implies that inflation will continue indefinitely. Suppose, for example, that the monetary authority pursues a pegging policy of the kind followed during the 1940s. Whenever a rise in the price level tends to raise the rate of interest, the monetary authority frustrates the rise by engaging in expansionary open-market operations.

Under the present assumption one can ignore the monetary sector and return to the simple world of Chapter 5 and undertake so called "inflationary gap" analysis.

Figure 17-3 differs from other diagrams in that the magnitudes measured are "nominal" or "money" rather than real. Between a money income level of zero and $p_0 Y^*$ it is assumed that increases in aggregate money demand raise the level of real income without affecting prices. Beyond $p_0 Y^*$, however, increases in demand leave real income unchanged but raise the level of prices. To simplify the exposition, we assume that the only components of aggregate demand are consumption and government expenditures. The consumption function is the schedule pC. It is assumed that the economy is initially in equilibrium at $p_0 Y^*$ with consumption expenditures of $p_0 C$ and government expenditures of $p_0 G$.

Next let us suppose that the government raises its demand for real resources to G'. Nominal government expenditures henceforth will equal pG' and therefore will be given by the pG' schedule. At p_0 the government spends $p_0 G'$. If the price level rises to p_1, the government spends $p_1 G'$; at p_2 it will spend $p_2 G'$; and so on. Clearly, if the government insists on obtaining the same quantity of real resources in all periods, it will have to make its nominal expenditures a constant proportion of money income.

Beginning at the initial equilibrium level, the additional government expenditure causes aggregate money demand to rise to D_0. But since the money value

[1] Of the many references that are pertinent to the discussion of this section we should at least mention A. Smithies, "The Behavior of Money National Income under Inflationary Conditions," *Quarterly Journal of Economics*, 57:113–128, 1942; J. M. Keynes, *How to Pay for the War*, Harcourt, Brace and Company, Inc., New York, 1940; T. Koopmans, "The Dynamics of Inflation," *Review of Economics and Statistics*, 24:53–65, 1942; and F. D. Holzman, "Income Determination in Open Inflation," *Review of Economics and Statistics*, 32:150–158, 1950.

of the supply of output is only p_0Y^*, there is an "inflationary gap" in an
amount E_0. The inflationary gap is defined as the excess of aggregate demand
over the available supply of output measured at the full-employment level of
money income and at the existing level of prices.

Since the level of output is fixed, the increase in aggregate demand causes
the price level to rise. If consumption expenditures fail to increase, the new
level of money income would be p_1Y^*. But the increase in money income that
accompanies the price rise causes consumption to rise by $\mathbf{b}'E_0$, where $\mathbf{b}'$ may
be defined as the marginal propensity to consume out of money income. In
addition, government expenditures now rise to p_1G' since the price level increase means that the government can no longer obtain G' worth of real
resources by an expenditure of p_0G' dollars. The consequence of the increase
in consumption and government expenditures is the creation of a new aggregate
money demand level of D_1 and a new inflationary gap of E_1. The price level
therefore increases again, and so do nominal consumption and government
expenditures.

Figure 17-3   A convergent inflationary process.

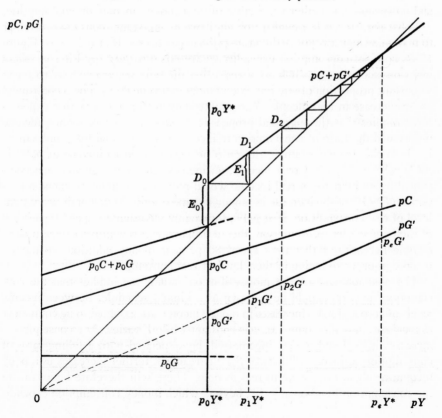

The inflationary process can be visualized as continuing in steps between the aggregate demand schedule and the 45-degree line. Observe that in the present example the gap tends to become narrower with time and ultimately to be eliminated. Thus the inflationary process comes to a halt and a new equilibrium level of money income is established at p_eY^*.

What are the characteristics of the new equilibrium point? Government expenditures at p_eY^* equal p_eG'. The government is now obtaining the real resources in amount G', whereas at the pre-inflation equilibrium point it obtained only G. For some reason, consumers must have been willing to release resources to the government. Observe in Figure 17-3 that the level of money consumption in the final equilibrium is a smaller proportion of money income than it was in the pre-inflation situation.

What have we been assuming about consumer behavior? Clearly, if consumers behave in the way outlined above, they must be subject to money illusion. Their level of real consumption has declined even though real income has remained the same. Apparently, consumers have confused an increase in money income with an increase in real income. Since an increase in real income is associated with a lower ratio of real consumption to real income, consumers end up spending a smaller proportion of their money income on consumption.

What sort of result would we obtain if we assumed that consumers attempt to maintain their level of real consumption expenditure? If at p_0Y^* (see Figure 17-4) nominal consumption expenditures are equal to p_0C^*, and if consumers insist on maintaining their level of real consumption, they would have to spend a constant proportion of any increase in money income that is not accompanied by an increase in real income. The maintenance of real consumption expenditures implies that the marginal propensity to consume out of money income must equal the ratio of consumption to income at the original full-employment level. In the present example the ratio of consumption to income at p_0Y^* is $p_0C^*/p_0Y^* = C^*/Y^*$. Consequently, an increase in money income unaccompanied by an increase in real income would require consumers to spend a proportion C^*/Y^* of the increase in money income in order to maintain a constant level of real consumption. If at p_0Y^*, for example, consumers spend 80 percent of their income on consumption, then a proportional rise in prices and money income necessitates that they spend 80 percent of any additions to money income in order to maintain their level of real consumption.

The abandonment of the money illusion assumption implies that the consumption function should be redrawn as a kinked schedule. Between income levels of zero and p_0Y^* increases in money income are assumed to be equivalent to increases in real income, i.e., p is constant while Y varies. As a consequence, increases in real and money income will be associated with a falling ratio of consumption to income. But once p_0Y^* is reached, further increases in money income result in no change in real income. There will therefore be a kink in the consumption function at p_0Y^*, beyond which money consumption expenditures remain proportional to money income. The new consumption function is shown in Figure 17-4.

If we begin at $p_0 Y^*$ and again assume that government expenditures rise to a level of $p_0 G'$, we have an inflationary gap of E_0. The bidding by the government against consumers for the available supply of output causes prices to rise to p_1 and money income to rise to $p_1 Y^*$. Now, however, consumers attempt to maintain their real consumption expenditures and therefore spend $p_1 C^*$ dollars; and the government, in trying to obtain real resources in an amount G', increases its money outlays to $p_1 G'$. Thus a new gap of E_1 is created. This in turn produces a further inflationary gap.

Under present assumptions the inflationary gap gets progressively wider in money terms and remains the same in real terms. Since consumers persistently try to buy a constant proportion of the available output and government persistently adjusts its expenditures to obtain G'/Y^* percent of real output, the two sectors in combination are persistently attempting to purchase more than 100 percent of the output that is available. There is therefore no end to the inflationary process.

Figure 17-4   A divergent inflationary process.

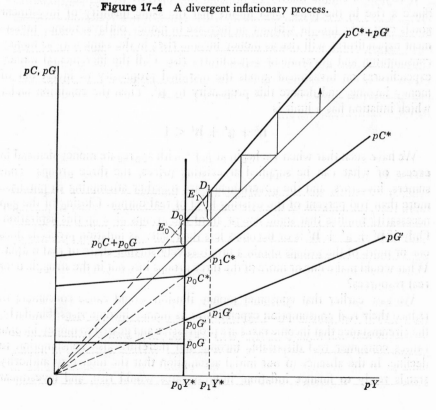

What general conclusions can be derived from this analysis? Figures 17-3 and 17-4 indicate that the inflationary gap will become smaller and that equilibrium will be attained if the aggregate money demand schedule cuts the 45-degree line at some point to the right of the original equilibrium point p_0Y^*. This implies that the slope of the aggregate money demand schedule must have a value of less than unity. But the slope of the aggregate money demand schedule is the sum of the slopes of the consumption function and the government expenditure schedules. The slope of the consumption function is the marginal propensity to consume out of money income b', and the slope of the government expenditure schedule may be termed the governmental marginal propensity to spend out of money income. If we denote the latter as g', then it is clear that the condition under which inflation has a limit is

$$b' + g' < 1$$

If instead
$$b' + g' \geq 1$$

there will be persistent inflation. In the latter case the aggregate demand schedule remains above the 45-degree line at all levels of money income in excess of the original equilibrium value p_0Y^*.

It is now a simple matter to broaden the analysis to include investment. Since a rise in the price level means that the same quantity of investment goods cannot be bought without an increase in money outlays, money investment expenditures will rise as money income rises in the same way as money consumption and government expenditures rise. Call the incremental money expenditures on investment goods the marginal propensity to invest out of money income, and denote this propensity by h'. Then the condition under which inflation has a limit is

$$b' + g' + h' < 1$$

We have seen that when we begin at p_0Y^* with aggregate money demand in excess of what can be supplied at existing prices, the three groups—consumers, investors, and the government—are together attempting to purchase more than 100 percent of the existing level of real output. Closing of the gap necessarily implies that some one or all of the groups give up this aspiration. Only if $b' + g' + h'$ is or becomes less than unity as inflation proceeds does one or more of the groups obtain a progressively smaller share of real output. What would make one or more of the three groups lose out in the struggle over real resources?

We saw earlier that consumer money illusion would cause consumers to reduce their real consumption expenditures as money income rises. Similarly, the circumstance that income taxes are progressive and geared to money income causes consumer real disposable income and therefore also consumption to decline. In the absence of our initial assumption that the monetary authority stands ready to finance inflation, interest rates would rise, and investment spending would be curtailed. Consumer installment credit would be more difficult to obtain. Thus gradual credit tightening might be viewed as a factor that reduces the marginal propensities to consume and to invest out of money income.

An effect similar to a fall in a marginal propensity to spend out of money income can be obtained by the existence of lags in the adjustment of expenditures to price level changes. As an example of the possible effect of such a lag, consider the case of government. At the existing price level p_0 the government attempts to get G' real resources, so that Congress appropriates p_0G' dollars. However, by the time the funds are spent, the price level may have risen to p_1. The appropriation subsequently rises to p_1G', but when the funds are spent, the price level may already have risen to p_2. As a consequence, the government's actual claim on real resources is not the planned level G'; instead, it is p_0G'/p_1 in the first period, p_1G'/p_2 in the second period, and $p_{n-1}G'/p_n$ in the nth period. The effective real governmental demand is therefore reduced by an amount proportional to the rate of change in the price level.

Similar lags appear elsewhere. During inflationary times wages lag behind prices, and this causes the effective marginal propensity to consume out of money income to decline. A similar effect results from the fact that the incomes of white-collar workers fail to keep pace with a rising price level and from the fact that many contracts, especially pensions and annuities, are fixed in nominal rather than in real terms.

Finally, as we saw in the last chapter, the full-employment level of real

Figure 17-5 Closing the gap by increasing output (all values in real terms).

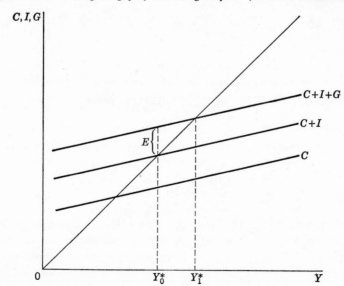

income grows over time. The inflationary push will be smaller the more rapidly Y^* can be made to increase relative to the rise in money income. One interesting aspect of this circumstance is that the less successful consumers are in the short run in maintaining their share of real consumption expenditure, the more successful they may be in the long run in attaining a higher level of real consumption. If business succeeds in bidding a share of real output away from the consumer sector, and if government uses its resources to build schools, the productive potential of the economy may grow more rapidly, and so also will the output of consumer goods.

Although output expansion tends to mitigate inflationary pressure, it is not true, as is sometimes supposed, that an excess of aggregate demand of E dollars over what can be supplied at current prices will be eliminated when E more units of output are produced by overtime work. Figure 17-5 shows a situation in which aggregate demand at full employment exceeds aggregate supply Y_0^* by an amount E. Can the inflationary gap of E be closed by increasing production by this amount? If output is to be expanded, workers must be induced to work overtime. Since they will want to spend **b** percent of any additional real income, the gap is reduced only by $E - \mathbf{b}E = (1 - \mathbf{b})E$ units of real output. To close the gap fully, therefore, output needs to be increased by the multiplier value $E/(1 - \mathbf{b})$, namely, by enough to shift the level of production to Y_1^*, where the aggregate demand schedule cuts the 45-degree line.

chapter 18

Business cycles

18-1 Introduction

The picture, in Chapter 16, of an economy moving steadily along an even growth path is a useful abstraction. Its value, however, is somewhat lessened by the fact that the periodic ups and downs in economic activity play an important part in determining the long-run trend. The trend, similarly, plays an important role in determining the nature, length, and amplitude of the ups and downs.

The study of these ups and downs is called the study of business cycles or the study of industrial fluctuations. Any reasonably adequate discussion of the causes of these swings would require at least another volume as long as the present one and would take us quite far afield. Yet because of the interrelationship between cycle and trend, it is important that we give some attention to the subject.[1]

Our approach in this chapter is to outline the bare bones of a theory of the cycle, to place the theory into the context of a growing economy, and to make

[1] There are many excellent surveys of the literature of business cycles. Among the most useful are J. A. Estey, *Business Cycles*, 3d ed., Prentice-Hall, Inc., Englewood Cliffs, N.J., 1956; A. H. Hansen, *Business Cycles and National Income*, W. W. Norton, New York, 1951; R. A. Gordon, *Business Fluctuations*, Harper & Brothers, New York, 1952.

such amendments and additions as seem necessary. Having accomplished this, we shall be in a position to examine the interrelationship between trend and cycle and to get a better idea of whether uninterrupted growth is possible.

18-2   A Modern Theory of the Cycle

Judging by the volume of discussion that has appeared in books and journals during the last few years, many economists seem to be quite impressed with the notion that a significant proportion of capital investment depends on *changes* in the demand for goods and services rather than on the absolute *level* of demand. Because increases in output necessitate increases in plant and equipment, while a constant level of demand can be produced with existing plants, it is changes in demand, rather than the level of demand, that "induce" net investment. This hypothesis, known as the acceleration principle,[1] permits us to make use of the third investment demand function of Chapter 7

$$I = I(i, \Delta Y) \qquad (18\text{-}1)$$

The way in which the acceleration principle generates business fluctuations can be illustrated as follows: Imagine an economy in which only one consumer good—a shmoo that satisfies all conceivable consumer needs is produced, and assume that the production of one shmoo per day necessitates the use of one shmoo machine. Suppose further that each time a shmoo machine is built, sufficient income to purchase three shmoos is paid out; that this income is spent in the subsequent day; that the marginal propensity to consume is $\frac{2}{3}$; that the life of one machine is 10 days; and that shmoo machines can be produced instantaneously. Given these assumptions, let us further suppose that the economy has been moving along a constant level of *NNP* of 20 for a number of days; that the level of current consumption during these days is 20 shmoos; and that the replacement rate of machines is even.[2] Thus, if 2 machines wear

---

[1] Actually, the principle has been well known for quite some time. The most famous early exposition is J. M. Clark, "Business Acceleration and the Law of Demand," *Journal of Political Economy*, 25:217–235, 1917. Interest in the principle was revived when it was found that the Keynesian consumption function and the acceleration principle could be combined into a self-generating cyclical mechanism. One such attempt was P. A. Samuelson, "Interactions between the Multiplier Analysis and the Principle of Acceleration," *Review of Economics and Statistics*, 21:78–88, 1939. R. F. Harrod, *The Trade Cycle*, Oxford University Press, London, 1936, developed a theory along similar lines. More recent works on the principle include J. R. Hicks, *A Contribution to the Theory of the Trade Cycle*, Oxford University Press, London, 1950, and R. M. Goodwin, "The Non-linear Accelerator and the Persistence of Business Cycles," *Econometrica*, 19:1–17, 1951.

[2] The assumption that the replacement rate is even is a heroic one, for it implies that investment has never fluctuated in the past and that all machines wear out in exactly the same number of years.

out each day, gross investment of 2 machines is required if the 20 shmoos are to be produced. Days 1 and 2 of Table 18-1 are two such constant income days.[1]

Table 18-1 should be interpreted as follows: In column 2 the level of current consumption is posted. Column 4 gives the number of machines that are available for use at the beginning of each day. Column 3 gives the number of machines required to produce the day's output. Column 5 gives <u>gross investment</u>, i.e., the <u>difference between the required number of machines (column 3) and the available number (column 4).</u>

Table 18-1

Time (1)	Con-sumption (2)	Required machines (3)	Available at start of day (4)	Gross in-vestment (5)
1	20	20	18	2
2	20	20	18	2
3	21	21	18	3
4	23	23	19	4
5	25	25	21	4
6	25	25	23	2
7	21	21	23	0
8	17	17	21	0
9	17	17	19	0
10	17	17	17	0
11	17	17	15	2
12	21	21	15	6
13	29	29	18	11

[Suppose that in day 3, consumers decide to increase consumption by 5 percent to 21 shmoos. Since only 18 machines are available at the beginning of the day, gross investment must rise by 50 percent to 3.] The increase in investment of 1 machine, however, creates sufficient income to buy 3 more shmoos. Since, however, the marginal propensity to consume is 2/3, consumption in day 4 rises by 2 to a new level of 23, which means that 23 machines are now required. Gross investment must therefore rise to 4, since only 19 machines are available at the start of the day. Income therefore again rises by 3 shmoos and consumption by 2, so that in day 5, gross investment must again be equal to 4. But since this is the same level of investment as took place in day 4, no further increase in income develops. Consumption therefore remains at 25, and

[1] This economy evidently is resting at the point of zero savings. Consumption expenditures are 20 shmoos, and, because net investment is zero, the level of *NNP* is 20 shmoos. Since gross investment of 2 shmoos takes place each year and since each machine is valued at 3 shmoos, depreciation is 6 shmoos and *GNP* is 26 shmoos.

investment falls to 2 since it is necessary to replace only the 2 machines that are worn out. Since investment drops by 2 machines, income drops by 6 shmoos and consumption by 4. This means that in day 7 only 21 machines are required; since 23 are available, gross investment now drops to zero. It is now apparently not even necessary to engage in replacement investment because there exists ample excess capacity.

The fall in gross investment to zero produces a further fall in consumption of 4 to a depression low of 17. At this level of consumption 17 machines are required; since 21 are available, gross investment again is zero. Since gross investment remains at zero—it cannot be negative—no further drop in income takes place. Consumption remains at 17 in day 9, and, since there are 19 available machines, there will again be no gross investment, so that consumption in day 10 again remains at 17. With just 17 machines available, gross investment still stays at zero. But in day 11 the wearing out of 2 more machines means that a situation has finally been reached in which the required number of machines (17) exceeds the available number (15). Since gross investment of 2 is therefore required, the level of consumption rises to 21; with 15 machines available (day 11), gross investment rises to 6 and the cycle starts its upward course.

It is apparent from the example that durability of equipment introduces a strong element of instability into the economic system. An increase in consumption of 5 percent (day 1) causes capital goods production to rise by 50 percent. If the machines have a life of 5 days instead of 10, the level of gross investment in days 1 and 2 would be 4, so that the 5 percent increase in consumption would cause gross investment to increase by only 25 percent. If the machines lasted only 1 day, consumption of 20 would require each machine to be replaced each day so that an increase in consumption of 5 percent would necessitate an identical percentage change in shmoo-machine production. The volatility of fluctuations is apparently intimately connected with the durability of equipment.

A second consequence of a trend toward greater durability is the fact that the economy will tend to languish in depression longer than would have been the case if equipment had depreciated rapidly. In the present example, if the length of life of a machine is 5 days, 4 machines instead of 2 would wear out in each of the depression days; thus the time it takes required equipment to catch up with actual equipment would be reduced.

A third consequence of durability is that it gives rise to the phenomenon of replacement waves. A good year for a durable-goods industry is apt to be followed by a good year x years later, if the average length of life of the good is x years, because buyers will be replacing more units of the good x years from the initial boom year than in the intervening years. In Table 18-1 we observe that 2 machines wear out each day up to the beginning of day 12. In day 13, however, 3 machines wear out because that is the number that was bought 10 days ago. Since 4 machines were bought on day 4, they will wear out and have to be replaced on day 14. As is obvious from the table, the backwash of the first boom serves to intensify the second boom. Once the purchase of durable goods proceeds at an uneven rate, there will be a tendency for it to continue doing so.

Replacement waves are likely to become diffused over time. All equipment, even of the same sort, does not last the same length of time. Moreover, different types of equipment have different life spans. Replacement waves tend, therefore, to wash out rather quickly for the economy as a whole. But for individual industries, in countries where a few major industries produce a significant proportion of the nation's output, and following a serious disruption such as a major war, replacement waves undoubtedly constitute a significant source of disturbance.

Returning to the acceleration principle, we may observe that since induced investment results from increases in output, an increase in investment, which is needed to keep income rising, means that consumption must not only increase but must do so at an increasing rate. Table 18-1 suggests that it is the failure of consumption to do so that causes the downturn in this model. The upturn, on the other hand, results from the fact that net investment cannot remain negative indefinitely as long as there is some positive level of consumption. When equipment wears out to the point where some replacement is required, gross investment rises, income and consumption rise, and expansion gets under way.

With some minor amendments, the type of model just described forms the basis of the most recent major cycle theory to be advanced. The theory, presented by J. R. Hicks,[1] changes the model in the following three ways:

1. Hicks points out that induced investment should depend not only on changes in consumption but on changes in output in general. In our simple model, investment was induced because increases in consumption required increases in consumer-goods capacity. If, however, investment increases, there will also be a need for added investment-goods capacity. Consequently, induced investment must be regarded as depending on changes in output in general, instead of merely on changes in consumption.

2. In the model above, the upper turning point resulted from the fact that consumption does not grow at a fast enough rate. While Hicks believes that such a downturn may occasionally occur—he would call such a cycle a "free" cycle—he believes that the values of the marginal propensity to consume and the acceleration coefficient[2] are such that expansion would tend to boom ahead indefinitely were it not for some outside interfering factor. This interfering factor Hicks calls the "ceiling of real resources," which is imposed by the full

---

[1] Hicks, *op. cit.*

[2] The acceleration coefficient is defined as the amount of extra capacity required to produce an additional unit of output.

employment of labor and other factors of production. A cycle that hits the ceiling Hicks calls a "constrained" cycle.

3. Hicks separates investment into two components: induced investment, which depends upon changes in output, and autonomous investment, which is not geared to present profit opportunities but depends on long-run trend factors such as the growth of population and advances in technology and is assumed to grow at a constant percentage rate.

In Figure 18-1 time is measured horizontally while the logarithm of output (real income) and investment is measured vertically. The lowest line describes the course of autonomous investment ($\log I_{at}$). The middle line describes the log of the time path of output when only autonomous investment materializes ($\log Y_{at}$). The highest line is the "ceiling," beyond which output cannot expand ($\log Y^*_t$). Since the full-employment level of output presumably depends on the growth of population and the rate at which advances in technology are made, Hicks assumes the ceiling rate of growth to be the same as the rate of growth of autonomous investment.

Suppose that the economy is in the midst of depression at times t_0 with output $\log Y_0$. Since long-run growth factors cause autonomous investment to rise, there results an automatic increase in the level of output, which, if excess

Figure 18-1 The Hicksian framework   (all values in real terms).

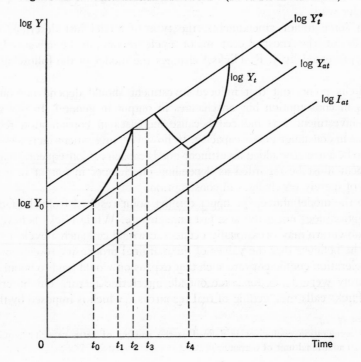

capacity has been substantially reduced by depreciation and obsolescence, induces investment. But the induced investment raises the level of output still further, so that more investment is induced through additional capacity requirements. Expansion, driven by the accelerator, continues to push output upward until the ceiling is reached at time t_2. At this point output can expand only at the ceiling rate of growth. But this means that the change in output that is possible between periods t_2 and t_3 must be less than the change in the preceding period. This, however, means that an absolute fall in investment must take place. Consequently output shrinks, gross induced investment falls to zero, and the economy enters a slump. In period t_4 the bottom of recession is reached. A new expansion must now await the wearing out of the excess equipment. When growth factors again produce a positive change in output or when gross investment rises because of the necessity of replacement, expansion proceeds once more.

The Hicks model, while highly oversimplified as presented here, serves as a useful framework of analysis which, with modification, yields a fairly good picture of cyclical fluctuation within a framework of growth. It serves especially to emphasize that in a capitalist economy characterized by substantial amounts of durable equipment, a period of contraction almost inevitably follows expansion. Since the rate of expansion of output is greater than the rate at which full-employment output grows (this must be the case or full employment would never be reached), the ceiling imposes an enforced period of slowdown; because induced investment depends on changes in output, this implies that there will be an absolute fall in the level of investment.

Hicks's model also pinpoints the fact that in the absence of technical progress and other powerful growth factors, the economy will tend to languish in depression for long periods of time. There are two reasons for this: First, without technical progress, autonomous investment may not rise over time, and thus a positive change in output, needed to set the accelerator in motion, will not take place until equipment has worn out to the point where some replacement investment is necessary. Second, if there is no technical progress, the time at which this replacement is necessary will be deferred because no help is obtained from the obsolescence of existing equipment. The whole burden of starting the accelerator going is thus placed on the wearing out (depreciation) of equipment. Small wonder that depressions are more severe and long-lasting during periods when long-run growth factors seem to be in abeyance.

Before moving on, one serious deficiency of the Hicks model should be brought out. The full-employment ceiling that Hicks defines is independent of the path of output. It depends rather on the growth of population, advances in technology, etc., and is thus assumed to grow at the same rate as autonomous investment. But the full-employment level of output depends on the magnitude of the resources that are available to the economy. The capital stock is one such resource. This implies that the ceiling is raised in any period during which the capital stock is increasing. Since the rate at which output increases determines the rate at which the capital stock changes, the ceiling level of output will differ depending on the time path of output. One cannot therefore separate the long-run full-employment trend from what happens during a cycle.

We move on now to supplement and amend the model by analyzing some sources of fluctuation other than changes in output.

18-3   Sources of Disturbance

1. **Innovation and fluctuations in autonomous investment.** In the Hicksian scheme of things, autonomous investment—investment not geared to the current level or changes in the level of output—plays a passive role. It can, however, be argued that in a highly progressive capitalist economy the driving force may be the periodic disruptions introduced by technical progress. Indeed, there is reason to believe that the placing of primary emphasis on induced investment, while ignoring fluctuations in autonomous investment, can be compared to the tail that wags the dog.

The chief exponent of the view that business cycles are a natural outgrowth of economic progress is J. A. Schumpeter.[1] Schumpeter draws a sharp distinction between invention (the discovery and development of new processes, new goods, and new methods by engineers and scientists) and innovation (the process whereby entrepreneurs put the invention to commercial use). The importance of the distinction between invention and innovation lies in the fact that while invention may proceed quite smoothly, innovation tends to move in fits and starts. It is this discontinuity in the rate of innovation that, in Schumpeter's view, causes fluctuations in economic activity.

Innovation does not proceed smoothly because people are by nature conservative. They tend to stick to tried methods and to eschew new ones until the value of the new methods has been proved by others or until their deteriorating competitive position forces them to take action. There are, however, a few bold innovators who, under favorable conditions, will lead the way. Once such an innovator starts the process, others begin to follow until ultimately there is a deluge of investment spending and a full-scale boom.

Why do others imitate? For one thing, competitors cannot afford to let themselves be outstripped by an aggressive rival. The more firms that follow the lead, the greater is the pressure on the remainder. In addition, the innovation, especially if it takes place in a situation of full or near full employment, causes prices to rise because bidding for the available supply of resources is intensified. Profit opportunities appear rosier, and investment is stimulated.

[1] J. A. Schumpeter, *The Theory of Economic Development*, Harvard University Press, Cambridge, Mass., 1934, and "The Analysis of Economic Change," *Review of Economic Statistics*, 17:2–10, 1935. See also Estey, *op. cit.*, Chap. 8.

If there is increased investment, prices again rise and investment is once more stimulated.

We need not go into the specific details of Schumpeter's theory. We should, however, note that a boom driven by innovation is apt to have a radically different type of upper turning point than Hicks's accelerator boom. There, it will be remembered, the full-employment ceiling made it impossible for output to grow more rapidly than the long-run rate of growth, and this implied that investment would fall and income would fall because induced investment depends on changes in output. But when investment is independent of output changes, the Hicksian ceiling need pose no obstacle to the further expansion of aggregate demand. The end of the boom may come about simply because ultimately the new factories will be completed so that investment spending begins to tail off. At the same time, the new factories begin turning out large volumes of consumer goods. Coming at a time when investment is falling or increasing at a decreasing rate, the added supply of consumption goods will not all be bought, prices break, widespread disappointment with respect to profits results, and recession begins. It appears, then, that the length of an innovation boom is largely determined by the period of gestation, i.e., the length of time required for the new factories to be built.

The most significant aspect of the Schumpeterian analysis is its demonstration that the same forces that create instability are the forces that also make for economic progress. Economic progress is impossible in the absence of innovation. But since innovation does not proceed smoothly, periodic ups and downs are the inevitable consequence.

2. Capital investment, interest, and money. Most present-day writers emphasize the importance of such "real" phenomena as the acceleration principle or changes in the marginal efficiency of capital due to innovation. Most would also agree that monetary effects may be important in accentuating or moderating swings, while some would go so far as to assert that monetary disturbances are the cause of all the trouble.

Recession produces a decline in borrowing and in the volume of transactions and therefore creates excess supply of money. Insofar as this is accompanied by a fall in interest rates, recovery will be facilitated. The increased borrowing that accompanies expansion, on the other hand, tends to raise interest rates, to make borrowing progressively more difficult and costly, and thereby to help to restrain expansion. Looked at in this way, the monetary system appears as a helpful stabilizer.

Might it not be the case that in the absence of monetary disturbances there would be no fluctuations in the first place? A prominent exponent of this view is F. A. von Hayek,[1] whose theory, dealing with variations in capital investment, follows our present line of inquiry.

[1] F. A. von Hayek, *Prices and Production*, 2d ed., Routledge & Kegan Paul, Ltd., London, 1951. See also Estey, *op. cit.*, Chap. 13.

As a starting point for an examination of Hayek's theory, let us postulate a full-employment economy, let us suppose initially that banks are required to maintain a ratio of reserves to deposits of 100 percent, and let us assume that no change takes place in the money supply or in the velocity of circulation. Under such conditions, all borrowing for investment must originate with funds released through current savings. In this situation the savings habits of the community will determine the amount of current output that can be devoted to expanding the future income stream. If the community decides to consume less today in order that future consumption might be increased, savings rise, resources are released from consumption, and, because this prompts the interest rate to fall, the resources are absorbed into investment.

Those resources that are devoted to the production of current consumption goods may be said to be utilized in the higher stages of production—i.e., those closest to the consumer—while those devoted to investment-goods production may be said to be devoted to the lower stages of production. At full employment an increase in investment involves a shifting of resources from the higher to the lower stages of production. This shift is known as a lengthening of the structure of production or an increase in the "roundaboutness" of production.

As long as such a change in roundaboutness occurs as a result of the voluntary behavior of savers, no harm can come of it. The difficulty arises when cheap credit creates the illusion that it is profitable to lengthen the structure of production. Since the illusion disappears in time, a vertical maladjustment—a situation in which there are more resources than can be profitably employed in the production of capital goods—results. A painful recessionary period of readjustment must follow, during which the structure of production is shortened.

Under a fractional reserve banking system it is possible for entrepreneurs to obtain resources for investment over and above those that are voluntarily released by savings. The process whereby this is accomplished is called "forced savings." Since banks are profit-making institutions, they will attempt to expand their loan-making operations the moment excess reserves appear. In so doing, they lower the market rate of interest below the natural rate (the rate that would maintain the proper balance in the structure of production);[1] therefore entrepreneurs are induced to use the artificially created bank credit to bid resources away from consumers. The resultant increase in consumer-good prices reduces real income and consumption, and thus "forces" the community to save.

The inflationary boom that is created by this process can be sustained as long as the artificially low market rate of interest prevails. But as money income rises as a result of the investment expenditures, consumers use this added income to purchase consumption goods. Consumer-goods prices therefore rise

---

[1] Hayek's "natural" rate of interest may be identified with the natural rate discussed in Chapter 13, which equates the demand for goods and services with the full-employment supply.

beyond the initial increase, and a tendency develops for resources to be bid back into consumption-goods lines. As long as ample bank credit is available, this tendency can be thwarted. But as reserves grow critically low relative to deposits, lending operations are curtailed, and the market rate of interest rises. This means that many of the new projects now appear unprofitable; a chronic vertical maladjustment develops; many of the projects are abandoned; and recession, viewed as the period during which the appropriate structure of production is restored, sets in.

One of the interesting features of Hayek's theory is its attempt to explain the extraordinary cyclical variation in the production of capital goods. The notion of forced savings and the theory that interest-rate changes may induce a lengthening of the structure of production may, in fact, help to explain this.

Resort to these esoteric doctrines is necessary only if full employment prevails throughout. The typical depression is marked by unemployed resources, and this makes possible the simultaneous expansion of consumption and investment goods. The fact that in the short run the percentage of income consumed falls as income rises is all that need be said to explain why investment-goods production rises in greater proportion than consumption. What the cycle would look like if unemployment existed at the outset is not discussed by Hayek, who regards any theory not starting at full-employment equilibrium to be methodologically unacceptable. Be this as it may, the fact is that interest rates will fall during recession; thus the lengthening of the structure of production, of which Hayek speaks, will, if it is brought about at all, almost invariably begin while unemployed resources are available.

Despite its rather severe limitations, Hayek's analysis serves to illustrate that once full employment is reached, a boom can be sustained by the action of the banking system. If the market rate of interest remains below the natural rate, attempts may be made to expand investment-goods capacity; this necessitates forced savings. Hayek's theory also suggests that an artificially sustained boom may make the subsequent collapse all the more serious if investment has been undertaken in areas where no true long-run profit opportunities exist.

We should note in passing an interesting similarity between the theories of Hayek and Schumpeter. Both writers begin their analyses with the economy assumed to be in a state of equilibrium at full employment. This means that if there are no changes in savings habits, expansion of investment-goods production must come about via forced savings. The forced savings, moreover, are made possible by the ability of banks to expand credit. But whereas the banks are the villains of the piece to Hayek, to Schumpeter they are the indispensable instruments of capitalist progress since it is they who make resources available to the innovating entrepreneur. Apparently, it all depends on the point of view.

3. Stocks, sales, and inventory fluctuations. The fluctuations in capital-goods production, with which we have been concerned, are not the whole story. During some recessions—mild ones to be sure—capital investment manages to remain fairly steady while the contraction in output is primarily the result of a shrinkage in consumption and of negative inventory investment. Indeed, it is quite possible to generate a pattern of cyclical behavior, despite constant capital-goods production, from the simple circumstance that merchants place orders not only to replace stocks of goods that have been sold but also to maintain inventories. These inventories are not at a constant level, but at levels that are related to current rates of sale, to the current rate of interest, and to price expectations.

A reasonable assumption to make about entrepreneurial behavior is that as long as the rate of interest is constant and price expectations are neutral, the desired level of inventory is just proportional to the level of current sales.

To illustrate the consequences of this kind of behavior, consider a model, shown in Table 18-2, in which the desired ratio of stocks to sales is 2:1 and the marginal propensity to consume is 0.5. Assume that the level of sales in day one is 100 shmoos. The desired level of inventory will therefore be 200 shmoos. If sales in day 2 are also 100, the desired level of inventory will remain at 200, so that orders in day 2 will be the 100 shmoos needed to replace the sales of the day.

Table 18-2

Time	Sales (consumption)	Desired stocks	Orders to adjust inventory	Total orders (income)
(1)	(2)	(3) = (2) × 2	(4)	(5) = (2) + (4)
1	100.00	200.00	0.00	100.00
2	100.00	200.00	0.00	100.00
3	112.00	224.00	24.00	136.00
4	130.00	260.00	36.00	166.00
5	145.00	290.00	30.00	175.00
6	149.50	299.00	9.00	158.50
7	141.25	282.50	−16.50	124.75
8	124.38	248.75	−33.75	90.62
9	107.31	214.62	−34.12	73.19
10	98.59	197.19	−17.44	81.16
11	102.58	205.16	7.97	110.55
12	117.27	234.55	29.39	146.66

Note: Detail may not add to total due to rounding.

Now suppose that in day 3 consumers decide to purchase 12 additional shmoos. Orders in day 3 must rise by the 12 shmoos needed to replace stocks at their old level plus an additional 24 because the desired level of stocks has risen to 224. Total orders in day 3 are therefore 136. Since this represents a change in income of 36 shmoos and since the marginal propensity to consume is 0.5, sales in day 4 rise by 18 to a new level of 130. The desired level of stocks now rises to 260; therefore orders in day 4 must be

$$130 + (260 - 224) = 166$$

Again this represents an income change, and therefore consumption again rises.

The cyclical upswing advances until day 6 when, despite an increase in consumption (from 145 to 149.5), orders nevertheless fall from 175 to 158.5. Since orders fall, income and consumption subsequently fall, and the cycle starts its downward course. Eventually it reaches a point (day 11) where, despite a fall in consumption, orders nonetheless rise so that expansion begins again.

What brings about these turning points? Orders consist of two components— the amount needed to replace the day's sales and the amount needed to adjust inventory to the desired level of stocks. The first component equals the *level* of sales, while the second depends on the *change* in the level of sales. Even though the absolute level of sales rises, thereby increasing the first component of orders, over-all orders may fall if the change in sales is less than it previously was. In day 5, sales are 145; since the change in sales between days 4 and 5 is 15, desired stocks rise by 30. But between days 5 and 6 sales rise by only 4.5, so that desired stocks rise by only 9. Orders to build up inventories therefore fall by 21; since this is not overcome by the positive change in sales of 4.5, there results an absolute decline in orders of 16.5.

Apparently, the fact that the marginal propensity to consume is less than unity makes it possible for the desired level of stocks to catch up to sales. Once this happens, there is no further need for upward inventory adjustment; the absolute volume of orders falls, and contraction sets in. Similarly, a marginal propensity to consume of less than unity means that sales do not fall as rapidly as orders; thus a time will come (day 11) when, despite a fall in sales, there is an absolute increase in orders because sales have fallen by less than in the preceding day. Contraction therefore is halted.

We may conclude that if entrepreneurs adapt their inventories to correspond with the level of sales in a manner similar to that postulated here, and if the marginal propensity to consume is less than unity, a self-generating inventory cycle may result. Certainly inventory fluctuations tend to intensify general cyclical swings.

The hypothesis presented above is a simplified version of the inventory-cycle analysis of L. A. Metzler.[1] In Metzler's view it is the marginal propensity to consume of less than unity that explains the turning points. If, for example, the marginal propensity to consume were equal to unity, there would be no turning point, as shown in Table 18-3. Sales would always rise by the exact

[1] L. A. Metzler, "The Nature and Stability of Inventory Cycles," *Review of Economic Statistics,* 23:113–129, 1941; and "Business Cycles and the Modern Theory of Employment," *American Economic Review,* 36:278–291, 1946.

amount of the change in orders; since this is always double the change in the preceding day, no downturn would result.

The eminent British economist R. G. Hawtrey[1] believes that the turning points result from the fluctuations in the desired level of stocks to sales, which are brought about by interest-rate changes. In a vein similar to that of Hayek, Hawtrey believes that if it were not for faulty banking policy, fluctuations would not take place.

Table 18-3

Time	Sales	Stocks	Orders
1	100	200	100
2	100	200	100
3	112	224	136
4	136	272	184
5	184	368	280
6	280	560	etc.

Our previous analysis of the transactions demand for money suggested that the average amount held idle for transactions purposes was likely to be inversely associated with the rate of interest. The higher the rate of interest relative to the cost of transactions (broker's fees, etc.), the more profitable it would be to enter the bond market and the lower average bank balances would be.

The demand for money is but one aspect of the general inventory problem. Weighed against the desirability of holding inventories is the cost of holding inventories—a cost that is partly dependent on the rate of interest. A high rate of interest raises carrying costs and is apt to lead merchants to try to get by on a smaller margin of inventory, while a low interest rate will have the opposite effect. It is in the relationship between inventory costs and interest rates and in the behavior of the banking system that Hawtrey finds the source of industrial fluctuations.

If by some means banks acquire excess reserves, they are moved to put the funds to work. The resulting fall in the rate of interest raises the desired ratio of stocks to sales; this leads entrepreneurs to borrow funds to increase inventory, and thus promotes expansion. The added income results in added consumption, which leads to further increases in orders, so that expansion billows upward as in the example of Table 18-3.

With a given volume of bank reserves, the time must come when the increased transactions impinge on the money supply. This process is aggravated, in Hawtrey's view, by the fact that during the later stages of expansion, the increased volume of transactions leads to a serious drain of cash from the

[1] R. G. Hawtrey, *Good and Bad Trade*, Constable & Co., Ltd., London, 1913. See also Estey, *op. cit.*, Chap. 12.

banks. As the ratio of reserves to deposits reaches a critically low level, banks restrict credit, interest rates rise, the ratio of desired stocks to sales falls, orders decline, and contraction gets under way. As orders decline, income and consumption shrink; orders decline still further, and so on in a cumulative contraction. If the banks realized that this process of contraction ultimately causes cash to move back to the banks, they would not contract to a significant degree. But since they show no such awareness, the contraction continues until the flow of cash back into the banks again produces excess reserves; this causes a lowering of the interest rate, at which point the process starts over again.

In addition to the physical volume of sales and interest rates, we would expect investment in inventories to be highly sensitive to price expectations. The expectation of an increase in the price level causes the desired level of stocks to sales to rise, while an expected decline in the price level has the opposite effect. Since the expectation of a rise in the price level leads to an increase in orders, the expected rise is likely to materialize and thus lead to further increases in orders.

Expectations play an important role, not only with respect to inventory accumulation, but with respect to capital investment and consumption as well. No theory of the business cycle is complete without some hypothesis about expectations. Let us turn to this problem.

4. Expectations. Little progress has been made by economists in formulating a theory of the movement of expectations during the course of a business cycle.[1] The hiatus is all the more unfortunate because all theories of the business cycle contain, explicitly or implicitly, a hypothesis with respect to expectations. Hayek's divergence of the money rate of interest from the natural rate would not produce an increase in investment if no one expected the money rate to remain below the natural rate for very long. Similarly, the increased capacity needs resulting from an increase in output would not, via the accelerator hypothesis, induce investment if the increase in output was not expected to be permanent; nor would merchants adjust their inventories upward if the increase in sales was not expected to be sustained.

The difficulty of formulating a suitable hypothesis about investment behavior in a world of uncertainty can be illustrated with the acceleration principle. The equation for induced investment is often written

$$I_t = \mathbf{v}(Y_{t-1} - Y_{t-2}) \tag{18-2}$$

---

[1] Expectations, however, are placed in a crucial role by many economists. Keynes believed that a prime cause of business fluctuations was the capricious nature of expectations. Other writers who emphasize expectations are A. C. Pigou, *Industrial Fluctuation*, Macmillan & Co., Ltd., London, 1927; O. Lange, *Price Flexibility and Full Employment*, Principia Press, Inc., Bloomington, Ind., 1944; and G. L. S. Shackle, *Expectations in Economics*, Cambridge University Press, Cambridge, Mass., 1949.

where today's induced investment is some constant $\mathbf{v}$ times the change in output between yesterday and the day before yesterday. The constant $\mathbf{v}$, known as the "acceleration coefficient," is the amount of additional capacity required to produce a unit change in output with optimum efficiency.[1] But there is a difficulty here: Suppose that there is sufficient capacity at the start of today (day t) to produce optimally the output of the day before yesterday (Y_{t-2}). If this is the case, yesterday's output (Y_{t-1}), must, in a period of growth, have been produced inefficiently. Thus, if entrepreneurs are not constantly lagging behind in their equipment needs, we would have to assume that capacity at the beginning of day t was sufficient to produce Y_{t-1} optimally rather than Y_{t-2}. If, however, investment is to take place in day t, it will do so only if output is expected to rise above Y_{t-1}. But this means that the investment that is made is not for the purpose of producing the observed change in output ($Y_{t-1} - Y_{t-2}$); rather, the investment results because the observed change in output indicates that capacity requirements are likely to increase. The two statements obviously are entirely different hypotheses—the one being mechanical, the other depending on expectations.

Put another way, if the desired ratio of capital to output is the constant $\mathbf{v}$, entrepreneurs will try to make the capital stock K_t equal to $\mathbf{v}Y_t$, which implies that investment, the change in the capital stock, will be

$$I_t = K_t - K_{t-1} = \mathbf{v}(Y_t - Y_{t-1}) \tag{18-3}$$

rather than $\mathbf{v}(Y_{t-1} - Y_{t-2})$. But Y_t is the flow of output during the current day, and this can only be guessed at at the beginning of the day. Accordingly, we should write

$$I_t = \mathbf{v}(\mathrm{ex}Y_t - Y_{t-1}) \tag{18-4}$$

where $\mathrm{ex}Y_t$ is expected output in day t, to obtain a sensible formulation of the investment equation.

How is $\mathrm{ex}Y_t$ to be estimated? One possibility is to suppose that the expected change in output between yesterday and today is some constant percentage $\mathbf{n}$ of the actual change between yesterday and the day before. In other words,

$$\mathrm{ex}Y_t - Y_{t-1} = \mathbf{n}(Y_{t-1} - Y_{t-2})$$

Substituting into Eq. (18-4), we now have

$$I_t = \mathbf{n}\mathbf{v}(Y_{t-1} - Y_{t-2}) \tag{18-5}$$

which indicates that new capacity needs are now gauged by taking the most

---

[1] By optimally efficient production we mean a situation in which long-run profits are being maximized. This means that the level of output must be such that marginal revenue is equal to long-run marginal cost.

recent observed change in output, multiplying this by the coefficient of expectations[1] to yield the expected change in output, and finally multiplying this by the acceleration coefficient.

Whereas the simple acceleration-principle hypothesis suggests that investment takes place to adjust capacity to changes in output, the more reasonable formulation above reduces the hypothesis to the much weaker statement that past observable changes in output indicate future capacity needs.

The problem is further complicated by the fact that capacity cannot be constructed instantaneously. Today's investment decisions are not translated into usable new capacity for some time. If the period involved is x days, output must be estimated x days ahead of time; thus the investment function would have to be

$$I_t = \mathbf{v}(\mathrm{ex}Y_{t+x} - \mathrm{ex}Y_{t+x-1})$$

where everything clearly depends on future output expectations.

None of this would pose a serious problem if it were always possible to anticipate demand correctly. But errors in forecasting in an industrial economy are practically inevitable. The fact that it takes a long time to construct plants and equipment means that entrepreneurs must try to see a long way into the future. The farther they have to look, the greater the chance of error and the more likely that intervening circumstances will throw off the calculation. If technical progress is rapid, many investment goods may grow obsolete before they are even ready to enter into production. If the level of per capita income is high, consumer tastes will be more diversified and capricious than would be the case in a primitive economy in which expenditures are concentrated on a few basic staples. As markets expand and as the structure of production becomes more and more involved with numerous tiers of producers, processors, fabricators, and middlemen, the likelihood of errors in forecasting is compounded.

As a general rule, forecasting becomes more difficult as an economy advances to a stage of highly developed capitalism. But along with the growth of heavy industry there is a compensating factor: competition usually declines in significant sectors of the economy. It is competition that gives rise to one of the most troublesome sources of errors in forecasting. In a competitive industry characterized by many small firms, none of the firms is likely to have a very good idea of what the others are doing. If demand increases and it appears profitable to invest, the end result may be one of disappointment because, all the others having also expanded operations, the resulting flood of goods depresses prices and inflicts losses. Since it takes time to bring the new plants and equipment into working order, the period during which expansion appears profitable is sustained; this increases the temptation to overexpand. Completion

[1] L. A. Metzler, "The Nature and Stability of Inventory Cycles," *op. cit.*, introduces the concept of a coefficient of expectations.

of the projects brings about the rude awakening. What would have been a correct forecast and a profitable investment for one firm, if none of the other firms had expanded, turns out to be an unprofitable move because the other firms are also busily engaged in expanding.

18-4   Steady Growth: Trend and Cycle

Apart from random shocks and seasonal variations, it seems likely that business fluctuations would not exist in the absence of three basic features of modern industrial life: the durability of many goods, the complicated and time-consuming structure of production, and the use of money. In the absence of durability, final goods production would be exactly equal to the level of consumer demand, and changes in consumer demand would lead to proportional changes all along the structure of production. A short gestation period would eliminate most of the errors of forecast; it would eliminate the period of construction during which money income is in excess of output and thus would eliminate the stimulus to overexpansion which the rising prices of this period present. In a barter economy, finally, there could be no forced savings, no divergence of the natural rate from the money rate, no speculation resulting from changes in the over-all price level, and none of the hoarding of cash balances which, as Keynes emphasized, has such damaging consequences.

But all three aspects listed above are vital and central features of industrial society. Even a highly controlled and planned socialist system is apt to suffer some dislocation from them.[1] Socialist planners must, for example, make up their minds whether they wish to introduce an innovation rapidly or slowly. If the new project is quickly built, many resources must be transferred from other areas. Completion of the project then brings about a second abrupt change and necessitates another large-scale transfer of resources. If this process is not effected smoothly and carefully—and it is difficult to see how even the most adept planners could make it so—the consequence is likely to be a temporary loss of income and production and a situation not unlike a capitalist recession. The alternative to this can only be a much slower introduction of the new method, and this implies a less rapid long-run rate of growth of output.

In the light of these considerations, and of some we have not touched upon, it seems likely that business fluctuations are an inevitable by-product of modern economic life. This being the case, it is not sufficient merely to consider steady growth economics. We must also pay attention to the interaction of trend and cycle.[2]

Let us begin by assuming that the economy grows at a constant rate at full

[1] See D. McC. Wright, *The Economics of Disturbance*, The Macmillan Company, New York, 1947.

[2] W. J. Fellner, *Trends and Cycles in Economic Activity*, Henry Holt and Company, Inc., New York, 1956, makes the interaction of trend and cycle his major theme.

employment with constant per capita income. There is no technical progress, so aggregate income and its components expand at the same rate as the growth of population. To facilitate the maintenance of this growth path, we suppose that the money supply also grows at the same rate as the growth of income and that the balance of international payments is in equilibrium.

Now let us suppose that an innovation is introduced and that the burst of investment spending which follows produces an innovations boom of the Schumpeterian kind. Although completion of the new projects, rising interest rates, the end of such acceleration effects as may exist, and the inevitable reversal of expectations bring an end to the boom and start the economy downward towards depression, the innovation will have raised the full-employment level of income above what it would have been in its absence. If it were possible to avert the downturn, per capita income might be considerably higher than otherwise.

The collapse can be serious or mild, depending partly upon the extent to which investment is oriented toward current profit opportunities or to long-run profit opportunities. Thus if the rate of technological change is rapid, there may be much long-range investment; if the rate of population growth is high, the demand for housing may serve to cushion the shrinkage in investment spending.

When the bottom of the slump is reached, the length of time required for recovery will again be conditioned by long-run growth factors. In the absence of any technological advance, recovery must await the wearing out of existing equipment and the time when inventories are adjusted to their desired levels. However, if innovations come on the scene, the day is hastened when desired capacity and actual capacity are again in line because the innovation renders some existing capacity and stocks of goods obsolete and because the innovation will increase the level of output. Insofar as the money supply is elastic, recovery will be hastened as borrowing for investment purposes is facilitated by low interest rates. If, furthermore, the economy responds to falling demand with a fall in the price level, investment may be stimulated both because the fall in the price level adds to the elasticity of the monetary system and because the cost of investment projects declines. The larger the percentage of the full-employment level of investment that is oriented toward the distant future, the more significant this latter factor is apt to be. The reason for this is that current output prices are likely to weigh much less heavily in long-run investment decisions than are current costs.

Expansion from depression now proceeds. Autonomous investment rises under the impulse of innovation, low costs, and interest rates. The change in output gives rise to favorable expectations and induces investment to take care of expected capacity needs. Orders exceed sales so that the ratio of stocks to sales will be maintained and even increased. All these and other factors interact to produce the boom.

The boom, however, encounters obstacles. Ultimately, if full employment is reached, output increases at a declining rate, and induced investment falls off. Other investment projects are completed so that investment expenditures slacken. In addition, interest rates rise, making borrowing progressively more costly.

If the boom is primarily an innovations boom and if it proceeds slowly, the level of output achieved at its peak will be higher than otherwise. This is so (1) because a slow boom makes available to the system in its later stages some of the new capacity that was constructed in the early stages; (2) because the innovation is labor- or capital-saving, and therefore a higher level of output per unit of capacity can be produced; and (3) because the innovation can lift the economy out of depression prior to the destruction of significant amounts of existing capacity.

It is not difficult to see that cycles condition the long-run growth path and that the long-run path conditions cycles. The key factor apparently is the rapidity with which technological advance takes place. As long as long-run growth factors are abundant, investment is less dependent on immediate profit opportunities. This implies that investment will be less sensitive to changes in demand; as a result recessions will be milder, recovery will occur more quickly, and recovery will be slower and smoother. It is not surprising that during periods of significant technical progress and growth the time spent in recession should be less than during periods of "stagnation."

Although Schumpeter emphasized that rapid growth was not possible without some instability, since such instability is a natural by-product of technical progress, it is also true that chronic instability resulting from innovation may reduce the rate at which the economy grows. For one thing, chronic instability produces a climate of uncertainty and must surely foster expectations that are not conducive to risk taking. Secondly, depressions reduce the full-employment output potential of the system because the capital stock grows less rapidly than otherwise, and in some cases (as in 1933) actually declines.

Failure to recognize the importance of this latter point—that depressions destroy productive resources—helps to explain the strange though widespread notion that recession, if not excessive, is helpful to the economy. Even a superficial glance at the statistics reveals the folly of this view. Imagine the additional output that could have been produced by the capacity that would have been accumulated had we not suffered the "mild" recessions of 1949 and 1954 and the "moderate" recession of 1958.[1]

In conclusion, although technological advance and innovation are vital to an improvement in per capita income, innovation may defeat its own purpose if it leads to such chronic instability that many of the economy's resources are destroyed or held idle for significant periods of time.

---

[1] The argument that "mild" recessions, which may result from the clumsiness of policy instruments, are a necessary result of attempts to halt inflationary spirals can be used to mitigate this conclusion.

part IV

*Problems in the Control
of Economic Activity*

chapter 19

Problems of fiscal policy

19-1 Introduction

In earlier chapters our interest was primarily directed toward the question of which policy, monetary or fiscal, would change the level of income or control the price level more effectively under differing economic conditions. However, to say that during recession fiscal policy is likely to be more effective than monetary policy and that during inflation the opposite is the case is not sufficient information for the policy maker. This part of the book is devoted to a consideration of some of the practical problems connected with fiscal policy, monetary policy, and the national debt; and to a discussion of such timely topics as "cost-push" inflation and structural unemployment.

The difficulties inherent in the utilization of various discretionary fiscal-policy devices are such that a good deal of reliance must be placed on automatic devices that provide the economy with considerable initial basic resiliency. As was pointed out in Chapter 1, the progressive income tax, unemployment compensation, and the system of farm price supports serve to stabilize disposable income by offsetting to some extent the effects of fluctuations in net national product.

Economic stability is fostered by other developments that have taken place in the last thirty years. The Federal Deposit Insurance Corporation, by insuring bank deposits up to $10,000, makes it extremely unlikely that we will experience banking panics, and the powers over security issue and stock-market speculation given to the Securities and Exchange Commission and to the Federal Reserve System, respectively, make a recurrence of the 1929 stock-market episode improbable. Another circumstance of importance is the sheer size of the government sector. There are stabilizing benefits to be derived from a huge Federal budget. Tax cuts can be used as a fiscal instrument to fight recession only if there are significant taxes available to cut. The Federal government expenditures component is a large and stable portion of the national income that does not shrink with the fall of disposable income and of profit expectations. Business confidence, moreover, must surely be enhanced by the announced policy of our government to take action on the economic front and by the feeling that we now know what to do about depression, which was not the case in 1929.

We are undoubtedly in a good position to avert economic disaster. We are not, however, doing very well in terms of fully achieving and reconciling our several economic goals. It has been argued that a policy of maintaining full employment will give rise to inflation because such a policy empowers unions and oligopolistic enterprises to push up wages and prices more or less at will. On the other hand, if we attempt to maintain a firm grip on the price level, we will be slow in taking action against recession. Since this means that we will not be making full use of our resource potential, our long-run rate of growth will be less than it might be. If we try to improve our rate of economic growth by pursuing policies that stimulate investment and suppress consumption, we may magnify an unstable component of aggregate expenditure at the expense of a fairly stable and more readily predictable one. In short, there is considerable difficulty in reconciling the three goals of full employment, price stability, and rapid growth. Some economists would go so far as to say that the goals are to a high degree incompatible in a free society in which control is exerted indirectly through monetary-fiscal action as opposed to the direct approach of administrative price control, rationing, and the allocation of resources by central direction.

Most Americans would agree that these latter alternatives must be shunned and that ways must be found to achieve adequate economic performance without direct control over economic life. It is therefore important to give careful consideration to the problem of policy making and to the preservation of a relatively free economy and a democratic society. In this chapter we shall discuss some problems of fiscal policy. For example: What kind of budget do we want? Are tax changes preferable to expenditure changes? What problems are raised with respect to the planning and execution of public-works projects?

19-2   Budgetary Policy and Stability

Various budgetary principles have been espoused from time to time. Among these the most prominent are the annually balanced budget, the "Swedish" or cyclically balanced budget, "formula flexibility," and the fully managed compensatory program. Let us consider these briefly.

The annually balanced budget. The principle of balancing the budget annually runs completely counter to the goal of economic stability. During an inflationary period a budgetary surplus is apt to arise because of increasing tax revenues. The principle of annual balance implies that an increase in government expenditures or a tax cut is required to bring the budget into balance; this obviously would add fuel to the inflation. Furthermore, the increased money income resulting from such a policy would further raise tax revenues so that in any case the budget would probably not be balanced without further tax cuts. During depression, on the other hand, tax revenues would fall so that, in order to eliminate the deficit, taxes would have to be raised and expenditures reduced. However, this would cause income to shrink still further and would cause tax revenues to fall. Thus the attempt to balance the budget annually is likely to be frustrated and will most certainly exercise a destabilizing effect on the economy.

There is little to be said for the policy of an annually balanced budget except that it may impose a restriction of sorts on government "extravagances" and may promote business confidence. These benefits are hardly likely to overcome the damage such a policy would do. Moreover, the rising tax revenues that result from inflation may lead to added government spending just at the time when the private economy is hard pressed to find sufficient resources; and it is really quite difficult to believe that business confidence is in the slightest bit bolstered by so-called "sound" fiscal policy.[1]

The "Swedish budget." A more sensible approach to fiscal policy is embodied in the principle of budgetary balance over the cycle. This type of program was first implemented in Sweden during the 1930s and has thus come to be called the "Swedish budget."[2] Its appeal is undeniable, and it serves as the basis for the program for economic stability espoused by the Committee for Economic Development.[3] The CED's version of the program calls for a programing of public expenditures purely on the basis of actual governmental needs. No public expenditure should be undertaken for the purpose of changing

[1] Although conservative businessmen vehemently deny that their confidence is bolstered by a government deficit, the stock market seems to indicate the opposite. During the Khrushchev visit of 1959 there developed some suspicion that peace might break out and that United States armaments expenditures would be reduced. As in all such cases, the stock market took a nosedive. Similarly, the stock market decline that began in the spring of 1962 and accelerated after the steel crisis was unquestionably attributable to the fact that a Democratic President made it clear that he is not a "spender" and that further inflation is unlikely. Despite professions on the part of our "rugged individualists" that the President's action in the steel crisis impaired that precious hot-house flower, business confidence, and therefore precipitated the collapse, it seems fairly clear that the steel incident merely proved conclusively that the administration means business on the inflation front.

[2] See G. Myrdal, "Fiscal Policy in the Business Cycle," *American Economic Review* (Supplement), 29:183–193, 1939.

[3] Committee for Economic Development, Research and Policy Committee, "Taxes and the Budget," New York, 1947.

the level of income. Once expenditures over the period of the cycle have been programed, tax rates would be adjusted in such a way that the surpluses during prosperous years would just balance the deficits during recession years. It is hoped that in this way the budget will achieve long-run balance, that restraint will be imposed on government spending, and that short-run stability will be fostered by the stabilization of disposable income.

An important element in the CED's program is the existing system of built-in flexibility that results from the progressive income tax and from government transfer-payment schemes. Given the proper income tax structure and transfer-payment programs, the CED's proposal would consist of an almost entirely automatic system of fiscal offsets to inflation and deflation.

The CED proposal has found widespread approval among economists and businessmen alike. It possesses, however, weaknesses that have led some to recommend going considerably beyond it. For one thing, it is quite unlikely that the deficits and surpluses that will occur over a cycle can be accurately predicted. Government expenditures must continually be adjusted to meet various emergencies and cannot be forecast with any degree of accuracy. If cyclical balance is to be maintained, tax rates would have to be tinkered with as often as government expenditures are changed. The CED's proposal, if cyclical balance is to be taken literally, may therefore involve less automaticity and more frequent tax changes than would a less rigid program. Finally, while the program may help to stabilize the level of economic activity, it cannot guarantee that the level at which income is stabilized will be the full-employment level. Automatic stabilizers serve to cushion the rise and fall of economic activity, but they do nothing to change the average level or to promote a reversal of movement. Cyclical balance may not be enough during some periods, while in other periods it may be too much.

Formula flexibility.   For those who place considerable value on automatically operating countercyclical devices, the scheme of "formula flexibility" has considerable appeal. Under our existing system a fall in income produces a reduction in tax revenues because there is less income available to tax and because taxpayers shift into lower brackets. While this helps to cushion the fall in disposable income, an even greater effect could be obtained if tax rates on all brackets were reduced at the same time as taxpayers were shifting into lower brackets. One answer would be to have an automatic reduction in tax rates when some sort of "peril point" is reached. When income shrinks, this peril point might be taken as a 5 percent fall in the Federal Reserve's index of industrial production, while in the upward direction it might be taken as a 3 percent rise in the consumer price index over an arbitrary period of time.

The advantages of formula flexibility are that it goes considerably beyond the scope of the present automatic stabilization schemes and that it removes stabilization policy from congressional muddling. On the other hand, the changes in tax rates are based solely on a set of indexes that are notorious for their lack of reliability. The indexes, moreover, incorporate the effects of strikes, crop failures, and other factors having little to do with whether aggregate demand is excessive or insufficient. Finally, it is conceivable that the two indexes could reach their respective peril-point levels simultaneously. Even without these technical drawbacks, it is unlikely that formula flexibility will become a part of the American scene because Congress will surely refuse to give up its role as the final fiscal authority.

Fully managed compensatory program. The policy that we have more or less adopted in the United States is a fully managed compensatory policy. Such a policy recognizes the importance of automatic stabilizers in fostering stability but goes beyond this by recognizing the need for such additional *ad hoc* tax and expenditure changes as may be necessary from time to time. Budgetary balance is placed in a secondary role. The major emphasis is placed on the maintenance of full employment and a stable price level, regardless of the measures that may be required to achieve these goals. Most economists would support such a policy, within limits. It is, furthermore the policy embodied in the Employment Act of 1946 and is espoused in the platforms of our two major political parties. The Democrats place heavier emphasis on full employment; the Republicans place primary emphasis on a stable price level. However, neither party has to date made a serious effort to implement the Act.

Critics of the managed compensatory program argue that the Federal government should not give a blanket guarantee against unemployment because such a guarantee would enhance the bargaining power of monopolistic groups and that this would cause inflation. Others argue that there is such a long lag between the time when a policy is needed and the time when its effects will actually be felt, that the policy might in practice turn out to be destabilizing. Since it is not fully automatic, it places major responsibility for the maintenance of stability on Congress, thereby allowing fiscal policy to become a political football and subjecting it to the arduous and slow-moving process by which congressional decisions are made. Since budgetary balance is placed in a secondary role, the policy may involve a long-run growth in the national debt. In addition, emphasis is placed on both the tax and the expenditure side, and this gives rise to new difficulties. A tax cut requires relatively little planning and no expansion of government activities. Additional disposable income is simply placed in the hands of the public, and economic activity is stimulated by the expansion of the private sector. Government expenditures also place additional disposable income in the hands of the public. In return, the government receives goods and services, but considerable planning must be undertaken to ensure that these goods and services have social utility.

19-3 Problems of Taxation and Expenditure

Tax changes will have an immediate effect on the level of disposable income and therefore on the level of consumption. This effect is more noticeable as increasing amounts of income become subject to pay-as-you-go taxation. There are, however, several obstacles to tax changes. Tax changes take the form either of changes in the rates of taxation or of redefinitions of income brackets. Once a tax change has been made to meet an emergency, Congress seems to find it difficult to revert to the original rates and brackets when the emergency has passed. In the case of government expenditure, Congress is not committed to a policy that is difficult to reverse. Congress appropriates funds for a particular project, and when the project is completed and the funds are exhausted, the matter is at an end. This is not so with taxes. Although emergency tax legislation often carries with it a stated expiration date, in the case of most taxes further painful legislation is required if rates are to be changed.

To remedy this particular disadvantage of a tax cut and to take advantage of the speed with which tax cuts affect disposable income, it might be possible to suspend tax collections for short periods of time. Imagine the result if Congress empowered the President to suspend tax collections for a period of one month. The impact on disposable income and expectations would undoubtedly be dramatic, and recovery might well be speeded up substantially. The effect, moreover, would be felt at the very time when it was most needed.

If there are pressing economic reasons why government expenditure changes are more desirable than tax and transfer payment changes, they stem from two facts: (1) tax changes are less high-powered, per dollar of deficit created, than are government expenditure changes; (2) recession seems like an ideal time to catch up on the construction of badly needed social capital. On these grounds and on those suggested previously, public expenditures may seem to be highly appealing alternatives to tax cuts.

The planning and execution of public works involve many problems.[1] The effect of public works is quite unlike that of a tax cut. The time required to make the income effects of public expenditures felt may be so long that the expenditures can do nothing to keep the economy from sliding into a serious recession. By the time the bottom is reached, the need for fiscal offsets may be far greater than those forecast at the beginning of the recession. On the other hand, if the slump is only a mild one and the economy bounces back quickly, or if expenditures are started as a result of a false alarm, the net effect may be inflationary. Public works are, in short, clumsy and slow-moving, requiring time to get ready and time to turn off. Although some speed-up of the process may be obtained by instituting a "shelf" of public works to be brought into

[1] Problems relating to the planning, execution, and economic effects of public works are discussed by J. M. Clark, *The Economics of Public Works*, National Planning Board, Washington, 1935. Suggestive papers on the subject are S. Slichter, "The Economics of Public Works," *American Economic Review* (Supplement), 24:174–185, 1934; J. Margolis, "Public Works and Economic Stability," *Journal of Political Economy*, 57:293–303, 1949; S. J. Maisell, "Timing and Flexibility of a Public Works Program," *Review of Economics and Statistics*, 31:147–152, 1949.

operation quickly, they are likely to be allotted little practical role in a stabilization program designed to cope with the type of recession we have had since World War II.

During more serious depressions public policy will undoubtedly focus on both the tax and the expenditure sides. During a serious depression, moreover, the problem of timing is apt to become less important. In the year 1933 it must have seemed highly unlikely that a public works project begun at that time could not be completed in time to avert inflationary pressures, and the consideration would in any case have been dismissed as irrelevant in the face of the pressing needs of the times.

But there are numerous drawbacks to the use of public projects as a countercyclical device, even in a serious depression. First of all, it is unlikely that the resources the government wishes to obtain for its projects will be those that are in most abundant supply. If the construction materials used by the government are substantially different from those used by private industry, the effect of public construction conducted on a countercyclical basis may simply be one of creating two unstable industries where formerly there was only one.[1] Even if the materials used for public construction are the same as those used in private construction projects, the construction industry may be overexpanded if private construction recovers while the public projects are still under way.

It is unlikely that all the resources unemployed by a fall in aggregate demand will find employment in public works projects. An advertising executive will probably not be a very good bricklayer, nor will it be possible to utilize the closed advertising agency on Madison Avenue for the purpose of making generators for a power project. If the executive is to be employed, it will be because the public expenditures produce secondary effects via the multiplier, because the government decides to go into the advertising business, or because the executive is put to work on some project such as leaf raking that does not require a specialized talent. If the government does go into the advertising business, there will be charges that it is competing with private enterprise. Leaf raking, on the other hand, will be denounced as a boondoggle having little social utility.

The vast literature discussing public works that appeared during the 1930s reflects the fact that in those days public works was virtually the only alternative to remaining mired in depression. Where there are few taxes available to cut, government contributions to aggregate demand must of necessity be in the form of expenditure increases. It is possible, however, because of the increasing leverage resulting from our present large tax bill, that future recessions will be fought with both barrels. If a public construction project is considered as only a small part of an integrated recovery program, the difficulties inherent in its planning and execution become somewhat less formidable. A program of recovery in which only part of the Treasury deficit results from inflexible and

[1] Margolis, *op. cit.*

immobile operations may nevertheless have considerable over-all flexibility when it is combined with such highly flexible measures as tax and transfer payment changes.

A managed compensatory program of stabilization assigns a secondary role to the maintenance of budgetary balance, both on an annual and on a cyclical basis. It seems, in fact, as if our government is content to balance the budget only during full-employment years and does not even attempt to plan for a surplus to balance the deficits of recession years. During the fiscal year of 1959–1960, a year of reasonable full employment, the administration was proud of its plan for a balanced budget. The preceding fiscal year, characterized by recession, produced a deficit in excess of $10 billion. If past experience is any guide, it looks as if we may be establishing a pattern of just balancing the budget during full-employment years while running a deficit in recession years. This means that we must expect to be faced with an ever-rising national debt throughout the future. In the following chapter we shall consider the importance of this debt—its burden on the present and future and its impact on monetary policy and on economic stability in general.

chapter 20

Financing government expenditures

20-1 Introduction

The national debt of a nation represents the effects of wars, depressions, productive public investments, "pork barrels," and all the times when it was undesirable or inexpedient to raise sufficient taxes. It therefore constitutes the sum of all the unrepudiated net deficits in the nation's history. In the United States the Federal debt stood at a level of $289.0 billion at the end of 1961 and gave every indication of rising higher in the foreseeable future. If the national debt is to continue to grow, it is pertinent to consider the problems the debt poses and whether, in the future, it might not be better to seek alternative ways of financing public expenditures.

The orthodox view of public debt, regarded by many contemporary economists as beneath contempt, holds that public debt is not fundamentally different from private debt. Failure to tax adequately today merely constitutes a shifting of the burden to the future, and government cannot indefinitely spend more than it takes in by way of taxes without ultimately bankrupting the country. Every man, woman, and child in the United States was in 1961 mortgaged to the tune of $1,573.

An extreme version of the opposite or "new"[1] view may be summarized as follows:

[1] The most extreme form of the new view can be garnered from the writings of A. P. Lerner. See especially "The Burden of the National Debt" in *Income, Employment, and*

1. Since it is impossible to borrow tanks, guns, bricks, steel, and human beings from the future, the burden, in terms of the real resources lost to the public cannot be shifted to future generations. The resources that the government desires must be obtained here and now if they are to be obtained at all.

2. What remains of past borrowings is a set of financial claims that are both owned and owed by the citizens.

3. The interest on the debt constitutes an internal transfer of funds from taxpayer to bondholder; since these are often the same people, debt service amounts to little more than a mild redistribution of income.

4. There is always enough taxable income to service the debt since the interest on the debt is itself taxable income; in any case, more debt can be issued to pay the interest.

5. These principles do not apply to an external debt since external debt gives foreigners a claim over real resources that must be paid back in the future.

Insofar as the orthodox views are correct, we must, when we go into debt, give due consideration to the welfare of future generations. Even if the new view is correct, we must still consider the difficulties created for economic policy by the existence of such a large volume of outstanding financial claims.

Although the new view has gained fairly widespread acceptance, recent dissent should warn us to take stock.[1] The question of the burden is well worth considering since it is part of the important question of how best to finance a public expenditure.

In this chapter we shall consider, first, the question of the burden of debt creation in terms of the real resource effect of a public expenditure and in terms of the burden imposed by the method of financing the expenditure; then the question of the burden itself, defined as the tax rate required to service the debt, over time; and finally the question of existing debt as it relates to economic stability.

20-2 Financing Public Expenditures and the Burden of the Debt

It will be useful if at the outset we separate the problem of the burden into two issues: (1) the effects of the government expenditures and (2) the burden imposed by the method of financing the expenditure. To do this, let us suppose initially that the expenditures are financed interest-free by the simple expedient of printing money. While such a policy may be regarded as an irrelevant alter-

---

Public Policy, W. W. Norton & Company, Inc., New York, 1948; and *Functional Finance and the Federal Debt,* Social Research, New York, 1943. There seems in fact to be little that is new about the "new" view for, as J. M. Buchanan, *Public Principles of Public Debt,* Richard D. Irwin, Inc., Homewood, Ill., 1958, pp. 16–18, points out, the modern principles were well known to economists of the nineteenth century.

[1] Buchanan, *ibid.*

native, there is in practice no difference between resort to the printing press and the sale of government obligations to the central bank.[1] When the Treasury induces the Federal Reserve System to purchase securities, the Treasury's account is increased by the amount of the sale. When the proceeds are then spent by the Treasury, the effect is to increase the money supply in exactly the same way as if the Treasury had merely printed money and spent it. If the Federal Reserve then returns the interest earnings on the debt to the Treasury, the analogy between money printing and the sale of bonds to the central bank is complete.

Under this method of financing, the question, "At whose expense are the resources purchased by the government obtained?" depends entirely on whether the resources are put to greater or less productive use than would have been the case in the absence of the expenditure. Three cases will make this clear.

Case 1a. Unemployed resources are available; the Treasury prints money that it spends at home. In this case the net effect of the expenditure is to activate otherwise idle resources. If the government enterprise is at all productive, there will be a net gain in real income both for the present and for the future since the return on idle resources is zero. The future gains because the restoration of full employment today increases future production and real income potential. A public expenditure under the conditions outlined here can have only beneficial effects on both the present and the future generation unless the public expenditure involves the exhaustion of irreplaceable natural resources.

Case 2a. Resources are fully employed; the Treasury prints money and makes purchases of goods and services at home. Because there are no idle resources available, the government expenditure raises prices and reduces real income and private demand so that resources are released to the government by forced saving. Printing money under these conditions is exactly equivalent to a tax and involves a one-for-one transfer of wealth from the private to the public sphere. Whether or not the future shares in the burden depends on whether the public expenditure is more or less productive than its alternative private use.

Case 3a. Resources are fully employed; a foreign country agrees to make 1,000 shmoos available to the economy subject to the requirement that in 20 years 1,000 shmoos will be returned. In this case the present generation receives a net addition to its stock of resources that it could not otherwise obtain, while the future generation must repay the real resources. But whether the future gains or loses depends on whether the resources are put to use in such a way that the value of the future income-stream net of repayment will be greater than or less than the value of the future income stream in the absence of the borrowing. It is of course entirely possible that society may be considerably better off throughout the future if the 1,000 shmoos required by the government are obtained from abroad.

It is a superficial view at best to believe that because imported shmoos must

[1] *Ibid.*, Chap. 10.

be paid back, external debt, even if interest-free, is burdensome and undesirable.[1] The issue of the burden, as Buchanan rightly points out, is not whether the future has to pay it but whether the future will be better or worse off, assuming the alternative of no present public expenditure at all.

Interest-free financing by sale of securities to the central bank or by printing money is not the typical method of financing government expenditures in excess of collected taxes, although the former was pursued to some extent during World War II. In the United States the most usual procedure is the sale of interest-bearing obligations to the public and to the commercial banking system. When this happens, the possibility arises that an additional part of the burden may be shifted to the future. When a generation decides to go into debt, it is deciding part of the tax bill of future generations. The lenders are members of the present generation who lend of their own free will because they see a profit, and therefore an increase in net worth, when the government offers bonds for sale. The borrowers, although they do not know it at the time, are future taxpayers who will receive a benefit in terms of real resources depending on whether the loan has made their real income greater than would otherwise have been the case. In any event, they must pay the taxes that are required to service the debt, and this involves a very real loss in satisfaction and net worth to the taxpayer. The lender of the past generation, although his children now own the bonds, initially avoided a reduction in net worth by virtue of the fact that he did not have to pay taxes. It appears then that the way government expenditures are financed is going to make a difference with respect to the burden of the debt. Let us consider this further by returning to our three cases, assuming now that the expenditure is financed by the sale of interest-bearing government obligations within the country and to foreign nationals.

Case 1b. Unemployed resources; domestic borrowing. The effect of the government expenditure in this case is identical to that in Case 1a. Both the present and the future stand to gain real income. But by selling bonds to individuals of the present generation, the government is, in effect, subsidizing the present generation at the expense of future taxpayers. Since the return on the idle resources used by the government would have been zero, the payment of interest in return for the use of these resources is an unnecessary and inefficient payment that constitutes a mere subsidization of today's citizens at the expense of future taxpayers. It is comparable to the case of an individual who borrows at 6 percent from a bank when he has no conceivable use for the funds. To avoid shifting any burden unnecessarily, the financing ought to be interest-free and should be accomplished either by direct currency creation or by sale of securities to the central bank.

Case 2b. Full employment; domestic borrowing. This case is somewhat more involved than Case 1b. When government expenditures are financed by the sale of bonds to the public and to the banking system in a full-employment

[1] *Ibid.*, Chap. 6.

situation, the market rate of interest is certain to rise, and private investment will be reduced. If, on the other hand, the expenditures are financed by printing money, there is a net increase in the money supply with no corresponding increase in the supply of bonds, so that interest rates are unlikely to be strongly affected. In this latter case a greater proportion of the resources desired by the government are likely to come from the consuming sector through inflation and forced savings, whereas if the funds are borrowed, they will come primarily from private investment. Bond financing therefore tends to reduce investment and the rate of growth of output while it maintains current consumption, whereas financing by currency creation has the opposite effect. On this score alone the future will be burdened by debt issue. But, in addition, the creation of debt again involves a subsidy to the present generation of bondholders from the future generation of taxpayers. The transfer, however, is not complete. The government expenditure, coming at full employment, raises the price level, thereby reducing the real value of the bonds as well as the real value of future tax payments; it thus effects a reverse transfer.

Case 3b. Full employment; foreign borrowing. Here the case is clear: the future pays both principle and interest out of real resources. But, as indicated before, borrowing from abroad makes available added resources, and this may make society in the future far better off than in either of the alternatives of Case 2b.

In summary, the present may preserve individual net worth at the expense of future taxpayers if it chooses to go into debt rather than to tax outright or indirectly via currency inflation. In the event that unemployed resources exist, the expenditure can be made without burden to either present or future. Bond financing, however, may create a burden in the form of a subsidy to present bondholders at the expense of future taxpayers. When resources are fully employed, this subsidy will be lessened because the price increases caused by the expenditure will transfer net worth from bondholder to taxpayer. Bond financing, on the other hand, is likely to reduce private investment and therefore economic growth to a greater degree than financing by currency creation; thus it is likely to constitute a burden on the future. If the debt is incurred abroad, future taxpayers will gain or lose depending on whether the capitalized value of the future income stream in the absence of the debt is less than or greater than the value of the income stream (net of debt service and repayment) that results if the debt is incurred.

Are there any "principles" of public finance to be garnered from this discussion? Clearly, we would not want to finance a government expenditure by taxation during a recession since that would reduce consumption expenditures, nor would we wish to borrow abroad when domestic resources will do just as well. In terms of the future, since the resources can be obtained at no cost, it seems foolish to subsidize bondholders at the expense of taxpayers.

In a situation of full employment, the case is somewhat clouded. Ideally, we should tax to cover the expenditure since taxes will help to negate the inflationary effects of the government expenditure, whereas borrowing from the public and borrowing from the Federal Reserve in particular would not have the same effect. Taxes, moreover, would involve no shift of burden to the future. There are, however, cogent reasons why, even at full employment, it may be undesirable to raise taxes. Tax increases may be difficult to achieve from a political point of view, and they may have incentive effects. Finally, there is no good reason why the future should not be asked to bear some of the expense of public investments, including both those that yield a real visible return and those such as wartime expenditures whose benefits can be measured only by the probable consequences of not having waged the war in the first place.

A little should perhaps be said about the incentive effects of taxation. In a community that has an income of $100 billion and no debt or taxes, an individual will keep all extra income he obtains from additional hours of work. If he works fewer hours and therefore draws less income, he will lose the total amount of the reduction in his paycheck. On the other hand, a community with income of $100 billion and a service charge on its debt of an additional $100 billion will require a 50 percent tax on all income. In this case an individual who works harder and gains an additional dollar will receive only an extra 50 cents for his pains; if he works fewer hours and earns $1 less, he will stand to lose only 50 cents.[1]

The implication of the incentive effect of taxation is that the creation of debt, by necessitating tax payments in the future, may reduce the willingness to work and the growth of real income in the future. What is not always recognized, however, is that the alternative of present taxation in lieu of debt creation may have the same effect. Whether to tax today or to tax tomorrow is a question that resolves itself about the issue of when the adverse incentive effects will be the greatest. During World War II it seemed clear that more work could be gained for the war effort by eschewing further taxation in favor of debt creation, thus taking the risk that the incentive effects of increased future taxation would not be significant.

With respect to bond financing as opposed to currency creation during the war, there can be little doubt that issuing bonds had less serious inflationary consequences and gave the public the feeling that its efforts in helping to win the war were not without reward.

Although, in general, debt creation seems the least desirable way of financing a government expenditure, there are enough exceptions to this rule to warrant the conclusion that the debt represents the wisdom of the past and its concern for the future every bit as much as it reflects its follies and its selfishness. When the past floated debt in order to combat depression, it performed an unmistakable service for the future even though the financing could have been

[1] J. E. Meade, "Mr. Lerner on the 'Economics of Control,'" *Economic Journal*, 55:47–69, 1945, as cited by Buchanan, *ibid.*, Chap. 3.

performed more effectively. When the past found it necessary to go into debt to protect the community from foreign aggression, the children have every reason to be grateful. When it invests in social capital that reaches fruition in the future, it does as a community what each parent does for his own children.

20-3 The Burden of the Debt Over Time

It seems clear that the national debt imposes a certain measure of burden on the economy. A relevant question might therefore be: under what condition will this burden become relatively milder or more severe in future years? In a highly suggestive analysis, Domar[1] has shown that the burden, defined as the tax rate applied to taxable money income that is needed to service the debt, depends not on the absolute size of the debt but on its growth relative to the growth of money income. The debt may grow whereas the tax burden of the individual members of the community may decline and become less significant.

Domar's analysis can most easily be expressed symbolically. Let us define:

$p_t Y_t$ = money net national product
i = the rate of interest
D_t = the debt in money terms at the beginning of year t
$U_t = iD_t + p_t Y_t$, taxable money income in year t
γ = the tax rate as a percent of taxable income needed to service the debt
α = the proportion of annual money income borrowed

Clearly,
$$\gamma = \frac{iD_t}{U_t} = \frac{iD_t}{iD_t + p_t Y_t}$$

Dividing numerator and denominator by iD_t gives

$$\gamma = \frac{1}{1 + (1/i)(p_t Y_t / D_t)}$$

from which it can easily be seen that the tax rate, given a constant rate of interest, depends uniquely on the ratio of money income to the debt.

It is clear from this expression that if the debt grows while money income fails to grow at all, γ will approach 100 percent. As shown in the appendix to this chapter at the end of the book, γ will also approach 100 percent even if money income grows at some absolute amount each year while borrowing continues at a constant percentage of money income. But if money income grows at a constant percentage rate r, γ approaches the constant rate,

$$\frac{1}{1 + (1/i)(r/\alpha)}$$

[1] E. D. Domar, "The Burden of the Debt and the National Income," *American Economic Review*, 34:798–827, 1944.

In this, the most relevant case, the burden will rise as the interest rate rises and as the annual percentage borrowed rises. Should the rate of growth of money income rise, the burden would fall. Even if real income were to remain constant, an increase in the price level would reduce the burden of the debt, while hyperinflation would wipe out the public as well as all private debt. Future governments could default on the debt by resorting to the printing press as surely as if they had repudiated the debt by fiat.

Table 20-1   The "burden" of the total gross debt for the United States, selected years, 1929–1961

Year (1)	Total gross debt (billions) (2)	Total gross debt per capita (3)	Interest payments on the total gross debt (billions) (4)	Interest payments as a percentage of net national product (5)
1929	$ 16.9	$ 139	$0.7	0.7
1933	22.5	179	0.7	1.4
1936	33.8	264	0.7	0.9
1938	37.2	286	0.9	1.2
1942	72.4	541	1.3	0.9
1944	201.0	1,456	2.6	1.3
1945	258.7	1,849	3.6	1.8
1946	269.4	1,905	4.7	2.4
1949	252.8	1,695	5.3	2.2
1951	255.2	1,653	5.6	1.8
1953	266.1	1,667	6.5	1.9
1956	272.8	1,622	6.8	1.8
1958	276.3	1,588	7.6	1.9
1961	289.0	1,573	9.0	1.9

Sources: Columns 2 and 3: 1929–1944, U.S. Department of Commerce, *Historical Statistics of the United States, 1789–1945*, Series P132–133, p. 305, U.S. Government Printing Office, Washington, 1949; 1945–1961, U.S. Department of Commerce, *Statistical Abstract of the United States, 1959*, 83d ed., Table 500, p. 380, U.S. Government Printing Office, Washington, 1961. Column 4: 1929–1955, U.S. Department of Commerce: *Historical Statistics of the United States, 1789–1945*, Series P102, p. 299; 1945–1961, U.S. Department of Commerce, *Statistical Abstract of the United States, 1959*, 83d ed., Table 501, p. 381. Column 5: Column 4 as a percentage of net national product. See Fig. 1–5 for source of net national product.

In the United States the ratio of debt to income, and therefore the tax burden of the debt, has fallen from its 1946 all-time high. The relevant data are given in Table 20-1, where column 2 gives the total gross Federal debt; column 3 gives the debt in per capita terms; column 4 gives the interest payments on the debt; and column 5 gives the interest payments as a percentage of net national product. Although column 5 is not exactly comparable to Domar's γ, it is close enough to be suggestive. Observe that while the debt increased from $269.4 billion in 1946 to $289.0 billion in 1961, interest payments as a percentage of net national product fell from 2.4 to 1.9 percent.

20-4   The National Debt and Economic Stability

The problem of income stabilization is complicated by the presence of the national debt both because the debt contains some inherent destabilizing features and because the effective pursuit of anti-inflationary monetary policy may conflict with the attempts of the Treasury to manage the debt. During the inflationary era of the 1940s and early 1950s no subject occupied economists more intensively than the problem of debt management and monetary policy. Today the issues that were raised at that time are less pressing. There is, however, the possibility that the future will bring about a similar era and that we may then look back to our past experience with profit.

On balance, the debt probably has an inflationary impact in that it constitutes a stock of liquid wealth for its owners, and liquid asset holdings are positively correlated with consumption expenditures. One of the fears held by economists during the late 1940s was that the public might at a moment's notice attempt to convert its large stock of liquid assets into physical assets, thereby creating severe inflationary pressure. Without a large accumulation of debt, it is doubtful whether consumers would have been able to increase their spending by as much as they did at the start of the Korean War.

There may also be stabilizing benefits to be derived from the existence of the national debt. When prices and incomes shrink, the Pigou effect is strengthened by the existence of a large stock of government obligations. When the price level rises, it is possible that the reverse effect may take place. These effects may be reversed by price expectations that are likely, in an inflationary period, to lead to attempted conversion of liquid into physical assets, while the reverse can be expected to occur during a period of falling prices. Both of these destabilizing movements are facilitated by the existence of public debt.

One of the most unfortunate aspects of having to live with the national debt was that an inflationary bias became built into public policy. There was an ever-present temptation to lower interest rates below the natural rate in order to make debt management easier.[1] As we have suggested before, this can be accomplished by forcing the Federal Reserve System to peg the market rate of

---

[1] Recalling the discussion of Chapter 7, if a long-term bond issued for a par value of $1,000 pays 5 percent interest on the par value, a rise in the market rate of interest to 10 percent will reduce the market value of the bond to approximately $500. At the maturity date the Treasury must pay the par value on the old issue, and, if it refinances (i.e., issues new long-term bonds to replace the old ones), it must offer 10 percent per $1,000 if it is to sell the issue. The service charge therefore doubles from $50 too $100 per $1,000 borrowed.

interest by buying up such quantities of bonds as are necessary to maintain their prices. The effect of such an operation is inflationary and therefore serves the added purpose of reducing the real value of the government debt.

This last point is worthy of special emphasis because it was rarely mentioned during the days, prior to 1951, when Secretary of the Treasury Snyder proclaimed himself the champion of an "orderly" bond market and the defender of widows, orphans, educational institutions, and other conspicuous holders of the Federal debt. Whether widows and orphans are protected by pegging operations is open to doubt. At any one time there will be some natural rate of interest that equates the demand for goods and services with the full-employment supply. At full employment, any attempt to lower the market rate below the natural rate by monetary expansion will produce increases in the price level. The bondholder thus has two unpleasant alternatives: (1) policy makers may allow the market rate to rise to the natural rate, in which case bondholders take an immediate capital loss; (2) policy makers may peg the rate so that bondholders take their capital loss in the form of a reduction in the real value of their bonds caused by a rising price level. In practice, the latter alternative is likely to be chosen since it creates the illusion of easing the day-to-day problem of Treasury financing and because wealth holders are apt to be more conscious of a quick and sharp capital loss than of the long-term attrition that results from a rising price level. Although there is no net benefit for bondholders inherent in this process, except in the short run, the pegged-interest-rate gospel was preached with a high degree of success during the years following World War II. By 1952 about all we had to show for the policy was a badly inflated price level and the expectation of further price increases.

The pegging policy of the postwar years went considerably beyond such Federal Reserve bond purchases as were required to maintain stable interest rates. On several occasions the Federal Reserve lowered member bank reserve requirements. Such action, during an inflationary period, might have been taken as prima facie evidence of insanity had it not been for the pressing need to find a resting place for Federal debt. A reduction in reserve requirements makes it possible for banks to substitute part of the public debt in place of the required reserves otherwise held idle in their reserve accounts. While this policy of subsidizing commercial banks helped to place the debt, it also presented banks with "secondary reserves" that they could convert into other forms of earning assets by simply allowing their short-term government obligations to mature. A reduction in reserve requirements at a time of full employment is obviously inflationary and can have no justification in terms of economic stability.

What can be done to reduce the conflict of interest between credit control and Treasury financing?[1] Most of the suggestions that were made were in the

[1] R. V. Roosa, "Integrating Debt Management and Open Market Operations," *American Economic Review* (Supplement), 42:214–235, 1952, provides a comprehensive survey of the issues.

form of gimmicks designed either to isolate portions of the debt from market fluctuations or to lengthen the average maturity of the debt so as to reduce the number of refunding operations in which the Treasury would have to engage. Proposals of the former sort involved recommendations that the commercial banking system be forced to hold a certain portion of required reserves in the form of short-term government debt and that part of the debt be converted into nonmarketable bonds such as the familiar series E bond, which could only be sold back to the Treasury. The proposal to freeze part of the debt in the hands of the banks was criticized on the ground that it would not affect the marginal holdings that banks switch into alternative uses when the opportunity arises. However, if such a freeze had involved an addition to required reserves rather than a mere substitution of debt for required money reserves, the policy would clearly have had a deflationary impact and would have served to quarantine a portion of the debt.

The proposal to convert marketable debt into nonmarketable bonds of the series E variety appears to have some merit. But if interest rates were to rise significantly under the impact of Federal Reserve credit restraint, these bonds would be sold back to the Treasury, and a drain of cash from the Treasury would take place. The tight money policy would thus be thwarted, and the Treasury would lose funds at the very time when added borrowing would prove to be most expensive. It is, moreover, unlikely that large investors in government obligations could be persuaded to hold nonmarketable bonds without an extremely high yield inducement. This is not to say that some progress might not be made with nonmarketable debt. It is possible, for example, to program a redemption schedule that puts a high penalty on early redemption and makes it more and more attractive to hold the bonds as maturity is approached. The fact remains, however, that as long as the debt is marketable at the Treasury, a rise in interest rates will lead to redemption and a drain of Treasury cash at a time when the Treasury's borrowing prospects from the public are the poorest. The Treasury may then be driven to borrow from the Federal Reserve System and thereby to negate the System's attempts at credit restraint.

The second type of proposal called for a concerted attempt on the part of the Treasury to lengthen the maturity of the debt. This was recommended in the hope that the number of times the debt had to be refinanced would be reduced and that more time would be left between funding operations during which credit restraint might be applied. The ideal situation would be achieved if all the debt were funded into consols since this would remove the necessity, once and for all, of refinancing maturing debt. The obstacles in the way of this policy are considerable. There are legal limits to the interest the Treasury may pay, and this makes it very difficult to issue long-term debt since the yield on such instruments is typically higher than on short-term debt, particularly if the expectation for the future is one of rising interest rates induced by the expectation of a rising price level. A start may, however, be made. It is not necessary to refinance all debt into consols immediately. The Treasury may undertake a gradual lengthening of the maturity on all debt until the market is willing to accept nonmaturing debt.

Is there any value to the debt as an instrument for fostering stability?[1] The debt consists of obligations of varying maturities. Long-term debt presumably competes with other long-term uses of funds, whereas short-term debt competes with other short-term uses. Thus it is argued that during recession the debt should be funded into short-term debt, in the hope that the long-term funds thus released will be driven into capital formation. During an inflationary period, on the other hand, the debt should be lengthened so that holding long-term debt becomes an attractive alternative to capital formation.

[1] H. C. Wallich, "Debt Management as an Instrument of Economic Policy," *American Economic Review*, 36:292–310, 1946.

chapter 21

*"Cost-push" inflation, structural
unemployment, and contemporary
stabilization policy*

21-1 Introduction

In Chapter 17 we attempted an analysis of "classical" or "excess-demand"
inflation. The homely notion of "too much money chasing too few goods"
applies very well to that sort of inflation. Since the termination of the Korean
War there has been much talk of a new kind of inflation, an inflation that
can occur in the absence of excess demand. According to one hypothesis, such
inflation is caused by changes in the structure of demand. According to the
more popular view, such inflation is caused by the excessive power over wages
and prices possessed by unions and oligopolistic business enterprises.

These theories have so taken hold of the public, the press, and our political
representatives, that the goals of full employment and rapid economic growth
have been shunted aside. It seems appropriate to end our discussion of macro-
economics with a consideration of these as well as some of the other pressing
current economic problems that are causing us to fall considerably short of the
goals of the Employment Act.

21-2 "Bottleneck" and "Demand-shift" Inflation

A rise in the price level may come about without an increase in aggregate
demand if the structure of demand changes more rapidly than resources can be

shifted. In the American experience, the year 1946 is one of the best illustrations of bottleneck inflation. With the close of the war there developed a simultaneous reduction in government expenditures and an increase in consumer and investment spending. In addition, during the year real net national product fell below the 1945 level, although money net national product continued to increase. Thus, while real output declined, the price level increased.

The source of the difficulty is not hard to find. The reduction in armaments spending drastically reduced the level of output in many industries. At the same time, the increase in consumption and investment demand, along with the relaxation of wartime controls, caused prices of consumer and investment goods to rise sharply. Had it been possible to reconvert instantaneously from wartime to peacetime production, no fall in real income (assuming aggregate demand to be the same) or rise in the price level would have taken place. Typically, however, it takes time to reconvert plants and to re-allocate resources in general. Consequently, it is possible for changes in the structure of demand to affect the general price level even though there is no increase in over-all aggregate demand.

The bottleneck thesis has reappeared under the new heading of "demand-shift" as a description of the 1955–1956 price increases.[1] The basic idea was that a shift in demand would cause wages and prices to rise in the areas in which demand had increased. But since wages and prices are inflexible in the downward direction, the rising wages and prices in some sectors are not matched by corresponding reductions in wages and prices in the sectors in which demand has declined. As a consequence, the general level of prices rises despite the absence of an increase in aggregate demand.

Demand shift might explain an increase in the price level during a given period, but it is doubtful if it can explain a long-run inflationary trend. Steady rises in the price level without corresponding increases in the money supply would result in ever-higher unemployment rates. An essential ingredient is missing, an ingredient that we shall attempt to uncover during the course of our discussion of "cost-push" inflation.

21-3 "Cost-push" Inflation

One of the most overpowering notions from the point of view of its influence on contemporary economic thought and policy is the concept of "cost-push," "wage-push," or simply "cost" inflation. Crudely stated, unions push up wages, and business pushes up prices. Inflation, in this view, is the consequence not of excess demand but of monopoly power.

[1] C. L. Schultze, "Recent Inflation in the United States," Study Paper No. 1, *Study of Employment Growth and Price Levels*, Joint Economic Committee, U.S. Congress, September, 1959.

The cost-push thesis has gained a vast following during the last decade despite the fact that the arguments in support of the hypothesis are, in the main, fairly shoddy. It has been impossible to keep analysis separate from prejudice and politics. Some of the proponents of the thesis are simply confused; others, unfortunately, have ulterior motives. Having warned the reader that there is more to the issue than economic analysis, let us proceed with the cost-push issue as we see it.

An example of crude cost-push theory is the argument that oligopolistic industries are capable of inflicting inflation on the economy by raising prices whenever they please. The most casual acquaintance with elementary economic theory exposes this view as nonsense. We expect business firms to attempt to maximize profits. If they make an attempt to operate at a maximum profit level of price and output, and if they increase prices, it may be because they misjudge the market, because the degree of competition has become less intense, or because demand has increased. If they misjudge the market, it would have to be explained why so many firms continuously misjudge the market and why the corrective reactions are always toward price increase. Second, there is no evidence that the degree of concentration has increased during the last decade, and even if there were such evidence, one would have to look for the cause of inflation in industries other than the traditionally heavily concentrated ones.[1] The crude cost-push theorist, however, seems to believe that steel prices are all that matters. Finally, if demand has increased, we can hardly attribute the price increase to anything other than excess demand. Although we may be distressed to learn that prices have increased, and although we may regard oligopolistic pricing practices as offensive to the ideal of competition, we should be careful not to confuse cause and effect and to attribute inflation to "administered pricing."

Another crude view is the notion that there is virtually no limit to the extent to which strong unions can force management to grant higher wages. If we had said the same thing about business pricing practices, we would have known that we were talking nonsense. Anyone except a pure competitor can charge a price different from the one that maximizes profits without losing all of his sales. Even if demand curves are highly inelastic, we would be at a considerable loss to understand why business has waited all these years to discover the fact and has only since 1953 begun to raise prices to the levels at which they could have existed all along. In the case of the union wage-push argument, the fallacy is a bit more difficult to expose because it is difficult to know just what it is that unions are trying to maximize. In general, however, unions can be thought of as faced with the need to choose between the alternative of higher wages and less employment, or lower wages and more employment. There will, presum-

[1] G. J. Stigler, "Administered Prices and Oligopolistic Inflation," *The Journal of Business*, 35:1–13, 1962.

ably, be some combination of wages and employment that is optimal from the point of view of the union, and when that combination is achieved, the union may be thought of as being in equilibrium.[1]

Only if unions are completely indifferent to the level of employment can it be argued that unions will always push for higher wages. And even if higher wages can be achieved without driving the hiring firms into bankruptcy, the question of why wages were not at the higher levels in the first place still remains.

Part of the confusion that surrounds the cost-push argument is attributable to the fact that wage-price behavior in key heavy industries is such as to make it appear as though cost-push inflation were in progress. Wage increases are granted in "rounds," and price increases rarely take place except after wage increases. It therefore appears as if aggressive union tactics "force" business to raise prices.

In competitive markets increases in demand cause prices to rise immediately. This is not, however, true in oligopolistic industries. According to Galbraith[2] the reason for this is that a price increase will invite a union wage demand, and wage increases, once granted, tend to be irreversible. Firms would therefore prefer to charge prices below profit-maximizing levels during prosperous periods in order not to be burdened with excessively high wage bills during periods of slack demand.

However, once unions succeed in raising wages, the objection to price increases no longer holds. As a consequence, wage increases are likely to be followed almost immediately by increases in prices. The naïve observer of the scene would therefore be tempted to infer that union wickedness has "forced" business to raise prices. Note, however, that none of this would have happened had demand not increased initially.

Unhappily, price increases that follow on the heels of wage increases in key industries cause the inflation problem to be dramatized in the public mind. The finger, moreover, tends to be pointed at unions as the instigators of inflation. Defenders of unions have not been very sophisticated in their response. Instead of attempting to trace inflation to its source, they have often met the "wage-push" argument with the counter charge that the wage increase merely serves as an excuse for business to raise prices and to place the blame for the increase on unions. Although ostensibly opposed to inflation, such persons seem to take particular satisfaction in pointing out that prices have not infrequently risen proportionately more than the wage increases they followed. In management's defense it should be pointed out that in the face of continual harassment by congressional committees and administration gadflys, heavy key industries

---

[1] For a discussion of "union indifference maps" see W. J. Fellner, *Competition Among the Few*, Chap. 10, Alfred A. Knopf, Inc., New York, 1949.

[2] J. K. Galbraith, "Market Structures and Stabilization Policy," *Review of Economics and Statistics*, 39:124–133, 1957.

can hardly ever "get away with" a price increase without the excuse of higher wage-induced costs. The steel crisis of the spring of 1962 would appear to confirm the point.

Having said a word in defense of management, we ought also to say a word in defense of labor. First of all, it is not really clear that business cannot raise prices in the absence of wage increases. Most large firms produce a wide variety of products. It would not be difficult to raise prices on one or a few items at a time. Such increases would be barely noticeable, whereas an announcement of an across-the-board increase, implemented by means of a nationally televised press conference, cannot help but produce a public outcry. The lack of subtlety in these matters on the part of some businessmen suggests that they are not at all averse to engaging in crude attempts to saddle unions with responsibility for inflation. The unions have little defense against the charge: They cannot very well admit that wage pressures are responsible for inflation. On the other hand, they cannot admit that price increases are due to excess demand because if that were the case, they could not call for expansionary monetary-fiscal policies to alleviate unemployment.

Returning to the economic implications of wage-price behavior in oligopolistic industries, observe that this kind of behavior implies that management would have been less reluctant to charge profit-maximizing prices in the absence of unions. And because wage increases are granted in rounds, it would appear that during inflationary periods the effect of unions is to keep the wage level below what it would have been in their absence. Indeed, there is evidence to suggest that this is just exactly what happens.[1] Unionized workers do lose ground relative to nonunionized workers during inflationary periods.

In view of these circumstances it is difficult to see how one can seriously argue that the kind of wage-price behavior that characterizes oligopolistic industries constitutes evidence of "wage-push" or "administered" inflation. It seems more reasonable to accept the view that union wage demands are based on what management can "afford" to pay; and what management can afford to pay is to no small extent dependent upon the level of demand.

The foregoing discussion leads us to a version of the argument that gets closer to the possible element of truth in the cost-push thesis. A shift in union preference in favor of higher real wages at the expense of some employment, or an increase in the degree of unionization, causes wages in the unionized sector to be pushed up. Employment therefore shrinks in the unionized sector, and the workers that are released from employment in the unionized sector then spill over into nonunionized sectors of the economy. But since wages are downwardly inflexible in all sectors, the net effect is to increase unemployment, while at the same time the price level rises because of the wage-price boost in the union sector.

[1] See the illuminating paper by Albert Rees, "Do Unions Cause Inflation?" *The Journal of Law and Economics*, 2:84–94, 1959, for a survey of the evidence.

There are several questions pertinent to the argument:

1. Can the labor transfer process implied by the thesis go on indefinitely? If the argument is true, we should expect employment in the unionized sectors to shrink and wage differentials to increase continuously. Studies of wage differentials between unionized and nonunionized sectors of the economy fail to support this version of the cost-push argument.[1]

2. Do wage increases in excess of productivity gains necessarily imply unemployment? If man-hour output is rising, wages will be increasing in all sectors. Therefore, the added supply of workers to the competitive sector may not imply that it is necessary for wages to decline absolutely if unemployment is to be avoided; it may mean, rather, that wages in the competitive sector will rise less rapidly than would otherwise have been the case. Insofar as the cause of unemployment is downward rigidity of wage levels, there is little reason to believe, except in the short run, that unemployment would have to develop from union-induced relative wage differentials. It is important to bear this point in mind because the coincidence of rising wages and prices with the development of unemployment has often been taken as evidence of cost-push inflation. As we shall show subsequently, such an inference is wholly unwarranted.

The foregoing argument applies to the long run. However, in the short run it seems clear that a rise in wages caused by a shift in union preference or an increase in union strength causes unemployment. Wage-price increases reduce the real value of the money supply, thereby raising the rate of interest and reducing the level of investment.[2] An increase in the price level makes the domestic market a better place in which to sell but a poorer one in which to buy. As prices and money income rise, the real value of tax collections increases, real disposable income declines, and consumption declines. As the price level rises, the real value of liquid assets declines, and the Pigou effect in reverse may be set in motion. All these circumstances mean that if unemployment is to be avoided, higher wages and prices must be "financed," i.e., offset by a proportional increase in the money supply.

3. If unions undergo a change in preference and if they do succeed in bargaining for higher wages, they will have achieved their goal, and there will be no reason to suppose that wages will continue to be pushed up. Thus we are confronted with the odd paradox that this cost-push argument is essentially a once-for-all (static, if you will) argument that cannot possibly explain a dynamic process of inflation. A shift in union preference can explain a once-over wage-price increase, but it cannot explain why the price level continues to creep upward over time. How, then, can this be a theory of inflation?

[1] Rees, *ibid.*, pp. 87–88.

[2] Unless, of course, the demand for money is infinitely elastic with respect to the rate of interest. Recall, however, that our analysis of Chapter 13 has shown this to be an untenable assumption when the economy is at, or near, full employment.

Because increases in wages and prices instigated by union wage pressures cause unemployment in the short run, some cost-push theorists argue that although the unemployment might eliminate itself over a longer period, the corrective forces are not allowed to operate because of the intervention of politically motivated, expansionary monetary-fiscal policies. Indeed, the cost-push theorist views the monetary authority as caught in a hopeless dilemma. Either the authority can maintain a lid on prices and wages by maintaining a tight rein on the money supply, or it can "legalize" the wage-price increase by expanding the money supply, thereby inviting further wage-price pushes.

It is the possibility of intervention by the monetary authority that makes the essentially static theory of price level increases due to union preference shifts a dynamic one. If the monetary authority intervenes to eliminate wage-push-induced unemployment, the general price increase will partly or wholly negate the initial attempt of the unions to raise the real wages of their members. Given the original preference shift, the unions now find that their efforts to increase real wages have been thwarted, and they are therefore tempted to try again. Consequently, a single once-for-all change in preference can produce steady wage pressure, provided the price level rises in such a way as to keep the desired level of real wages from being attained and provided the monetary authority attempts to maintain full employment. The action of the monetary authority therefore is what allows cost-push to become a dynamic inflation-generating process. Unions may wish to gain a real wage increase at the cost of some unemployment. But if the monetary authority refuses to permit unemployment to develop, and if price increases keep real wages from rising, unions never reach their subjective equilibrium levels of real wages and employment.

If inflation is made possible only because of the action of the monetary authority, some economists feel it pertinent to ask whether this should not be regarded as old-fashioned demand pull. The important question, however, is whether the monetary authority really behaves in the manner prescribed by the theory. Although there is always argument about the consequences of particular monetary policies, it does not seem to us that the authority has behaved in a way that would lend credence to the theory. The present Chairman of the Board of Governors of the Federal Reserve System continues to make it clear that he does not feel impelled to increase the money supply the moment wages increase in some major industry. And the consistently tight monetary policy under which we have been laboring for several years indicates that the System does not operate in a manner that would allow cost-push to be generated.

The behavior of the monetary authority illustrates why the cost-push message is so bleak. The thesis implies that the expansionary effects of increases in the money supply will not raise output and employment but rather will be frittered away in the form of wage-price increases. Unhappily, the Federal Reserve, on the basis of virtually no evidence, has accepted the thesis. Meanwhile, the economy struggles along at considerably less than full employment and with substantial excess capacity. Abstracting from cyclical changes, the trend percentage of the labor force that is unemployed has been rising ever since 1956, and even this measure could well be an understatement in view of the fact that discouraged workers appear to have been leaving the labor force.

21-4 The Measurement of Price Level Changes[1]

When the cost-push theorist is confronted with the various arguments that show his position to be a flimsy one, he plays his remaining trump card. He will point out that during much of the 1950s the economy operated with substantial levels of unemployment and excess capacity despite the fact that the consumer price index (CPI) crept up steadily, if slowly. He is especially likely to call our attention to the recession of 1958 during which unemployment rose to a postwar high while the consumer price index continued to advance.

The plain fact of the matter, however, is that constancy of the CPI has virtually no relationship to any meaningful concept of price stability in a growing economy. Indeed, constancy of the CPI really means that the general price level is falling. The counterpart of a constant price level under conditions in which technical progress is absent is a rise in the price level under conditions of growth. And this does *not* mean that the purchasing power of the dollar is being eroded. These are strong statements; let us try to back them up.

Part of our confusion on the score of price stability arises from our preoccupation with the relationship between wages, prices, and productivity. The average cost of production, AC, can be defined as

$$AC = \frac{w}{AP}$$

where w is the money wage rate and AP is the average product of labor, i.e., the number of units of output produced by the average worker. If the average worker produces 5 units of output per day, and if his daily wage is $10.00, the average cost of production per unit of output is $2.00.[2] If the average product

---

[1] The discussion of this section has benefited greatly from R. Ruggles, "Measuring the Cost of Quality," *Challenge*, 10:6–9, 1961; and the previously cited paper by Rees, "Do Unions Cause Inflation?" as well as from lectures by Rees and Zvi Griliches which one of the authors was privileged to attend at the University of Chicago.

[2] As any text on price theory makes clear, the ratio of factor price to average product must be the same for all factors if the firm is minimizing cost. In other words,

$$AC = \frac{P_a}{AP_a} = \frac{P_b}{AP_b} = \cdots = \frac{P_n}{AP_n}$$

where the subscripts refer to factors $a,b, \ldots, n$, respectively. If these ratios are not equal, average costs could be reduced by substituting one factor in place of another until equality is reached.

of labor increases by 3 percent and if money wages also rise by 3 percent, the ratio w/AP will remain unchanged. Consequently, average costs do not rise, and there is therefore no reason why prices should change unless there is a shift in the demand schedule that confronts the firm.

It is reasoning of this sort that lies behind the notion that "noninflationary" wage increases are increases that are equal to the rate of productivity growth.[1] It is also reasoning of this sort that leads us into confusion on the issue of whether price indexes are appropriate measures of price stability.

Wages can increase in proportion to productivity without raising costs. But what about cases in which the cost of the input is identical to the price paid for the output? Assuming constant prices elsewhere, there can be no such thing as a noninflationary increase in the income of a doctor. Although their productivity may have increased greatly, any increase in the compensation of such professional persons shows up as an increase in the *CPI*.

The major increases in the *CPI* that have taken place during the last ten years are due to the kinds of items that were mentioned above. The cost of medical care, especially, has risen rapidly. But is the increase in these costs pure inflation, or have there been productivity increases? If there have been such increases, how are the providers of this improved service to be compensated except by an increase in price? If we consider medical expenses, not in terms of the cost of an hour of medical consultation, but in terms of the benefit that can be derived from the consultation, it is no longer quite so clear whether we are really paying more for the consultation. Similarly, it is not clear whether we are paying more for an hour's worth of classroom instruction or for an hour spent in the dentist's chair. Only if there had been no productivity increase would it have been legitimate to conclude that the increase in the nominal cost of these services implies inflation.

In general, it is true that the *CPI* will rise if wage increases are in excess of the rate of growth of productivity. But there is a logical fallacy in reasoning from this circumstance that any rise in the *CPI* implies an increase in compensation in excess of productivity gain, and therefore inflation. Doctors, teachers, lawyers, and other providers of services not unreasonably expect to be compensated for improvement in the quality of the service they perform. If we rule out the fact that such compensation can accrue indirectly through price declines elsewhere in the economy, the compensation must take the form of higher nominal returns for services. Such increases, however, quite unreasonably raise the *CPI*, whereas wage increases that are proportional to the rate of growth of productivity do not. Productivity increases, in combination with price stability,

---

[1] In *The Economic Report of the President* for 1962 the Council of Economic Advisors has set forth "guideposts for non-inflationary wage and price behavior." The Council states (p. 189) "The general guide for non-inflationary wage behavior is that the rate of increase in wage rates (including fringe benefits) in each industry be equal to the trend rate of overall productivity increase."

when that concept is used in a meaningful sense, therefore imply increases in the *CPI*. By the same token, stability of the *CPI* implies deflation.

Another way in which productivity gains accrue to the economy is in the form of improvements in the quality of the physical commodities that we buy. In a highly significant study Griliches[1] has computed the effect on automobile prices of different specifications. The effects of changes in horsepower, weight, and length were evaluated for the "low priced three."[2] Over the period 1954–1960 list prices of cars rose steadily. The *CPI*'s "new automobile component" index rose from a value of 129.7 in 1954 to a value of 144.3 in 1960. However, Griliches' method of computing the index yields a fall from 128.9 to 111.3. Consequently, if quality changes are taken into account, it is by no means clear whether a rise in the price of products necessarily means that price inflation is under way.

Submit yourself to the acid test: Assume that you are given a choice of buying only the goods and services that were available in 1953 at 1953 prices or the goods and services that were available in 1962 at 1962 prices, and do not forget such items as the Salk vaccine that were not available in 1953. Only if you genuinely prefer the 1953 bundle of goods and services can you assert in any significant way that inflation has characterized the years since the Korean War. And even if you do prefer the 1953 bundle of goods and services, you will have to admit that the price increases that have taken place since that time do not represent nearly as much "pure inflation" as is commonly supposed.

If we are concerned about the general level of prices rather than just consumer prices, we might properly be concerned with the *GNP* deflator rather than the *CPI*. But the *GNP* deflator suffers from the same drawbacks as the *CPI* and some additional ones as well. To cite one problem, the *GNP* deflator includes government, and the price of government services is measured at cost. Thus anytime government employees receive a pay increase, the *GNP* deflator records this as a price increase. This means that the *GNP* deflator is based on the assumption that there are never any productivity increases in the provision of public services. Although it is common to make jokes to the effect that this is not an unwarranted assumption, it is nevertheless a fact that even such a relic as the postal service has done much to streamline its operations.

The inadequacy of our price indexes is very serious business. The *CPI* is widely regarded by economists, businessmen, and public officials as *the* measure of the price level. If it is true that we have erroneously been led to believe that the price level has risen during periods characterized by high levels of unemployment (assuming without justification that this is evidence of cost-push

[1] Z. Griliches, "Hedonic Price Indexes for Automobiles: An Econometric Analysis of Quality Change," National Bureau of Economic Research, *The Price Statistics of the Federal Government*, No. 73, 1961.

[2] Until 1961, when compacts were introduced into the *CPI*, the low-priced three—Chevrolet, Ford, and Plymouth—were the cars included in the *CPI*.

inflation), and if, because of the upward creep in the *CPI*, we have become so fearful of inflation that we have failed to take measures to reduce unemployment and excess capacity, then we have been paying an intolerably high price in the form of unemployment and lost production as the consequence of a faulty statistical construction. Ruggles estimates that "we waste through underutilization an amount equal in size to two or three times what we now spend on defense, or 20 to 25 times as much as we now are giving in foreign aid." He suggests, moreover, that "these wasted resources could rebuild our cities and automate our factories within a few short years; they could raise our rate of growth to equal or surpass that of any other nation."[1]

We have been suggesting that price stability means one thing in a context of stagnation and no technical progress and something quite different in an atmosphere of growth and productivity increase. Unhappily, many people have confused the two very badly, a confusion that is prodigiously costly. Perhaps it will not be possible to revise our price indexes along the lines suggested by Griliches; but we ought at least to be aware that constancy of the *CPI* implies, if anything, a deflationary trend.

21-5   Structural Unemployment

Contemporary stabilization policy is complicated not only by widespread acceptance of the cost-push thesis and by the balance-of-payments problems, but also by a new ogre known as "structural" or "hard-core" unemployment. Automation, it is argued, has caused the skills of workers to become obsolete so rapidly that an ever-increasing number are unemployable without substantial retraining and relocation. Although technical progress is always causing existing skills to become obsolete, many people have come to believe that the process has been accelerating in recent years. The implication of this belief is that at fairly high levels of employment, additional employment is becoming steadily less elastic with respect to increases in aggregate demand.

A useful tool for the analysis of this problem is the "Phillips curve" shown in Figure 21-1.[2] On the vertical axis the percentage change in wage rates is recorded, while the percent of the labor force that is unemployed is measured on the horizontal axis. The Phillips curve slopes downward and to the right. Periods of substantial relative unemployment are associated with loose labor markets and small increases in wage rates. Periods of low relative unemployment, on the other hand, are periods of tightness in the labor market and therefore of rapidly rising wage rates.

The structural unemployment thesis implies that the Phillips curve has been shifting to the right. Consequently, the percentage wage increase associated

---

[1] Ruggles, *op. cit.*, p. 9.
[2] A. W. Phillips, "The Relation between Unemployment and the Rate of Change of Money Wage Rates in the United Kingdom, 1862–1957," *Economica*, 25:283–299, 1958.

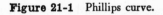

Figure 21-1 Phillips curve.

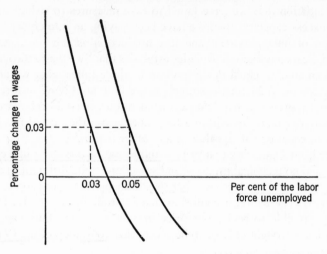

with a particular relative level of unemployment is growing larger. In Figure
21-1, for example, the shift to the right of the Phillips curve means that a 3
percent increase in wage rates is associated with 5 percent of the labor force
unemployed as opposed to 3 percent prior to the shift. Therefore the implication of the structural unemployment thesis is that in order to obtain an increase
in the level of employment, society must pay more in the form of wage and
price increases than it has paid in the past.

The structural unemployment thesis suggests that the unemployment problem is less one of inadequate demand than one of providing means for retraining
and relocating workers. Policies of the latter kind are not only worthwhile but
are desperately needed in the United States. But it is also possible that significant
strides can be made with monetary-fiscal policy and that such policies can be
pursued with little risk of inflation (although not without risk of a rise in the
CPI).

To date we know of no evidence that supports the structural unemployment
thesis. In fact, the only careful study of the issue that has been made[1] fails to
reveal any change in the proportion of the labor force that may be said to be
structurally unemployed. Moreover, a straight line of best fit for interwar data
compared with a similar computation for the postwar years reveals no difference in the two Phillips curves thus obtained.

To the West Virginia coal miner and other skilled workers who have been

[1] J. W. Knowles and E. D. Kalacheck, "Higher Unemployment Rates, 1957–1960:
Structural Transformation or Inadequate Demand," *Subcommittee on Economic Statistics of
the Joint Economic Committee*, U.S. Congress, 1961.

permanently displaced by machinery, it may seem cruelly unrealistic to suggest that the structural unemployment thesis is erroneous. But the question here is not whether structural unemployment exists, which it undoubtedly does, but whether or not the problem has accelerated in magnitude. We may not be able to re-employ the coal miner by expanding demand; but we will certainly not be able to re-employ him without demand expansion. To quote Ruggles again, "Those wishing to restrict demand have labeled the unemployment 'structural,' and thereby have succeeded in removing it from their own conscience. This rationalization may satisfy them, but it is not much help for the unemployed— since it is obvious that the only cure for unemployment, whether structural or any other kind, is more jobs, and you don't get more jobs by restricting demand, no matter how much retraining you do."[1]

21-6 Conclusion

The evidence in support of the cost-push hypothesis is unconvincing. Of the versions of the theory we have examined, some are pure nonsense; sometimes cost-push is confused with excess-demand because of oligopolistic pricing practices; and the "dilemma model" simply has not been a description of reality. As the result of our examination of the consumer price index, we found that the simultaneous appearance of unemployment and a rising *CPI* did not constitute evidence of cost-push inflation. Although it is true that expansion of demand and production may cause the *CPI* to rise, this does not imply that demand expansion is inflationary. Anytime we increase aggregate output per man-hour, the *CPI* is going to rise. But we now know that this has nothing to do with inflation when the term inflation is used in a meaningful way.

The structural unemployment thesis, which serves as a second excuse for ignoring the unemployment problem, appears also to be unsupported on the basis of acceptable evidence. However, even if there is some validity to the thesis, which implies that demand expansion will not cure the employment problem, the problem still cannot be solved without such demand expansion. There is absolutely no point in retraining and uprooting people if there are no job prospects for them anywhere. Similarly, there is no sense in wringing our hands over the "waste" that results from having a surplus of farmers as long as we do not provide adequate opportunities for farm people in the cities.

The unholy trinity of cost-push inflation, structural unemployment, and the balance-of-payments crisis has so mesmerized our political representatives that we are in the continuing throes of a complete policy paralysis. Any proposal to expand demand is denounced as inflationary and as "fiscal irresponsibility." We talk about growth and are worried because the Soviets are moving ahead at a faster pace, yet do nothing either to utilize the resources that are available

[1] Ruggles, *op. cit.*, p. 9.

to us or to invest in the future, preferring rather to allow our slums to continue to fester and our children to continue to be badly educated. The need to balance the budget and to "maintain the integrity of the dollar" remains, for some inexplicable reason, more important than the welfare of our citizens. It all goes to show that there is as yet much to be learned and to be done in connection with "the economic problem."

Mathematical appendices

These appendices are presented for the benefit of the reader who has a mathematical bent and who may, therefore, find it both interesting and useful to have the verbal and diagrammatic exposition of the text supplemented by mathematical methods. We wish to emphasize that nothing is added by these appendices; the reader who is unfamiliar with the calculus and with the few other mathematical methods that are employed should not feel that he is missing anything. The contents of these appendices simply represent mathematical verification of what was said in the text.

Appendix to Chapter 10

The policy results derived in Chapter 10 may all be derived mathematically. However, let us confine ourselves to the simple model of Section 10-2. Ignoring taxes, but including government expenditures, product market equilibrium is given by

$$I(i) + G = Y - C(Y)$$

which for convenience can be rewritten as

$$G = Y - C(Y) - I(i) \tag{10-1}$$

Monetary equilibrium is given by

$$m = kY + L(i) \tag{10-2}$$

The effect of an increase in the money supply can be observed by differentiating the equations totally with respect to m. This yields

$$0 = (1 - C_y)\left(\frac{dY}{dm}\right) - I_i\left(\frac{di}{dm}\right) \tag{10-3}$$

$$1 = k\left(\frac{dY}{dm}\right) + L_i\left(\frac{di}{dm}\right) \tag{10-4}$$

where C_y is the partial derivative of consumption with respect to income (the marginal propensity to consume); I_i is the partial derivative of investment with respect to the interest rate (the reciprocal of the slope of the investment demand schedule); and L_i is the partial derivative of the speculative demand for money with respect to the interest rate (the reciprocal of the slope of the speculative demand function). Evidently

$$\frac{dY}{dm} = \frac{I_i}{L_i(1 - C_y) + kI_i}$$

and

$$\frac{di}{dm} = \frac{(1 - C_y)}{L_i(1 - C_y) + kI_i}$$

In the Keynesian case, L_i is infinite, so that

$$\frac{dY}{dm} = 0$$

and

$$\frac{di}{dm} = 0$$

In the classical case $L_i = 0$, so that

$$\frac{dY}{dm} = \frac{1}{k}$$

and

$$\frac{di}{dm} = \frac{1 - C_y}{kI_i}$$

The change in the interest therefore depends on the slope of the savings function, the transactions demand for money function, and the investment demand schedule.

The effect of an increase in government expenditures can be observed by differentiating Eqs. (10-1) and (10-2) totally with respect to G. This gives,

$$1 = (1 - C_y)\left(\frac{dY}{dG}\right) - I_i\left(\frac{di}{dG}\right) \tag{10-5}$$

$$0 = k\left(\frac{dY}{dG}\right) + L_i\left(\frac{di}{dG}\right) \tag{10-6}$$

so that
$$\frac{dY}{dG} = \frac{L_i}{L_i(1 - C_y) + kI_i}$$

and
$$\frac{di}{dG} = \frac{-k}{L_i(1 - C_y) + kI_i}$$

In the Keynesian case L_i is infinite so that

$$\frac{dY}{dG} = \frac{L_i}{L_i(1 - C_y) + kI_i} = \frac{1}{(1 - C_y) + \dfrac{kI_i}{L_i}} = \frac{1}{(1 - C_y)}$$

i.e., the ratio of the change in income to the change in G equals one divided by the marginal propensity to save. Again, since L_i is infinite,

$$\frac{di}{dG} = 0$$

In the classical case $L_i = 0$, so that

$$\frac{dY}{dG} = 0$$

and
$$\frac{di}{dG} = \frac{-1}{I_i}$$

which implies that the change in the interest rate depends uniquely on the slope of the investment demand schedule. As we saw before, the rate of interest must rise by enough to just choke off investment in an amount equal to the change in government expenditures. The amount of the rise in the interest rate needed to reduce investment by exactly this amount must obviously depend uniquely upon the slope of the investment demand schedule.

Appendix to Chapter 11

In this appendix we attempt to analyze the effect of a cut in money wage rates on the level of employment. Including government expenditures, but excluding taxes, the model of Chapter 11 can be written

$$G = Y - C(Y) - I(i) \tag{11-1}$$

$$\frac{M}{p} = kY + L(i) \tag{11-2}$$

$$Y = X(N,K^*) \tag{11-3}$$

$$\frac{w_0}{p} = X_n \tag{11-4}$$

To simplify matters, write Eq. (11-3) as $Y = X(N)$ and substitute Eqs.

(11-3) and (11-4) in Eqs. (11-1) and (11-2). This gives

$$G = X(N) - C[X(N)] - I(i) \tag{11-5}$$

$$\frac{MX_n}{w_0} = kX(N) + L(i) \tag{11-6}$$

To observe the effect of a money wage cut, we differentiate the last two equations with respect to w_0. This gives

$$0 = (X_n - C_y X_n)\left(\frac{dN}{dw_0}\right) - I_i\left(\frac{di}{dw_0}\right) \tag{11-7}$$

$$\frac{-MX_n}{w_0{}^2} = \left(kX_n - \frac{M}{w_0}X_{nn}\right)\left(\frac{dN}{dw_0}\right) + L_i\left(\frac{di}{dw_0}\right) \tag{11-8}$$

from which it follows that

$$\frac{dN}{dw_0} = \frac{-(1/w_0{}^2)(MI_iX_n)}{X_n(1 - C_y)L_i + I_i\left(kX_n - \dfrac{M}{w_0}X_{nn}\right)} \tag{11-9}$$

and

$$\frac{di}{dw_0} = \frac{-(1/w_0{}^2)MX_n{}^2(1 - C_y)}{X_n(1 - C_y)L_i + I_i\left(kX_n - \dfrac{M}{w_0}X_{nn}\right)} \tag{11-10}$$

The Keynesian case is the simplest. Here L_i is infinite so that

$$\frac{di}{dw_0} = 0$$

and

$$\frac{dN}{dw_0} = 0$$

Notice also that an infinitely inelastic investment demand schedule, i.e., $I_i = 0$, will make

$$\frac{dN}{dw_0} = 0$$

and

$$\frac{di}{dw_0} = \frac{-MX_n}{L_i w_0{}^2} \tag{11-11}$$

By writing Eq. (11-4) as

$$p = \frac{w_0}{X_n}$$

and differentiating with respect to w_0, we have

$$\frac{dp}{dw_0} = \frac{X_n - w_0 X_{nn}(dN/dw_0)}{X_n{}^2} \tag{11-12}$$

In the Keynesian case, $dN/dw_0 = 0$, so that

$$\frac{dp}{dw_0} = \frac{1}{X_n} = \frac{p}{w_0}$$

which means that the price level falls in proportion to the wage cut so that no change in real wages materializes.

The classical case is more complicated. Here $L_i = 0$ so that

$$\frac{dN}{dw_0} = \frac{-MX_n}{w_0{}^2[kX_n - (M/w_0)X_{nn}]} < 0 \qquad (11\text{-}13)$$

and

$$\frac{di}{dw_0} = \frac{-M(X_n)^2(1 - C_y)}{w_0{}^2 I_i[kX_n - (M/w_0)X_{nn}]} > 0 \qquad (11\text{-}14)$$

An understanding of this can be obtained by noting that Eq. (11-14) may be substituted in Eq. (11-13). This yields

$$\frac{dN}{dw_0} = \frac{I_i}{X_n(1 - C_y)}\left(\frac{di}{dw_0}\right) < 0 \qquad (11\text{-}15)$$

Notice that $I_i/(1 - C_y)$ is the simple multiplier that translates a change in investment into a change in income. Multiplying the denominator by the marginal product of labor converts this into an employment multiplier. Notice also that no change in employment can take place unless the wage cut stimulates an investment expenditure increase via a change in the rate of interest. Observe finally that since $X_{nn} < 0$, the denominator of Eq. (11-13) is necessarily positive so that $dN/dw_0 < 0$; since $I_i < 0$, the denominator of Eq. (11-14) is negative so that $di/dw_0 > 0$.

Referring back to Eq. (11-12) and rewriting the expression as

$$\frac{dp}{dw_0} = \frac{p}{w_0} - \frac{w_0 X_{nn}}{X_n{}^2}\left(\frac{dN}{dw_0}\right)$$

we note that, since $dN/dw_0 < 0$,

$$\frac{dp}{dw_0} < \frac{w_0}{p}$$

which means that the real wage will change in the same direction as the money wage.

Appendix to Chapter 13

1. The neutral money case

The model of Section 13-3 can be represented by the equations

$$I(i) = Y^* - C(Y^*) \qquad (13\text{-}1)$$

$$\frac{M}{p} = L(i,Y^*) \qquad (13\text{-}2)$$

When we differentiate the equations with respect to M, we obtain

$$I_i\left(\frac{di}{dM}\right) = 0 \tag{13-3}$$

$$\frac{1}{p} - \left(\frac{M}{p^2}\right)\left(\frac{dp}{dM}\right) = L_i\left(\frac{di}{dM}\right) \tag{13-4}$$

From Eq. (13-3) it is apparent that the interest rate does not change. Consequently, Eq. (13-4) becomes

$$\frac{1}{p} = \left(\frac{M}{p^2}\right)\left(\frac{dp}{dM}\right)$$

or

$$\frac{dp}{p} = \frac{dM}{M}$$

The percentage change in the price level is therefore equal to the percentage change in the money supply, and the rate of interest is unchanged.

2. Consumption depends on the level of wealth

When consumption becomes a function of the real value of privately held wealth, we have

$$I(i) = Y^* - C(Y^*, W) \tag{13-5}$$

$$\frac{M}{p} = L(i, Y^*) \tag{13-2}$$

$$W = \frac{aY^*}{i} + \frac{M}{p} \tag{13-6}$$

Let us assume first that the money supply is increased by gold production or that money is simply dropped out of airplanes. We assume also that this miracle somehow comes to pass without increasing the level of disposable income. Differentiating the three equations with respect to M gives the set of simultaneous linear equations

$$0 = I_i\left(\frac{di}{dM}\right) + C_w\left(\frac{dW}{dM}\right) + 0 \tag{13-7}$$

$$\frac{1}{p} = L_i\left(\frac{di}{dM}\right) + 0 + \left(\frac{M}{p^2}\right)\left(\frac{dp}{dM}\right) \tag{13-8}$$

$$\frac{1}{p} = \left(\frac{aY^*}{i^2}\right)\left(\frac{di}{dM}\right) + \left(\frac{dW}{dM}\right) + \left(\frac{M}{p^2}\right)\left(\frac{dp}{dM}\right) \tag{13-9}$$

When we use these equations to solve for a change in the rate of interest we obtain

$$\left(\frac{di}{dM}\right)\Delta = \begin{vmatrix} 0 & C_w & 0 \\ 1/p & 0 & M/p^2 \\ 1/p & 1 & M/p^2 \end{vmatrix} = 0 \tag{13-10}$$

where

$$\Delta = \left(\frac{M}{p^2}\right)\left(\frac{C_w \mathbf{a} Y^*}{i^2} - I_i - C_w L_i\right) \tag{13-11}$$

Notice first of all that since I_i and L_i are both negative while C_w is positive, Δ must be positive. Second, when we evaluate the determinant in Eq. (13-10) we find that it has a value of zero. Consequently, if $di/dM = 0$, it follows immediately from Eq. (13-8) that

$$\frac{1}{p} = \left(\frac{M}{p^2}\right)\left(\frac{dp}{dM}\right)$$

so that

$$\frac{dp}{p} = \left(\frac{dM}{M}\right)$$

and from Eq. (13-9) that $dW/dM = 0$.

Apparently, then, an increase in the money supply that is brought about in the way specified above yields the classical conclusions. The rate of interest does not change; the price level rises in proportion to the increase in the money supply; and the level of wealth remains constant.

The foregoing analysis suggests that the results obtained by Metzler are independent of the amount of money that is pumped into the system. They depend, rather, upon changes in the value of privately held securities. Consequently, we may ignore the money supply and see what happens when the quantity of securities held by the public declines. The constant $\mathbf{a}$ has been assumed to be the proportion of Y^* that is in the form of corporate profits. An open-market operation that transfers private security holdings to the monetary authority will reduce the proportion of total profits accruing to private individuals. Consequently, the effect of the open-market operation can be analyzed by examining the consequences of a change in $\mathbf{a}$.

Differentiating Eqs. (13-5), (13-2), and (13-6) with respect to $\mathbf{a}$ yields the set of simultaneous linear equations

$$0 = I_i\left(\frac{di}{d\mathbf{a}}\right) + C_w\left(\frac{dW}{d\mathbf{a}}\right) + 0$$

$$0 = L_i\left(\frac{di}{d\mathbf{a}}\right) + 0 + \left(\frac{M}{p^2}\right)\left(\frac{dp}{d\mathbf{a}}\right)$$

$$\frac{Y^*}{i} = \left(\frac{\mathbf{a} Y^*}{i^2}\right)\left(\frac{di}{d\mathbf{a}}\right) + \left(\frac{dW}{d\mathbf{a}}\right) + \left(\frac{M}{p^2}\right)\left(\frac{dp}{d\mathbf{a}}\right)$$

In this case,

$$\frac{di}{d\mathbf{a}} = \frac{(M/p^2)C_w(Y^*/i)}{\Delta} \tag{13-12}$$

where Δ has exactly the same value as before. Since we know that $\Delta > 0$, and since the denominator of the above expression is positive, $di/d\mathbf{a}$ must be positive. A fall in $\mathbf{a}$ therefore causes the rate of interest to fall.

Similarly,

$$\frac{dW}{d\mathbf{a}} = \frac{-(M/p^2)I_i(Y^*/i)}{\Delta} \tag{13-13}$$

Since $I_i < 0$, $dW/d\mathbf{a}$ is positive, and this means that a fall in $\mathbf{a}$ reduces the value of privately held wealth.

Finally,

$$\frac{dp}{d\mathbf{a}} = \frac{C_w L_i(Y^*/i)}{\Delta} \tag{13-14}$$

Since $C_w > 0$ and $L_i < 0$, $dp/d\mathbf{a} < 0$, which means that the price level rises as $\mathbf{a}$ falls. Observe from Eqs. (13-12) and (13-14) that the interest rate and price level would not change if C_w were zero.

In conclusion, in a sense money is still neutral. An increase in the money supply, in and of itself, does not affect the rate of interest. But if the method of increasing M results in a transfer of earning assets from the public to the monetary authority, the rate of interest will decline.

Appendix to Chapter 15

To follow the argument of this appendix, the reader should be familiar with the concepts of a differential equation and its solution and with the concept of Taylor's expansion.

The static model that underlies the analysis of Chapter 15 consists of the two equations

$$I(i,Y) = Y - C(Y) \tag{15-1}$$

$$m = L(i,Y) \tag{15-2}$$

It will be useful for future reference to know the equations for the slopes of these functions. Differentiation with respect to i and Y gives

$$\left(\frac{di}{dY}\right)_{IS} = \frac{1 - C_y - I_y}{I_i} \tag{15-3}$$

$$\left(\frac{di}{dY}\right)_{LM} = \frac{-L_y}{L_i} \tag{15-4}$$

All the symbols except I_y, the marginal propensity to invest, are familiar. We assume that $I_y > 0$, although beyond this we know very little about it. Since $L_i < 0$ and $L_y > 0$, the slope of the LM function is definitely positive. Since $I_i < 0$, the slope of IS will be negative if $(1 - C_y) > I_y$, i.e., if the marginal propensity to save is greater than the marginal propensity to invest, and it will be positive if the reverse is the case.

If we increase the money supply, we obtain the familiar set of simultaneous linear equations

$$0 = (1 - C_y - I_y)\left(\frac{dY}{dm}\right) - I_i\left(\frac{di}{dm}\right)$$

$$1 = L_y\left(\frac{dY}{dm}\right) + L_i\left(\frac{di}{dm}\right)$$

From these equations it follows that

$$\frac{dY}{dm} = \frac{\begin{vmatrix} 0 & -I_i \\ 1 & L_i \end{vmatrix}}{\Delta} = \frac{I_i}{\Delta}$$

and

$$\frac{di}{dm} = \frac{\begin{vmatrix} (1 - C_y - I_y) & 0 \\ L_y & 1 \end{vmatrix}}{\Delta} = \frac{(1 - C_y - I_y)}{\Delta}$$

where

$$\Delta = \begin{vmatrix} (1 - C_y - I_y) & -I_i \\ L_y & L_i \end{vmatrix} = L_i(1 - C_y - I_y) + I_iL_y \quad (15\text{-}5)$$

Observe that the sign of Δ is ambiguous. $L_i < 0$, but $(1 - C_y - I_y)$ may be either positive or negative depending upon whether the marginal propensity to invest is greater or less than the marginal propensity to save. Consequently, we cannot tell whether the increase in the money supply will raise or lower the level of income and the rate of interest. Notice also that if we had retained our assumption of Part II that investment is not a function of the level of income, $I_y = 0$, we would have

$$\Delta' = L_i(1 - C_y) + I_iL_y \quad (15\text{-}6)$$

which is definitely negative. Thus an increase in the money supply would unambiguously raise the level of income and lower the rate of interest. But when $I_y > 0$, our comparative static analysis no longer gives unambiguous results, especially since we know very little about the value of I_y.

In this situation dynamic analysis can help us out. Let us assume, as we did in the text, that the rate of change of income is equal to the difference between intended investment and savings and that money market adjustments are instantaneous. This permits us to write the dynamic model

$$\frac{dY}{dt} = I(i,Y) - Y + C(Y) \quad (15\text{-}7)$$

$$m = L(i,Y) \quad (15\text{-}8)$$

where dY/dt is the rate of change of income.

To make further headway, we need to find linear approximations to these equations. What we can do is to assume that in the neighborhood of equilibrium the functions are linear. Accordingly, we apply Taylor's expansion and retain only linear terms. Eqs. (15-7) and (15-8) are therefore rewritten as

$$\frac{dY}{dt} = -(1 - C_y - I_y)(Y - Y_0) + I_i(i - i_0) \tag{15-9}$$

$$0 = L_y(Y - Y_0) + L_i(i - i_0) \tag{15-10}$$

where $Y - Y_0$ and $i - i_0$ are the deviations of income and the rate of interest from the equilibrium values Y_0 and i_0, respectively.

By substituting Eq. (15-10) into (15-9), we can reduce Eq. (15-9) to a linear first-order differential equation in Y. Such an equation has a solution of the form

$$Y = Y_0 + \mathbf{a}e^{\mathbf{q}t} \tag{15-11}$$

where $\mathbf{a}$ and $\mathbf{q}$ are constants and e is the base of the natural logarithmic system. If the term $\mathbf{a}e^{\mathbf{q}t}$ is to disappear and Y is to return to Y_0, the root, $\mathbf{q}$, must be negative.

By differentiating Eq. (15-11) with respect to time, we obtain

$$\frac{dY}{dt} = \mathbf{q}(Y - Y_0) \tag{15-12}$$

Using this expression to replace dY/dt in Eq. (15-9) allows us to rewrite Eqs. (15-9) and (15-10) as

$$0 = -(1 - C_y - I_y + \mathbf{q})(Y - Y_0) + I_i(i - i_0) \tag{15-13}$$

$$0 = L_y(Y - Y_0) + L_i(i - i_0) \tag{15-14}$$

If these equations are to be valid for all values of the variables, the determinant formed by the coefficients must be zero. Accordingly,

$$0 = \begin{vmatrix} -(1 - C_y - I_y + \mathbf{q}) & I_i \\ L_y & L_i \end{vmatrix} = [L_i(1 - C_y - I_y) + I_iL_y] + L_i\mathbf{q}$$

Now observe that the term in square brackets is nothing other than Δ.

Hence $$\Delta + L_i\mathbf{q} = 0$$

or $$\mathbf{q} = \frac{-\Delta}{L_i}$$

Since stability, i.e., a return of Y to Y_0 after a disturbance, requires that $\mathbf{q} < 0$, and since we know definitely that $L_i < 0$, it follows that Δ must be negative.

Since we now know definitely that Δ must be negative if the system is stable, the logical step is to examine the properties of Δ and see what the negativity condition implies. We know that

$$\Delta = L_i(1 - C_y - I_y) + I_iL_y < 0 \qquad (15\text{-}15)$$

This expression can easily be rearranged to read

$$\frac{(1 - C_y - I_y)}{I_i} + \frac{L_y}{L_i} < 0$$

From Eqs. (15-3) and (15-4) it is apparent that this is equivalent to

$$\left(\frac{di}{dY}\right)_{IS} - \left(\frac{di}{dY}\right)_{LM} < 0$$

In other words, the slope of the IS curve plus the slope of the LM curve with its sign changed must be negative. Recalling the three cases of the text, the first case, in which IS had a negative slope, clearly meets the stability condition. IS has a negative slope and LM has a positive slope. When we add the slope of the IS curve to the slope of the LM curve with its sign changed, the sum must be negative.

In the second case IS had a positive slope, but we still found the equilibrium to be stable. According to our condition for stability, this would imply that the positive value of the slope of IS must be absolutely less than the value of the slope of the LM curve. If we check back again to Figure 15-4, we can see that this is indeed the case.

In the third case the slope of the IS curve was greater than the slope of the LM curve. We found this situation to be unstable, a result that is confirmed by the mathematical analysis. In this case the sum of the slope of the IS curve and the slope of the LM curve with its sign changed will be positive. This means that Δ is positive; q, will therefore also be positive; and the term ae^{qt} of Eq. (15-11) will grow progressively larger. The static equilibrium values Y_0 and i_0 are therefore irrelevant. Although the system may lodge at this point for a time, any disturbance will make the variables of the system deviate progressively from the equilibrium levels.

In summary, Samuelson's analysis shows that there are cases in which comparative static models give ambiguous results. One needs, therefore, to examine the underlying dymamic processes in order to be sure that the results of the static models are meaningful. Notice also that if we are willing to assume that the system is stable, Δ must be negative; and if we know the values of L_i, C_y, I_i, and L_y, about all of which we can get some information, then we can infer the range of values within which I_y must lie. Assuming that $I_y \geq 0$, it can readily be inferred from Eq. (15-15) that

$$0 \leq I_y \leq (1 - C_y) + \frac{I_iL_y}{L_i}$$

if the stability condition is to be met.

Appendix to Chapter 20

Domar performs his mathematical analysis of the burden of the debt with the help of differential equations. His results can also be obtained with the simple mathematics employed in Chapters 5 and 7 if we assume that magnitudes remain the same during a time period but change between time periods. Let the symbols used in the analysis be the same as in the text. The burden then will be

$$\gamma = \frac{iD_t}{iD_t + p_t Y_t} = \frac{1}{1 + (1/i)(p_t Y_t / D_t)} \tag{20-1}$$

from which it can easily be seen that the tax rate, given a constant rate of interest, depends uniquely on the ratio of money income to the debt. Assuming that α is the proportion of each year's income borrowed, the debt at the beginning of year t will be

$$D_t = D_0 + \alpha(p_0 Y_0 + p_1 Y_1 + p_2 Y_2 + \cdots + p_{t-1} Y_{t-1}) \tag{20-2}$$

One possibility considered by Domar is the case in which money income fails to grow at all. In this case Eq. (20-2) becomes

$$D_t = D_0 + \alpha p_0 Y_0 t$$

so that the ratio of debt to income,

$$\frac{D_t}{p_t Y_t} = \frac{D_0}{p_0 Y_0} + \alpha t$$

approaches infinity as time goes on. If money income fails to grow while the debt mounts, the tax rate needed to service the debt will ultimately approach 100 percent.

If the level of money income grows at a constant absolute amount β each year, income in year t will be

$$p_t Y_t = p_0 Y_0 + \beta t$$

so that, substituting in Eq. (20-2), we have for the debt

$$D_t = D_0 + \alpha p_0 Y_0 + \alpha[(p_0 Y_0 + \beta) + (p_0 Y_0 + 2\beta) \\ + \cdots + (p_0 Y_0 + (t-1)\beta)]$$

or $\qquad D_t = D_0 + \alpha p_0 Y_0 t + \alpha\beta[1 + 2 + 3 + \cdots + (t-1)] \tag{20-3}$

The term in the brackets is an arithmetic series which has the sum $t(t-1)/2$. Consequently Eq. (20-3) becomes

$$D_t = D_0 + \alpha p_0 Y_0 t + \frac{\alpha\beta t(t-1)}{2} = D_0 + \alpha t\left(p_0 Y_0 - \frac{\beta}{2}\right) + \frac{\alpha\beta t^2}{2}$$

and the ratio of debt to income becomes

$$\frac{D_t}{p_t Y_t} = \frac{D_0 + \alpha t \left[p_0 Y_0 - (\beta/2)\right] + (\alpha \beta t^2/2)}{p_0 Y_0 + \beta t}$$

Because the square term dominates, the ratio of debt to income approaches infinity, and the tax rate approaches 100 percent of taxable income.

Finally, if income grows at a constant percentage rate r,

$$p_t Y_t = p_0 Y_0 (1 + r)^t$$

Substituting in Eq. (20-2), we have

$$D_t = D_0 + \alpha p_0 Y_0 [1 + (1 + r) + (1 + r)^2 + \cdots + (1 + r)^{t-1}]$$

The term in the brackets is a geometric series that has the sum $[(1 + r)^t - 1]/r$ so that

$$D_t = D_0 + \frac{\alpha p_0 Y_0 (1 + r)^t}{r} - \frac{\alpha p_0 Y_0}{r}$$

and the ratio of debt to money income becomes

$$\frac{D_t}{p_t Y_t} = \frac{D_0 + \dfrac{\alpha p_0 Y_0 (1 + r)^t}{r} - \dfrac{\alpha p_0 Y_0}{r}}{p_0 Y_0 (1 + r)^t}$$

As t grows larger and larger, this expression approaches the constant term α/r, so that the tax burden becomes

$$\gamma = \frac{1}{1 + (r/i\alpha)}$$

which increases as i, the rate of interest, increases and as α, the percentage of annual money income borrowed, increases and decreases as r, the rate of growth of money income, increases.

Index